The Nature of Historical Knowledge

To my wife
in gratitude

The Nature of
Historical Knowledge

Michael Stanford

Basil Blackwell

© Michael Stanford 1986

First published 1986

First published in USA 1987

Basil Blackwell Ltd
108 Cowley Road, Oxford OX4 1JF, UK

Basil Blackwell Inc.
432 Park Avenue South, Suite 1503,
New York, NY 10016, USA

British Library Cataloguing in Publication Data
Stanford, Michael John Goring
 The nature of historical knowledge.
 1. Historiography
 I. Title
 907'.2   D13

 ISBN 0-631-14373-4
 ISBN 0-631-15291-1 Pbk

Library of Congress Cataloging in Publication Data
Stanford, Michael John Goring, 1923–
 The nature of historical knowledge.

 Includes bibliographical references and index.
 1. Historiography.   2. History–Methodology.
 I. Title.
 D13.S79 1986   907'.2   86–14696
 ISBN 0-631-14373-4
 ISBN 0-631-15291-1 (pbk.)

Typeset by System 4 Associates, Gerrards Cross
Printed in Great Britain by Billing & Sons Ltd, Worcester

Contents

Prologue

1 Towards a Better Understanding of our Understanding of History

There is some confusion about both the nature and the aims of historical knowledge. The almost infinite number of facts and ideas demands some kind of meaningful arrangement. The ordering of these facts and ideas is done in many ways. History, as its critics often remark, lacks the formal theoretical structure of most academic disciplines. But it does not lack structures. It has, perhaps, too many.

This book attempts to identify the structures involved in history, and to see how they relate to one another. It offers one comprehensive overall arrangement of all these structures in order to bring some clarity to the confusion. Moreover, this clarification may help solve some of the methodological, and even some of the philosophical, problems that are commonly encountered in the practice of history. In addition to that of structure, three other ideas are emphasized and in some part explored here: the role of models or representations in historical understanding; the importance of language in any kind of knowledge but especially in historical knowledge; and the literary aspects and functions of historiography.[1]

My main purpose, however, is to provide a simple and intelligible overview of the whole of history – in both senses of the word. It is to show the interaction between history-as-events, or *res gestae*, and history-as-story, or *historia rerum gestarum*.[2] It is to suggest that the speculative and the analytic approaches to the philosophy of history are not mutually exclusive but interdependent. Thus I hope to outline a sort of map or schema of history which shows where every element is located – archive and lecture course as much as war or civilization. Many have written on various aspects of the theory or practice of history, as well as on the human past, of course, but few have tried to show how all the topics can be brought together.

---

[1] The first two of these are developments of ideas explored in my Ph.D. thesis 'Knowledge as structure: some problems' (University of Bristol, 1977).

[2] See G. W. F. Hegel, *The Philosophy of History* (Dover Publications, 1956), p. 60.

This essay should help anyone coming for the first time to the philosophy of history to find his or her bearings.

Perhaps, more ambitiously, this study may point the way to that long-awaited 'Critique of Historical Reason' that Kant omitted, and Dilthey failed, to write. To do so it would be necessary, first, to demonstrate how historical understanding is possible and, second, to point to the limits of that understanding. These limits include the lack of empirical data – because the past has irretrievably gone; the inevitable subjectivity of a form of action that must be performed by everyone for him- or herself; the difficulties of symbolic communication (that is, the use of language of some kind); and the dilemma that all thought is for the sake of action, but that true historical thinking must be essentially contemplative. We should not forget that history (in both senses) involves thinking at many levels – in acting, in reporting, in interpreting, in understanding, in representing, in writing, in teaching, and in learning – and therefore cannot ignore certain philosophical considerations. Indeed, we may venture to assert that the discipline of history is part of the great preoccupation of the twentieth-century mind: the effort to understand itself.

Finally, this book is primarily descriptive in purpose, not prescriptive – though I shall make no attempt to hide my own views. It aims to bring out what is hidden, to clarify what is obscure, to make the implicit explicit, and to assist us to act more rationally. It should give us a clearer understanding of what we are doing as well as of what we may choose to do, whether as students or as agents of history. It will not, however, tell people what they ought to do. A great deal of time and energy is expended in trying to know and to understand the past. I make no claim to prescribe how this is to be done. I wish rather to increase our insight into the nature of our efforts both to do and to make history.

2   An Example: Fritz Fischer's *Griff nach der Weltmacht*

I now turn to a concrete illustration of what may be involved in the structure of history. In 1961 the German historian, Fritz Fischer, published a massively documented work on Germany's aims in the First World War. Much to the surprise and indignation of many of his countrymen, he showed that imperial Germany was pursuing an aggressive and expansionist policy in Europe throughout the course of this war. As he put it:

> The meaning and purpose of this book is to show that the age of imperialism did not end, as most historians make out, in 1914, but reached its first climax in Germany's colossal effort to weld continental 'Mitteleuropa' into a force which would place Germany on equal terms

with the established and the potential world powers: the British Empire, Russia and the United States.[3]

This is an important example of historical activity, in both senses of the word 'history' (events, and the historian's account of these events). Several elements may be distinguished in Fischer's activity. There is, first, his book, the work of history that we hold in our hands. Second, there are the events (of the years of the First World War) that he relates in his book. Third, there is his interpretation of these events, an interpretation that caused a scandal in German academic circles in the 1960s. Fourth is the documentary evidence that he used, which connects the events to the world of today and was the object of his massive researches. Fifth is his 'audience', or the 'public mind', first of Germany, but then also of Europe and the wider world. The book had, and still has, considerable impact on this mind, and we should not suppose that changing the public mind has no effect on the course of history. Fischer's book is only one of many studies of imperial Germany which demonstrate how much the ideas and outlooks of Germany's rulers and patriotic citizens of that era were formed by the works of the German historical school – Treitschke, von Sybel, Delbrück, and so on.[4] The link between history-as-account and history-as-events is obvious. Less obvious at the moment, but surely not to be doubted, is the further connection between Fischer's book and subsequent historical events. In so far as he has successfully demonstrated that Germany's aims in the First World War were not so very different from those of Hitler's Third Reich in the Second,[5] the subsequent behaviour of German governments and of foreign governments towards Germany (whether East or West) can hardly be unaffected. Certainly this was what has been feared by many of Fischer's critics. Thus historical actions, by governments and people, are a sixth element in this analysis. And historical events are made up of two parts: the human acts resulting from human decisions, and the given situation within which those acts are performed. The situation, as Marx comments in a famous passage, is often not of their own choosing. Then, as we see, historical actions become part of historical events.

[3] Fritz Fischer, *Germany's Aims in the First World War* (Chatto and Windus, 1967), p. x.

[4] 'No German historian of note, not even such critics as Gustav Schmoller, Friedrich Meinecke, or Karl Lamprecht, questioned the positive value of the nation and its need for political and military power and aggrandisement': G. G. Iggers, *The German Conception of History: the national tradition of historical thought from Herder to the present* (Weslyan University Press, 1968), p. 130.

[5] See, for example, the map of 'Mitteleuropa' proposed by Bethmann Hollweg and printed on p. 107 of Fischer, *Germany's Aims in the First World War*.

3 The Elements of Historical Activity

Having identified six elements in the activity associated with Fischer's book, I shall place them in the order in which they occurred. First came the events of the years 1914–18. Next came the evidence, which consists largely of memoirs and state papers deposited (after a temporary sequestration by the Americans at the end of the Second World War) in the archives at Bonn, Koblenz, Merseburg, Potsdam and Vienna. These documents were created in the years 1914–18, but survived into the late 1950s when Fischer saw them (and there is no reason to suppose that they do not exist today). Thus the evidence spans the gap in time between the events and the historian – the gap between the acts of the historical agents and the thoughts of the historical observer or student. These thoughts form the third element. In studying these documents and other existing historical material, Fischer arrived at a new understanding of the events under review; in short, he made a radically different construction from the evidence. Although he probably discussed his ideas with friends, colleagues and students, this fresh and challenging, and doubtless slowly evolving, view remained for some years a part of Fischer's mind. When, however, he produced a book (in 1961) his mental construction took on an objective, material and public form. It was enshrined in certain words and phrases in the German language, and the book took its place within the tradition of German literature. It was a historical work. Such a work is defined by Hayden White as 'a verbal structure in the form of a narrative prose discourse that purports to be a model, or icon, of past structures and processes in the interest of *explaining what they were by representing* them'.[6] This definition draws attention to the fact that a work of history, once written, is not only a contribution to historical science but also a literary product susceptible to literary and linguistic analysis. More of this later; at the moment it is sufficient to note that the book is the fourth element in our analysis, and it is a direct product of the third element.

The fifth element, as we have seen, is the mind of the public. It is difficult to surmise exactly what constitutes popular belief about the past. There seems to be a wide range of both interest and knowledge, extending from those who are almost totally lacking in any awareness of, or concern with, what has already happened, to those professional historians or retired politicians and generals who are obsessed by the past almost to the exclusion of the present. Between the two, there are, in any civilized country, a large number of people who are interested in the past for its own sake,

---

[6] Hayden White, *Metahistory: the historical imagination in nineteenth-century Europe* (Johns Hopkins University Press, 1973), p. 2. The italics are White's.

and many who also desire some historical information to guide them in current decisions of business and politics. Some fairly relevant and accurate knowledge of history is as important to the businessman, journalist or politician as is a knowledge of geography, economics or sociology. This fifth element, then, was undoubtedly affected, and perhaps changed, by the appearance of Fischer's book. Finally, we come to the actions, wise or foolish, that are performed in business, diplomacy, politics, travel, the performing arts, and so on, and that are based partly upon historical beliefs. (The behaviour of governments and peoples in 1914, not only in Germany and Britain, but in Ireland, the Balkans, the USA and the Middle East, best illustrates this point.) Historical belief, then, is an important constituent of historical action. And historical actions, the sixth element in our analysis, form part of historical events, the first element in another cycle.

It is to this cycle that we now turn.

4 The Structure of Historical Activity

Many books and articles have been published on the philosophy and methodology of history, and most historians have at some time let fall *obiter dicta* on this or that philosophical or methodological point. Few of these works, however, have taken a sufficiently broad view. In this large and confusing field it is, perhaps, easier to get one's bearings if one stands a long way back and tries to include all that is relevant in one perspective.

In considering historical activity it is necessary to include both thoughts and actions, both beliefs (however false or superstitious) *and* firmly based, authenticated knowledge, and to take into account not only the past but also the present and the future. We must look at thought and language, deeds and words, arts and sciences. Some of the objects of our concern are fully visible; others are, by their very nature, always unseen. We have to deal with both the material and the ideal, yet the distinctions are not always clear. What is this book I am holding? Is it material? It occupies space and weighs several hundred grams. Is it ideal? It contains the thoughts of a historian, which formed themselves in words in his mind, appeared on the paper on his desk, took legible form in the consequent typescript, were printed and published in Hamburg in 1961 in German, and were translated, reprinted and published in England. Surely the book that made such an impact is not this yellow and red object before me?

However, if we must take a broad view, we must also simplify and clarify what we see in order to apprehend it. Any model is a falsification. Equally any map that plotted every detail of the landscape would be perfectly redundant (as well as enormously unwieldy). Having already identified what

Prologue

I take to be the more significant elements in historical activity, I propose a schema to suggest how they come together. The arrows indicate relationships

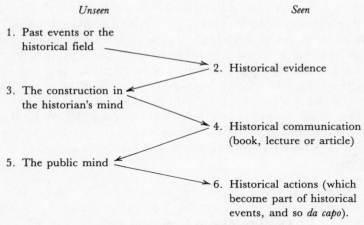

Figure 1   The structure of historical activity

of cause and effect. They do not, however, represent all these relations; for example, the construction (3) results not only from evidence (2) but also from earlier interpretations of evidence as found both in existing historical works (4) and in existing public beliefs (5), which the historian, to some extent, shares. This schema may be taken as an acceptable, if simple representation of the structure of historical activity. Both the structure and its elements should be more closely examined. First, however, it would be profitable to discuss the concept of structure. In the succeeding chapters I shall go on to discuss the various structures of history.

1

The Concept of Structure: Structures in History

1 Structure Defined and Introduced

Among the definitions of structure in the *Shorter Oxford English Dictionary*, two are especially appropriate: '3. The mutual relation of the constituent parts or elements of a whole as determining its peculiar nature or character...6. An organized body or combination of mutually connected and dependent parts or elements.' It is the former, more abstract, use 3 upon which I shall concentrate, though the more concrete sense 6 will sometimes be relevant.[1]

There are two main points: 'structure' is defined as a relationship; and such relationship determines the character of the whole. The first, if taken alone, would hardly distinguish a structure from a pattern (for either may be seen as a relationship). A pattern, however, does not necessarily determine. According to the *OED*'s definition, a structure is more than a pattern; it is that relationship which determines the character of the whole. This distinction must be stressed, for sometimes a mere arrangement of parts is wrongly referred to as a structure.

A distinction should also be made between a pattern that is inherent in the subject matter and one that is imposed upon it. The former is discovered to exist in the world, or in the part of it we are thinking about; the latter is brought to the objective world by our thinking. 'To discern a pattern in' and 'to impose a pattern upon' are conceptually distinct, though the two activities may not always be easily distinguished in practice. When we recognize a figure 5 in green dots in a colour-blindness test, we are discerning a pattern *in* the dots. When we look at the stars and, like our ancestors, descry bulls and bears and maidens in them, we are *imposing* patterns, since the stars can be arranged in different ways – the Great Bear, for example, is sometimes called the Plough.

[1] I have discussed the concept more fully in my Ph.D. thesis, 'Knowledge as structure' (University of Bristol, 1977), pp. 271–318.

As has already been remarked, history is a subject with few theories, but many structures. This may seem at first sight paradoxical, for it is often taken as a mark of a well-developed intellectual discipline that it should have a firm theoretical structure. History, however, although a long-established and in many ways intellectually developed discipline, notoriously lacks such a theoretical frame; yet it does have many structures – that is, firm and permanent or semi-permanent relations of elements that determine the character of the whole.

There are several reasons why it is useful, in any intelligent activity, to have a grasp of the relevant structure. First, it enables us to see how the various parts are related to each other and to the whole; a convenient example is the skeleton of the human body. Second, a knowledge of structure facilitates a study of relationships rather than of the things related; here we may think of an anthropologist's account of kinship within a primitive society. Third, it enables us to think more formally, less concretely. This is the advantage of algebra over arithmetic; many of us can recall the sense of power with which we grasped for the first time that, for example, the expansion of $(x^2 - y^2)$ to $(x + y)(x - y)$ was true for all values of x and y. Similarly, once the relationship between strength and weight has been understood, one can immediately see why the thickness of an animal's legs must increase in proportion to its weight, not its height. A gnat could never be the size of an elephant; conversely, the largest dinosaurs (like whales today) were possibly too heavy to emerge completely from the supporting medium of mud or water. Fourth, a grasp of structure enables us to pick our way through vast fields of information. A railway timetable is more comprehensible if one knows the layout of the lines. One can, with such a grasp, select the relevant information (from, say, a handbook on gardening or cookery), simplify one's knowledge in order to convey it or explain things to others, and distinguish the more from the less important, the permanent from the ephemeral. Finally, and significantly, one knows how to construct and to reconstruct, whether in engineering, art restoration, historiography, or composing a symphony or a sonnet.[2] In short, as Aristotle argues, 'wisdom is the knowledge of first principles.'[3]

2   Types of Inherent Structure Relevant to History

I now turn to the structures that may be relevant to history, whether as a sequence of actions and events or as a form of knowledge. In this section I discuss the structures that are inherent in the subject matter, rather than

[2] See also this chapter, section 2.
[3] *Metaphysics, book A.*

those that are imposed upon the subject matter in the course of our thinking about it.

Basic to the universe, we may suppose, are various logical structures. These include the structures of mathematics and formal logic. (So, at least, it is generally believed. The intuitionist philosophy of mathematics has the contrary view.[4] If it turned out that these were man-made, they would come under the heading of imposed structures.) There are also, though more debatably, the various permanent relationships between minds, symbols and referents that have been the concern of much of the past century or so of Western philosophy, from Frege and Wittgenstein onwards. Within the philosophy of knowledge, in hermeneutics, in semantics, there is still much debate over the precise nature and extent of such relationships, but I wish to argue that, while some of these connections are arbitrary, others are permanent and inherent in the nature of things,[5] and therefore to be counted among the structures of the universe. Probably there are other philosophical structures of this kind. That they are still the subject of debate as to both nature and extent indicates their importance. Questions of the relationships in knowledge, thought, communication and meaning are widely considered to be of profound importance. Of such structures we may affirm at least two things: they are rational (that is, they appeal immediately to reason rather than to experience), and they are inherent (that is, they emerge from the way the universe is constructed). Although they are discovered by the human mind, they were not invented by it, nor are they alterable by human wills. They may be understood and described in different ways, they may be studied or ignored, but they cannot be changed.

Secondly, one can identify neurological and psychological structures, those of the brain or the mind. The former comprise the functioning of the senses or other cerebral faculties as put forward in the theories of J. J. Gibson, J. Z. Young, Sir John Eccles and Richard Gregory.[6] Examples of the latter are the deep structures of the mind that are suggested, for language, by Noam Chomsky, or for this and other activities by such social structuralists as Claude Lévi-Strauss.[7] Kant's theories of what we may call the inherent structures of the understanding are still being fruitfully pursued, not least

[4] Stephan Körner, *Fundamental Questions of Philosophy: one philosopher's answers* (Penguin, 1971), pp. 64–7.

[5] Cf. Arthur C. Danto: 'There is, in brief, between men and the world, as between language and the world, a space of an extra-worldly sort'; Preface to *Analytical Philosophy of Knowledge* (Cambridge University Press, 1968), p. ix.

[6] See J. J. Gibson, *The Senses Considered as Perceptual Systems* (Allen and Unwin, 1968); J. Z. Young, *A Model of the Brain* (Oxford University Press, 1964); Sir John Eccles, *The Understanding of the Brain* 2nd edn (Blakiston/McGraw Hill, 1977); Richard Gregory, *The Intelligent Eye* (Weidenfeld and Nicolson, 1970).

[7] See John Lyons, *Chomsky* (Fontana/Collins, 1970); N. Chomsky, *Language and Mind* (Harcourt Brace Jovanovich, 1972); Edmund Leach, *Lévi-Strauss* (Fontana/Collins, 1970); C. Lévi-Strauss, *Structural Anthropology* (Allen Lane, 1968 and 1977), vols I and II.

in what is called 'genetic epistemology'. An early use of Kantian ideas in biology is quoted by Chomsky from the ethologist, Konrad Lorenz:

> In the case of animals, we find limitations specific to the forms of experience possible for them. We believe that we can demonstrate the closest functional and probably genetic relationship between these animal a priori's and our human a priori. Contrary to Hume, we believe, just as did Kant, that a 'pure' science of innate forms of human thought, independent of all experience, is possible.[8]

We need not here trace out the arguments about the nature and extent of the a priori and the empirical elements in learning and knowledge. So long as we have reason to believe that these activities are, at least in part, shaped by the permanent forms of the brain or of the mind – that the mind is something more than a mirror or a *tabula rasa* – structures of this second type too are inherent rather than imposed. Unlike the first type, they do not belong to the universe as a whole, but to the form and functioning of the human mind. Nevertheless they belong to the world that we discover; they are not themselves the product of our wills or of our choices. If they are, indeed, a part of our thinking, they are an inescapable not a chosen part.

The third category of structures includes those of the universe as a whole, of 'the nature of things'. These are structures neither of pure reason nor of the human mind, but of objective reality, of the world 'out there'; they are neither philosophical nor psychological, but cosmological. Whether distance, direction and time are fundamental, as Euclid supposed, or whether they are relative to the observer, as Einstein thought, depends not on Euclid or Einstein but on how the universe really is. So does the question whether mind or matter is fundamental, whether the universe is ultimately ideal or material. So does the question whether matter is being continually created or whether the cosmos is running down after an initial explosion. Are the relations of production basic to human society, as Marx thought? Is the universe moved by an eternal mover, as Aristotle believed? All these are problems about the nature of the universe, not the thinkers whose names are often attached to the theories. It is also worth bearing in mind the possibility that, though the universe has these fundamental structures, they may be now, and perhaps will for ever remain, beyond the scope of the human intellect. This was essentially the view of Kant, though he did allow for several breaks in the curtain.

To sum up, I have now identified, or at least gestured towards, three types of inherent structure, which belong to reality as we find it. Before going further it is worth making two points about inherent patterns and structures in history. First, one may correctly identify an inherent pattern but wrongly

---

[8] Quoted by Chomsky, *Language and Mind*, p. 95.

take it to be a structure – that is, a pattern that determines the character of the whole. The second point is that structures are especially important for the historian, whose task it is to construct a model or icon of the whole from a few given parts – much as the archaeologist re-creates whole pots from a few sherds – and who therefore needs to know what shape or pattern to expect; still more, to know the forces and tensions that go to make a society or a war, for example. The aim of historical understanding must be to grasp the underlying structure, not as an ideal of perfection, but because accurate construction and representation are not possible without it.

3 Why We Impose Structures

I now turn from inherent to imposed structures, the structures of human origin that the mind creates and imposes upon the world in an attempt to understand it and to change it. It is worth asking why this occurs. Animals presumably take the structure of the world as it is; for them there are only inherent structures, and they impose nothing. Exactly the opposite with God: for a creator, to think the structures is to give the structures. We might say that the structures *inherent* in the universe are precisely those that God *imposed* in creating the universe. Humans, like the beasts, have not created the universe; yet they insist on imposing their own being (thoughts, patterns, meanings, priorities) upon the universe. In this respect, as in so many others, it has been said that human attempts to usurp the prerogatives of God can only lead to trouble. ('Of Man's first disobedience and the fruit...'). So it is pertinent to enquire for what reasons and in what circumstances the human mind imposes structures.

First, I make the rather Kantian point that the mind can make little or no sense of its percepts unless it arranges them in some sort of pattern.[9] Spatial and temporal arrangements are the most obvious of these. A good deal of the psychology of perception, especially *Gestalt* theories, supports this, as does the work of J. J. Gibson.[10] Benjamin Lee Whorf and others have suggested that our perceptions are patterned by our language.[11] However, the basic idea may be traced from Giambattista Vico in the early eighteenth century, through German historicists like Hamann, Herder and Wilhelm

[9] 'Thoughts without content are empty, intuitions without concepts are blind.' From the opening of the Transcendental Logic in *Immanuel Kant's Critique of Pure Reason*, trans. N. Kemp Smith (Macmillan, 1963), p. 93.

[10] See, for example, M. D. Vernon, *The Psychology of Perception* (Penguin, 1962), pp. 51 ff. Also J. J. Gibson, *The Senses Considered as Perceptual Systems*, esp. chapter 13.

[11] See *Language, Thought and Reality: selected writings of Benjamin Lee Whorf*, ed. and introd. by John B. Carroll (Massachusetts Institute of Technology Press, 1956).

von Humboldt, to Ernst Cassirer and Edward Sapir.[12] 'We cut nature up,' wrote Whorf, 'organize it into concepts, and ascribe significances as we do, largely because we are parties to an agreement to organize it in this way – an agreement that holds throughout our speech community and is codified in the patterns of our language.'[13] Other social conventions – myth, ritual, labour arrangements, for example – may also affect the way that we see the world. We see it not as William James's 'booming, buzzing confusion', but as an articulated, differentiated and constructed pattern. This patterning is supplied partly by the senses, brain and mind of the individual, and partly by what we may call the common or public mind of the community, as represented in language and other conventions. Our original, naïve view is that the world is exactly as we perceive it; a little enquiry, however, reveals that other people frequently see it differently. Moreover, it is never easy to determine which, if any, of us is correct. Lévi-Strauss, in his *Structural Anthropology*, shows two quite dissimilar plans of a village as described by members of either the upper or the lower phratry of the Winnebago tribe of North American Indians. The discrepancy, he suggests, is because each moiety would tend to conceptualize it differently, depending upon their position in the social structure.[14]

So far we have been talking of the imposition of *patterns*, but (as was noted above) a structure is more than a pattern. It determines the character of the whole. Although this may not be explicit in the various kinds of patterning that are imposed in perception, nevertheless in the arrangement of parts there is also an assumption of the whole, as well as an emphasis on some elements as being more significant than others. As both Whorf and Lévi-Strauss assert, agreements about social significance are incorporated in the language used. Language thus has an evaluative, as well as a purely descriptive, character. Since language ascribes significance, as Whorf says, to some elements rather than to others in relation to the value of the whole, we may properly say that it is structures, not merely patterns, that are being imposed. The concept of structure implies that some elements are, or are seen to be, more important than others, and such distinguishing of importance is a kind of evaluation. Moreover, the relationship of 'structuring' or 'being the structure of' is reciprocal. If the structure is that relationship between the parts which determines the character of the whole, it may also be the character of the whole which determines the relationship between the parts. Which seems to come first may depend on no more than which of the two first captures our attention.

[12] See George Steiner, *After Babel: aspects of language and translation* (Oxford University Press, 1975), pp. 75 ff.

[13] Whorf, *Language, Thought and Reality*, p. 213.

[14] Lévi-Strauss, *Structural Anthropology*, vol. I, pp. 134–5.

In a second type of patterning the mind imposes structures by means of inner representations of the outside world – 'cognitive' or 'mental maps' which extend far beyond any single perception. For example, I can find my way about my own house or village without ever having had one individual perception of the whole house or village; that would, indeed, be impossible. Yet this is no very sophisticated skill. Even laboratory rats running a maze exhibit such a capacity.[15] By contrast with the first type of patterning, which is a 'concrete structure' wholly contained in one perception of how the world (or a part of it) empirically is, the second type is not contained in any single sense-perception. It is a mental patterning produced by, or at least accompanied by, a number of similar, repeated experiences. So it seems for rats, and it is probably little different in principle for other animals, including humans. In so far as the pattern, however it is built up, must be distinct from any one experience, it is an abstract pattern or structure. However, to speak of the structure as 'abstract' is not to subscribe to the 'abstractionist' theory of learning; on this I consider Geach's arguments to be conclusive.[16] The pattern is not necessarily built up by inductive or abstractive processes, but may be formed by applying existing a priori concepts (Plato, Kant), or by constructing concepts (Piaget).[17]

Thirdly, there are the patterns that we ourselves deliberately create out of the world itself, or parts of it. From a child playing with sticks and stones or toy bricks to a sculptor or engineer, from carpets to concertos, a wide range of human activities consists of rearranging the way things are. Sometimes these patterns that we impose on the world are not merely patterns but structures ordering the objects that come to hand.

A fourth type of structuring goes beyond mathematics or music or micro-electronics. We also deliberately construct and impose patterns on the human world. The many organizations that make up a society, however primitive or sophisticated, have their own recognizable structures of power, privilege, function, and so on. Obvious examples are hunting groups, fraternities, courts, armies, priesthoods, trading companies, industries. It is not always easy for the investigating social scientist (economist, anthropologist, social psychologist) to determine how far the structures of these groups are deliberately designed (as one might design a house or a sonnet), and how far they have emerged in response to economic, social or psychological pressures. To employ the distinction already made, how

[15] For another kind of 'inner representation', see Peter Gould and Rodney White, *Mental Maps* (Penguin, 1974).
[16] See P. Geach, *Mental Acts: their content and their objects* (Routledge and Kegan Paul, 1971), *passim*, but esp. pp. 18–38.
[17] See J. Piaget, *Structuralism*, trans. and ed. Chaninah Maschler (Routledge and Kegan Paul, 1971): 'Now observation and experiment show as clearly as can be that logical structures *are* constructed' (p. 62); 'There is no structure apart from construction' (p. 140).

far are they inherent in, and emergent from the social world, or how far
have they been first planned and then imposed upon that world? There is
arguably a trend among anthropologists to regard these social forms as
constructions from ways of thinking about and evaluating the world (that
is, ideas), rather than inevitable responses to needs or pressures, as Marxist
or functionalist theories would maintain.

The fifth kind of structuring arises when social scientists, whether
Marxists, functionalists or structuralists, have doubts about their own
understanding of the society under investigation. Both the anthropologist
trying to unravel the complexities of the kinships within a tribe of South
American Indians and the economist examining the structure and functioning of the North American stock market are likely to have the same sort
of doubts. They cannot make sense of their data unless they understand
how the items combine to make the whole: that is, the kinship grouping
of the tribe, and the stock market. As their work proceeds, they may sense
a growing clarity and cohesion, and will thus try to construct a mental picture
of the whole. Social scientists often explain their ideas by sketching the
structure on paper, in order to represent, however crudely, a complex social
reality in a two-dimensional diagram. (Textbooks of anthropology or
economics often contain such sketches.) However, the scientists will tend
to doubt, on the one hand, whether any such social phenomenon can be
adequately represented in this way, and, on the other, whether the structure
of the phenomena has been accurately represented (that is, whether the
structure demonstrated is, in fact, inherent), or whether a structure or pattern
has been imposed and the data hence arranged according to the scientist's
own ideas. These ideas spring partly from the structure of the mind, and
in any case cannot transcend its limitations.

This brings me to the sixth reason for, or occasion of, structuring
experience. Good scientsts will not stop at describing what they see, but
will go on to formulate and test theories about their observations. Indeed,
it is false to say that they will 'go on'. It is widely agreed that in scientific
investigation (in both natural and social sciences) observation and theoriza-
tion go hand in hand. All observations, however simple, are informed by
theory, however rudimentary or provisional, and all theories must ultimately
be tested against observation. Theories, of course, purport to deal not with
a specific experience or phenomenon, but with a whole range. They bring
masses of data under one set of abstract ideas. It used to be believed that
the 'laws of nature' lay hidden in nature, like a vein of gold in the rocks,
to be unearthed by the persistent investigator. Scientists today are concerned
not with laws, but with theories or even only hypotheses; they believe that
theories are of human rather than divine origin and that, far from being
eternal, they are subject to constant revision. Nevertheless, to bring our
observations under a set of rational and publicly validated concepts and

theories is obviously advantageous in many ways; so much so that we seek no further reason for structuring our experience beyond this final one.

4 Types of Imposed Structure Relevant to History

Now that I have examined why and when structures are imposed on experience, I can more easily discusss the kinds of imposed structures that may be involved in historical knowledge, and hence are of concern to every historian and teacher and student of history. The first three kinds we looked at (in section 2) were apparently inherent in the world as we find it and exist there independently of human will or choice; the second three seem to be of human origin.

Structures of the social type, while certainly of human origin, are not of conscious human design. It seems that we, like other animals, have the ability to build up internal representations of our environment[18] which are social as well as spatial. Most people 'know their way around' not only in the locational sense; they also know, at least roughly, how their society works – including, for example, how to go shopping, post letters, attend school, vote, pay taxes, worship and travel. It is arguable that these social abilities are backed by a similar sort of inner representation to that which, according to many investigators, enables a rat to run a maze. If we do have some sort of inner representation of the various structures of society, then it is almost certain that language – which is perhaps essential to social skills – plays a large part in both building it up and in employing it, in so far as these functions can be distinguished. On the other hand,, it may be argued (as I suspect Gilbert Ryle would have done) that the possession of social skills in no way necessitates the possession of any kind of cognitive map or picture. In reply it may be urged that, since the skills that include language skills are readily transferred and adapted to other societies, the existence of some sort of structure of other social behaviours is suggested. That these skills not only can be applied to the situation where they have been learnt, but also can be adapted to quite dissimilar situations, seems to point to some sort of abstract structure in our minds. This structure is abstract because it is not contained in, or derived from, one situation (that is, it is not a 'concrete' structure), but is applicable to many occasions – like statements in algebra instead of arithmetic. It is of human origin because it lies in us rather than in the world (where the 'world' is defined as the object of human speech, knowledge and actions). In our speech, knowledge and actions we *apply* this structuring to the world.

To make quite clear the distinction between this kind and the first three

---

[18] See this chapter, section 3.

kinds of structure, I must emphasize that these abstract structures of social behaviour have been built up from experience of the world; they are creations of the mind, not frameworks of the mind. There are based on our beliefs *about* the world, and such beliefs (which may well be erroneous) are not found *in* the world. Of course, in these, as in most other mental activities, there must be an innate or a priori element – if only because we have to do our thinking with physical bodies (brains, nerves, senses, etc.). But it is not argued here that such abstract structures of social behaviour are part of our initial mental equipment like the mental structures postulated by a Chomsky or Lévi-Strauss. Abstract structures, I believe, are imposed upon the world in our attempts to talk about it, understand it and change it. They are, however, rarely consciously and deliberately designed. More often they are an accepted part of our culture.

What is the relevance of this to history? Surely it is these very social skills that are required for the study of history, for our thinking about past societies. When people move from one town to another, from town to country, from Britain to the USA, when they join the army or start a new job, they must learn their way about in a different social situation. So it is when one researches into English Tudor government or Victorian working-class housing. It is not enough to read the documents; one must make a mental reconstruction of that sixteenth- or nineteenth-century world. In doing so one inevitably brings one's individually acquired cognitive structures to historical understanding. The resulting problems of accuracy, distortion, misunderstanding, omissions, and so on, are obvious and enormous. The historian is under a particular obligation to grasp the inherent, objective structures of that world, as I have already remarked.[19] Moreover, structures derived from one's own social experience seem to be imposed both in understanding history and in enjoying works of fiction – the novel, the drama, the short story, the narrative poem. Indeed, it has often been argued that there is a great similarity between following a narrative in fiction and doing so in history.[20] This similarity is surely not unrelated to Vico's distinction between *factum* and *verum*. Both historical 'truth' and fictional 'truth' belong to the sphere of the former.

Children and uneducated people may imagine the narrated events taking place in a society very like their own – as in medieval paintings of biblical subjects. More educated or sophisticated readers make allowances for the different material environment and the different customs of a distant age.

[19] See this chapter, section 2, last paragraph.
[20] See W. B. Gallie, *Philosophy and the Historical Understanding* (Chatto and Windus, 1964); Hayden White, *Metahistory:* (Johns Hopkins University Press, 1973); P. Munz, *The Shapes of Time: a new look at the philosophy of history* (Wesleyan University Press, 1977), p. 25 and n. 6. On the recent revival in narrative history, see Lawrence Stone, *The Past and the Present* (Routledge and Kegan Paul, 1981), chapter 3.

Yet neither type of reader finds much difficulty in following the story.[21] A great deal of history has been cast in the narrative mode, largely because narrative, whether in fiction or in history, rests heavily on our experience of social being.

The second kind of imposed structure, the theoretical, differs from the first in that it is based not on direct, unconsidered experience but on a conscious plan. Much of twentieth-century historiography is characterized by the analytical approach, whose roots go back at least to the eighteenth century. This approach breaks down the description of the historical situation, event or process into its constituent parts.[22] Although there are no rules about what constitutes those parts or how the analysis is to be performed, there are fashions, even conventions. Yet it is a mark of the vitality of historiography that these fashions are continually changing and the conventions are frequently breached, as historians devise fresh ways of analysing a period or process. New methods are often connected with the discovery of new sources of historical material. In general, however, analysis is preferred to narrative when historians wish to concentrate on a factor (or factors) present on several occasions. If, for example, the role of the cavalry seems to be decisive in several battles, or the attitude of the press to be influential in political crises, then a historian may analyse the military or political situations by focusing on the cavalry or the press. This may spur him or her to look for other factors (for example, the artillery, the infantry, the terrain, the quality of the generalship, the morale of the troops) whose roles may also be singled out for attention in other battles, and a full analysis can thereby be made. In practice, however, the historian often neglects or avoids this, and instead tells a narrative of one analysed factor. Thus we get histories of the cavalry or histories of the press or a particular newspaper. Such books, by turning an incomplete analysis into a narrative, distort both narrative and analysis. It is undeniable, however, that this approach is more popular with both writers and readers. The basic fact of all historiography is that not all the material can be presented at once; it has to be offered and consumed seriatim, and read page by page. This takes time and energy. After a while the attention begins to wander. A well-made narrative is much more effective in holding the attention than a mere list of relevant factors.

From the point of view of intellectual enquiry, the idea of analysis leads to the concepts of structure and synthesis. According to the notion of

[21] Macaulay's remark, 'I shall not be satisfied unless I produce something which shall for a few days supersede the last fashionable novel on the tables of young ladies', is well known: letter to Napier of 5 November 1841, in Sir George Otto Trevelyan, Bt, *The Life and Letters of Lord Macaulay* (2 vols, Oxford University Press, 1932), vol. II, p. 52. Perhaps he was echoing his great predecessor, Edward Gibbon, who boasted in his *Autobiography*: 'My book was on every table, and almost on every toilette' (Everyman edition, (Dent, 1911), p. 145).

[22] Some discussion of what these parts may be follows in the next chapter.

structure, the process of historical analysis bears some resemblance to carving a fowl. It can be best cut up if one knows the bones and the joints. Is it possible to know the structure of a piece of history – an event, a process, a period – in such a way that one can analyse it into the distinct and significant parts? Otherwise an inept method of analysis is like trying to serve a chicken by sawing across the breastbone.

But what of synthesis? It is obvious that (although one rarely needs to put a chicken together again) a bird well carved and dissected along the joints would be more readily put together than one that has been chopped and mangled. The function of synthesis in historiography is to restore the historical whole – the event, process, and so on. When making complete analysis a historian breaks the subject down into what he or she considers to be its constituent parts. Yet it is a commonplace that history is all of a piece: events coincide; people and things interact. One cannot meaningfully concentrate on the cavalry in the battle without considering at least the generalship and the terrain; a factor isolated for detailed scrutiny must not be kept apart. To understand a battle, both the historical writer and the reader must be able to put it all together in their minds. Only by under-standing how the pieces acted upon one another will they be able to grasp the total event. Good historians should be able to help their readers to do this, though ultimately all must do it themselves.

What if the historian is writing a history of, say, the cavalry, one of those bastard analytical narratives referred to above? Since the cavalry is almost unintelligible outside its military, political and social contexts,[23] the history of the cavalry demands in addition a history of the army, a history of warfare, a history of foreign affairs and a history of class structures and relations, at least. On the other hand, because time, knowledge, paper, printing costs and the reader's attention all impose limitations, the historian will normally devote a chapter each to the three or four most essential contexts and then proceed with the story. Again, but less satisfactorily this time, readers are left to make the synthesis for themselves as best they can. (Colleagues well versed in nineteenth-century military history, who may be reviewing it, can do this pretty well; school students or average readers much less well.) But the dilemma is a real one. If historians try to describe everything, their narrative will make no progress; if they stick to a thin but elegant story they will entertain readers but do violence to the 'seamless web of history'. A story told out of context is only a story; it is not history.

Although there is no way out of the dilemma, the problems of analysis can be partly solved by considering the structure and synthesis: before you cut it up, think how you will put it together again. If the structure of

---

[23] These were skilfully brought together by Cecil Woodham-Smith, in her account of the Charge of the Light Brigade, *The Reason Why* (Constable, 1953).

something is known, the more important can be distinguished from the less important constituent parts, and the way in which those parts come together to determine the character of the whole can be perceived. Thus, if something is analysed according to a perception of the structure – that is, if it is broken up along the lines of the more important parts – then the resultant synthesis can be more easily and correctly carried out. This becomes apparent when the analytical approach to history is made, not according to fashion or momentary inspiration, but in accordance with a pre-existing theory, when a more orderly procedure is likely to be followed. There are, however, virtually no accepted theories in history at the moment except for the several variations of Marxism. Otherwise the theory adopted is likely to be taken from another discipline – from law, in the case of constitutional history; from economics, sociology, political science or, more rarely, anthropology, in most other kinds of history that are at all theoretically based.

One of the commonest and most prestigious modes of historiography, the writing of political history, still makes very little use of theory. It tends towards the narrative mode; where it uses analyses these tend to be *ad hoc*. The point is exemplified in two major works of political analysis, Sir Lewis Namier's *England in the Age of the American Revolution* and Professor John Vincent's *The Formation of the British Liberal Party, 1857–68*, published in 1930 and 1966 respectively. Both divide up their subject under such headings as 'The Unreformed House of Commons', 'The Social Structure', 'The Upper Classes', 'The Land as Basis of Citizenship', 'The State' (Namier); or 'The Parliamentary Liberal Party', 'The Rank and File', 'Leadership', 'Policy' (Vincent). Neither author states why he has chosen to divide his book in this way. Neither indicates whether he has listed all the constituent parts or only some. Neither explains how the parts he has identified combine to form the whole. Neither makes clear whether the chosen topics are comparable and totally constitutive of the whole, or whether they are of different logical categories. Are they guilty of a category-mistake like saying 'In my hand I hold three things: a right glove, a left glove and a pair of gloves'?[24] In Vincent's case one may agree that the parliamentary party, the rank and file and the leadership together constitute the party, though the first and third categories are likely to overlap. But what of 'Policy'? Clearly this belongs to quite a different category, that of ideas rather than of people. Although Vincent is well aware of this, he does not explicitly state that a party is made up of people and ideas and nothing else. (Is this true?) Nor does he suggest that at either level he has comprehensively enumerated the parts. Rather, the topics chosen are almost certainly the most important, the most interesting, or even the best endowed with copious and available

[24] For category-mistakes, see Gilbert Ryle, *The Concept of Mind* (Hutchinson, 1949), p. 18 and *passim*.

source material. These are all very proper considerations for the historian, but would it not be helpful if they were made explicit? I shall deal with considerations of the evidence, the analysis of events, the structure of the finished book and the need to relate to a reading public in succeeding chapters.

Vincent's arrangement of the material and his analysis of the subject matter, however, are both more systematic than Namier's, to whom all my criticisms of Vincent's book apply with greater force. Possibly Namier was led astray by his admiration for aristocratic insouciance. 'English civilization,' he averred, 'is essentially the work of the leisured classes.'[25] I have no desire to denigrate what are widely recognized as two masterpieces of analytical political history. Their merit lies in the writing, in the thorough research which supports the conclusions, but above all in the insights resulting from great intelligence and labour. The authors may very well maintain that they write their books according to their own ideas, not in deference to mine. Indeed. I simply wish to maintain that, in works of analytical political history, more systematic analysis, carried out on more explicit principles, not only makes it easier to understand the works themselves, but leaves readers better informed of just what they know and what they do not know. Finally, such analysis enables other scholars to see exactly where their own work might dovetail in with what has already been done. If Namier and Vincent's works exhibit the limitations of *ad hoc* analysis, it is not surprising that most works of this kind, being written by lesser historians, are even more open to these criticisms.

Whether analysis follows the private designs of the individual historian, or whether it is guided by accepted theories (usually those of another discipline), a set of discrete, abstract structures, originating outside the material, are applied to a particular historical situation or series of events. These structures are distinct and abstract, of human origin, and imposed upon the data. Unlike those of the fourth type, however they are deliberately designed. They are human artefacts, like a chisel or a house; they are not unintended or subconscious adaptations of the mind, like a mode of speech or a habit. As is well known, they play an increasing part in twentieth-century historiography. Perhaps the most widely used is the Marxist approach, but there are many others, both formal and informal. The narrative and analytic modes of writing history correspond roughly to vertical and horizontal sections of the subject; they are complements rather than alternatives to the fourth and fifth types of structures. The narrative approach usually makes more use of our unconscious, apparently (though not literally) instinctive ability to structure the social setting. Theories and other deliberate and

[25] Sir Lewis Namier, *England in the Age of the American Revolution*, (2nd edn Macmillan, 1961), p. 14.

explicit structurings are usually found rather in the analytical approach. Both the fourth and the fifth types of structuring are also very much the concern of the social sciences – with the inevitable repercussions upon historiography.[26]

Finally, there is a set of structures that are by contrast primarily, if not entirely, historical – that is, they originate among historians or others thinking about the past. First, certain chronological conventions divide historical time by dynasties, reigns, centuries or periods. Then, equally convenient, there are spatial divisions of history, such as histories of Europe or South-East Asia or the Caribbean, where geographical considerations partly determine the subject areas. Much orthodox historiography, especially since Ranke, divides history into nations – a practice that owes much to the European preoccupation since the seventeenth century with the nation-state. From this it has not been difficult to write histories of institutions, organizations and, more recently, social groupings, because they have been seen to play an important part in national histories. Examples are histories of the East India Company, Parliament, trade unions, the working class, churches and sects. History can also be divided by abstract subjects (rather than by these concrete objects), such as military history, local history, art history, intellectual history, and so on. These are not distinguished by or developed according to any recognized principle. Such subjects (or sub-subjects) come into existence when working historians decide to concentrate on new areas. Once enough sound work seems to have been done, a new historical territory is laid out for development. (One suspects this is decided as much by ambitious publishers and university administrators as by practising historians.)

All these conventional divisions hardly imply a coherent, structural view of history. Apart from these conventions, most historical work (as I have suggested) is done on an empirical and *ad hoc* basis. It is rather in the field of speculative philosophy of history – an area much scorned or, at best, neglected today – that one finds at least a recognition that a more coherent and systematic approach is desirable. Pre-eminent here are Hegel, Marx, Spengler and Toynbee, though simpler attempts to structure history are found in innumerable writers from Joachim of Flora, Ibn Khaldoun and Sir Walter Ralegh, through Voltaire, Vico, Herder and Comte, to Reinhold Niebuhr and Jacques Maritain. Such artificial structures or models of history try to make the past easier to comprehend. Of the first four names, Marx and Toynbee are perhaps the most interesting because they purport to describe at least five things: the articulation of historical events; the driving forces of the historical process; some, at least, of the interrelationships of the parts; the expected future course of history; and, most important of all,

[26] See, for example, Peter Burke, *Sociology and History* (Allen and Unwin, 1980).

the meaning and significance of the whole human story. Without going into these and other overarching theories of history in any more detail here, I would observe that in all these questions the appetite is greater than the sustenance provided. We really should like to know how history is actually articulated, what are the driving forces, what it all adds up to finally.[27] But most people (Marxists again excepted) who have read these massive works hopeful of answers to these vital questions have come away still unsatisfied.

It would seem that the fundamental problem here, too, is a dilemma. Philosophers of history are rejected or neglected by almost all historians on the grounds that they *are* philosophers; that is, they are experts in ideas. If they are not historians, their comparative ignorance of (so-called) historical facts (historians claim) vitiates much of their argument. If, on the other hand, they *are* historians they are attacked for their ideas – as, for example, Toynbee was attacked by the Dutch historian, Pieter Geyl.[28] Historians argue further that before one can speculate about the whole of human history one should know it. However, most of it is and must be for ever unknown, and, even if one confines oneself to that small part of the past which is known, there is far more to be mastered than any one human mind can grasp. This also assumes that knowing history is a simple, positivistic business of 'knowing facts'. As I show later, this is far from being the case. One can usually recognize good historians not by their precise knowledge (like the dates of battles or the clauses of constitutional documents) as by their imprecise knowledge; they know the limits of possibility. They may not know exactly what a historical agent did on a given occasion, but (unlike non-experts) they know within closely defined limits what that agent could not have done. Beyond this, good historians (like experts in other fields) have a 'feel' for their subject and can make inspired guesses, without being able to state explicitly how they know. Of course, experts are sometimes wrong, but not nearly so often or so badly as amateurs. Philosophers of history commonly lack not only a knowledge of the facts but also, and perhaps more gravely, historians' implicit understanding of historical processes. So the sort of rational structures of history offered by Hegel, Marx or even Toynbee may not be of use to practising historians.

On the other hand, one must apply some sort of intellectual patterning to a chaos, or it never becomes a cosmos. Unless facts, perceptions and the mass of evidence are ordered in some way, they remain unintelligible. This has been a commonplace of philosophy and science since the ancient Greeks. So how do we order the chaos of history? History is often charged with lacking a firm, theoretical structure – without which, it is suggested, it can hardly

---

[27] I give these points some further consideration in the next chapter.
[28] See Pieter Geyl, *Debates with Historians* (Fontana/Collins, 1962).

be considered an intellectually respectable discipline. But equally no attempt to give such a structure to history (Marxism once again excepted) is likely to be granted any intellectual respectability among historians. That is the dilemma. Non-historians argue that without a firm theoretical structure history lacks intellectual respectability; historians claim that with any such structure so far on offer (Marxism partially excepted) history ceases to be history and becomes metaphysics or sociology.

5   The Many Uses of Structure in History

As with many dilemmas the difficulty decreases if the alternatives are not posed so starkly. In practice, as I have pointed out, history has many structures, which cope adequately with the small-scale, immediate problem of ordering facts, although they are less successful in dealing with the larger-scale questions of what concepts, methods, theories and logical structures may be valid and acceptable throughout the whole discipline. It is easier to achieve conceptual and methodological uniformity in a discipline where the important entities (like gravity or electricity) underlie the observable phenomena than in one like history where what is significant is the phenomena that are concrete, apparent and perceptible to all. Whether or not this is true, history has many structures, rather than a single one, for other reasons, including the almost limitless range of the subject matter (almost everything that has occurred in the past is potential material for the historian) and the ease with which what passes for history can be written. In addition, since historical events are never present for examination, the 'facts' must always be inferred rather than directly apprehended, yet (by contrast with the physical sciences) everyone believes he or she is capable of such inferences. Moreover, as Gibbon remarked, 'history is the most popular species of writing, since it can adapt itself to the highest or lowest capacity.'[29] Finally, the word 'history' has several distinct, if connected, meanings.

I do not intend to argue that history should be forced under one structure, or even to urge that the number of structures should be reduced. My aim is to identify the many structures that do exist in history, to show that they are relevant to the historian, and to suggest how they may themselves be seen to form one comprehensive structure. I offer no master theory but rather a kind of map of the whole terrain of history, in order to remind workers in one field that other fields exist alongside theirs, and to indicate the way to and from them.

First, as I explained in section 3, any form of knowledge needs some sort

[29] Gibbon's *Autobiography*, p. 144.

of structure before the mind can make much sense of it. Second, history as a discipline consists largely of propositional knowledge, which implies a complex structure involving both language and society.[30] Third, historical thinking rests neither on a priori judgements (as in mathematics) nor on empirical observations (as in natural history) but, as in science, on judgements that, though *sui generis*, are seen to be more or less reliable. (Of course, the reliability of any particular judgement is never a closed question in either history or science.) However, in the natural sciences such judgements generally rest on observation, experiment and theory. It is a peculiarity of history that both observation and experiments are, by the very nature of the subject, out of the question, and that theory is either non-existent or, at best, not acceptable to most Western historians.

On what, then, do historical judgements rest? Briefly, they rest upon historical evidence as interpreted by human understanding of human experience. Human experience takes place almost entirely in a social context, much of which consists of language, and the rest of which is *described* (or misdescribed) by language. Further, most of the insight that one age brings to the understanding of another is mediated by language. Our historical knowledge is based largely, if not entirely, upon written documents, and even some of the non-written evidence (tapes, films recordings, memory) is still expressed wholly or partly in language. It is not surprising that hermeneutics plays an increasingly important role in the discipline of history – a role that goes back to the work of Wilhelm Dilthey (1883–1911), if not to Giambattista Vico (1668–1744).

Structures, then, occur at many levels. When a historian who is compiling an account of the past evaluates and selects the evidence to be used, not only the reliability but also the importance of that evidence must be assessed. The historian should have a mental picture of the society and of how the historical agents themselves saw it, some notion of the nature and causes of the changes in that society, and, finally, some idea of the form the account will take. He or she will probably be intending to publish the results, and will try to present the account in a literary form that meets the expectations of, and is likely to please, his or her readers. A good deal of critical attention is sometimes given to the literary aspect of historiography,[31] because the message has to be conveyed by the historian to other people, whose understanding of history, especially when filtered via the popular press, school memories or barroom gossip, is likely to have its own, very different shape. Yet it is this public understanding, not that of the historian, that in turn shapes the political and economic events that make history.

[30] See my 'Knowledge as structure', sections IIIB and IVA.

[31] See, for example, Hayden White, *Metahistory*, and *Tropics of Discourse: essays in cultural criticism* (Johns Hopkins University Press, 1978), or R. H. Canary and H. Kozicki (eds), *The Writing of History: literary form and historical understanding* (University of Wisconsin Press, 1978).

Each stage in the process I have just sketched requires a definite structure, since the mind can think about only one thing at a time (I speak very loosely here, without defining terms).[32] If the object is fairly simple, like a person or an event, the thought can be concrete. But if the object is fairly complex, like a constitution or a symphony or a battle, then the mind has to pass over the details and concentrate on the main features that give it shape. These features, of course, are not very different from the *Oxford English Dictionary*'s definition of structure quoted earlier: 'The mutual relation of the constituent parts or elements of a whole as determining its peculiar nature or character.' And so I proceed to a proposed structuring of the structures of history.

[32] More precisely, the mind is said to be able to deal with a maximum of eight concepts at a time, which is few enough. See C. H. Waddington, *Tools for Thought* (Jonathan Cape, 1977), p. 32.

2

The Events of the Past,
or the Historical Field

It was remarked in the Prologue that history has many small-scale structures, but yet lacks one single structure that comprehends the whole. I suggested there a schema of six stages which may have the merits of being clear, logical and reasonably close to the facts. In the succeeding chapters I propose to describe each of these stages in turn, with the connections between them.[1] One may then judge whether this proposed schema can be one way of meeting the requirements for such a comprehensive structure of history.

1 Identifying the Field

I shall begin with the subject matter of history, the events of the past. This is stage 1 in my schema. The 'historical field' may be defined as that which contains all historical occurrences. Another way of looking at is to say that it contains all human life in the temporal mode, that is, as extended through time. There is an inescapable ambiguity in this concept of historical field. Does it contain all occurrences or is it constituted by them? It is analogous to the familiar problem of time: does time exist independently of everything that happens in time? Both are a matter of debate; neither need delay us here.

There are three preliminary points to be made, however. First, this book is based on the assumption that there was a real past for historians to study – a past that existed quite independently of our knowledge of it. Like a distant galaxy, it remains beyond our reach but not beyond the possibility of our knowing it better. To suppose that what is present, either spatially or temporally, is more real than what is remote seems mere parochialism.

Second, I wish to emphasize the distinction between this real past and whatever is thought, said or written about it. The word 'history', which can be used for either, is therefore sometimes ambiguous, though usually the

---

[1] See the Contents list, p. v.

context makes clear which meaning is intended. If necessary I shall adopt the convention of writing 'history$_1$' for the former (*res gestae*) or 'history$_2$' for the latter (*historia rerum gestarum*).

The third point concerns the historical field and the past. For most purposes these can be taken as the same, but strictly they are not, for the following reasons.

1 Much of the past antedates human existence on earth.
2 Many past events are natural not human, and enter history only if they affect men and women – like the eruption of Vesuvius in AD 69.
3 Even many human occurrences remain unreported and forgotten, and so (probably but not certainly) vanish from human knowledge.

The dilemma of historians is that they want to see the past 'as it actually was', but can see it only through the medium of their own and other people's ideas: 'The central problems of a historical methodology or epistemology hinge upon the fact that an objective knowledge of the past can only be obtained through the subjective experience of the scholar'.[2] It may help if we try to see the past as a series of presents; for this is how it was actually experienced, each present with its own past and its own future. These terms (past, present, future) are not chronologically fixed but relate to a moment of consciousness, a moment that paradoxically seems to stand outside the flow of temporal succession. Hence

> — history is a pattern
> Of timeless moments.[3]

The future has a place in our hopes, fears and plans; the past has a place in art, religion, tradition and history. But only in the present do we experience and act. Thus if we are to understand the experiences and actions of a given moment in the past we must invest that moment with all the immediacy, ignorance and urgency of the present. For the present, however vivid, is often more perplexing, yet exigent: we have to do something. Like the generals in *War and Peace*, we act in ignorance not only of the future but also largely of what is happening now. An obvious but neglected truth about the past is that people acted with so little knowledge, and missed so many opportunities because they did not know all the choices they had. Now the matter is settled; it is the course of history. Like the owl of Minerva which 'spreads its wings only with the falling of the dusk', historical knowledge comes too late.[4]

[2] Hajo Holborn, *History and the Humanities* (Doubleday, 1972), p. 79.
[3] T. S. Eliot, 'Little Gidding', *Four Quartets* (Faber, 1944), p. 43.
[4] *Hegel's Philosophy of Right*, trans. T. M. Knox, (Clarendon Press, 1952), p. 13. Hegel is discussing philosophy, but his point applies equally to history.

2   The Range of the Historical Field

How far does this historical field extend? Spatially it covers the whole surface of the earth, with certain modifications. First, during mankind's existence on earth the habitable surface has changed in two ways: partly because areas of land have risen above the sea (the Nile Delta) or sunk below it (Thera); but more significantly because climatic changes or technological advances have rendered large tracts less habitable (the Sahara and Sahel) or more so (Siberia). Secondly, historical activity has extended over and under the sea, which covers three-quarters of the earth. Seafaring is at least 10,000 years old, but purposeful ocean travel hardly existed before Columbus, only five centuries ago. In this century we have also begun to utilize the sea-bed – for example, with oil wells and pearl- and fish-farming. Thirdly, Montgolfier and the Wright brothers extended the range of human activity (and hence of history) into the air, and in the second half of the twentieth century Yuri Gagarin and Neil Armstrong were pioneers of a much greater extension into space and on to the surface of other worlds. Nevertheless, most human lives have been lived in comparatively restricted areas.

With regard to the temporal range of the historical field, according to the common assumption that 'history' means 'written history', history begins with the invention of writing in Sumeria and Egypt in the late fourth millennium BC. Another criterion of history – the existence of distinguishable individuals – gives us a similar date. Probably the first man we can name was Nar-mer, the king of Upper and Lower Egypt shortly before 3000 BC.[5]

There are, however, several objections to this conventional view. Such a recent starting date for history excludes some of the most notable and characteristically human attainments; fire, religion, art, language, self-consciousness, farming, seafaring, pottery, metallurgy, war, dance, song and social organization were already part of the inheritance of these early civilizations. Admittedly we do not know the individuals responsible, but this seems to matter less now that so much history is based on statistics rather than biographies.

Another objection is that the use of writing spread very slowly over the earth, and has been only recently acquired by some peoples. The distribution of 'history' thus becomes very uneven, and there are good reasons why not only the literate should be included in history. From a political point of view, as peoples emerge into self-conscious nationhood they demand a history;

---

[5] Note the title of one book, Samuel N. Kramer, *History Begins at Sumer: thirty-nine firsts in man's recorded history* (University of Pennsylvania Press, 1981). See also Cyril Aldred, *Egypt to the End of the Old Kingdom* (Thames and Hudson, 1965), pp. 43–8; Alan Gardiner, *Egypt of the Pharaohs* (Oxford University Press, 1961), p. 404.

what Palacky or Mickiewicz did for Czechs or Poles in the last century is being done in Asia and Africa today. In addition, as I have mentioned, many historians are concerned more with groups or classes of people than with individuals; David Landes's *The Unbound Prometheus* (1969) or Marc Bloch's *French Rural History* (1931) mention hardly any individuals, and this trend continues. Further, with changes in methodology, many historians now make greater use of unwritten evidence, such as religious, artistic, archaeological, linguistic or geographical material.[6] Above all, great advances have been made in oral history.[7]

The strongest objection to holding that history began with writing is, however, that by doing so we limit the historical field by a factor (that is, writing) of our knowledge of that field, not by an element of the field itself. This is to confuse history-as-account with history-as-event. Unless we hold a strictly idealist philosophy of history, like Hegel's, there is no reason to confuse history$_2$ with history$_1$. If, as I have argued, the events of the past occurred quite independently of our knowledge of them, then the fifth millennium BC was as real as the fourth or the third, whether or not we decide that history begins with King Nar-mer in the late fourth. We may arbitrarily impose limits on what we call the 'historical field', but the field itself is neither a creation of our minds nor subject to our wills.

Finally, time and space not only draw the boundaries but also limit the events in the historical field. For most of history the vast majority of men and women lived close to where they were born. If one watches a child learning to walk, one can see how the conquest of even a small space is bought at the expense of time, energy and skill. This is true of all travel. Such limitations have had a profound effect on war, government and trade. For example, the administration of Louis XIV's France (that is, the time for correspondence between centre and periphery) took a matter of weeks, and that of the Spanish Empire took months or even years. Communication is a central theme of Braudel's study of the Mediterranean and the Chaunus' work on Seville and the Atlantic.[8] Time and space are the inescapable dimensions of human life, and hence of history. Time is the harsher; once lost it can never (unlike space) be recovered. The whole enterprise of historiography, from Egyptian king-lists and Hittite chronicles onwards, is in conflict with time. Trying to push open a little the doors that time has slammed behind us, historians seek 'le temps perdu'.

---

[6] Cf. the well-known pronouncement of the age of historical positivism, 'History is only the utilisation of documents': C. V. Langlois and C. Seignobos, *Introduction to the Study of History* (Duckworth, 1898), p. 316.

[7] See chapter 4, section 3.

[8] Fernand Braudel, *La Méditerranée et le monde méditerranéen à l'époque de Philippe II* (Armand Colin, 1949), 2nd rev. edn (1966); Pierre and Huguette Chaunu, *Séville et l'Atlantique de 1504 à 1650* (Armand Colin/SEVPEN, 1959).

3 The Constituent Elements of the Historical Field

Having identified the historical field and suggested what its limits may be, I now turn to its possible structure. In any complex object one may distinguish the whole, its parts, and the characteristic relationship between them.[9] In this case, where things are not static, but where actions are performed and events occur, there is a fourth element – the driving forces of change. I shall begin with the constituent elements of the historical field.

What men and women do and suffer, make up the events of history. And these events, or rather a select few of them, 'make history', as we say. They 'make history' either in their own right or in the imagination of a historian, either as part of history$_1$ or as part of history$_2$. Natural events (earthquakes, tidal waves) form part of history in so far as they affect mankind; so does the knowledge of natural events (the extinction of the dinosaurs, the explosion of a distant star), even if the events themselves are not part of history. But everything else that affects mankind flows from human actions.

A fully rational human action may be divided into the object or the aim, the assessment of the relevant situation, the choice of means, and the drive or motive to act; old-fashioned psychology used to refer to corresponding faculties – evaluative, cognitive and conative. A modern psychologist's view of assessment is that 'all, or at least most, of what are termed (rather indiscriminately) affects, feelings, and emotions are phases of an individual's intuitive appraisals either of his own organismic states and urges to act or of the succession of environmental situations in which he finds himself.'[10] There is also a social dimension, for an action has a meaning in its appropriate context (as described later in this section). Although each feature of human action is of interest to the historian in attempting to understand why things happened as they did, perhaps the cognitive aspect offers most scope. Aims are not always achieved; why they are frustrated is also important.

No one, of course, acts alone; and many actions that make up history are seen as the deeds of various collectivities – especially governments – rather than of individuals. Most atrocities have arisen from a failure to distinguish between the man or woman of flesh and blood and the race, class, party, religion or nation to which he or she is held to belong.

Are such collectivities also elements of the historical field? Since most historians write as if they are, it may be useful here to adopt a sociologist's distinction between groups and quasi-groups:

[9] See chapter 1, section 3.
[10] John Bowlby, *Attachment and Loss* (Penguin, 1971), vol. 1: *Attachment*, p. 138.

a social group has at least a rudimentary structure and organization (including rules, rituals, etc.), and a psychological basis in the consciousness of its members. . . . A quasi-group, on the other hand, is an aggregate which lacks structure or organization, and whose members may be unaware, or less aware, of the existence of the grouping.[11]

On this basis, I should be inclined to consider that groups (families, trade unions, nation-states) are elements in the field, but that quasi-groups (classes, races, age-, sex- or blood-groups) are not. The puzzle remains, however. For example, does E. P. Thompson's famous book describe the transition of a quasi-group to a group?[12] And did the English working class become a constitutive element of history at a definite point in the last century? Under the pressure of historical events, perhaps quasi-groups may become groups.

Another possible candidate for inclusion in the field is the 'state of affairs'. In his second book Herodotus interrupted his narrative to describe Egypt, and Gibbon began with two chapters of description (the Roman Empire in the second century AD). The state of affairs may cover many years (as in these cases) or only a few seconds, like the scene in Dallas where John F. Kennedy was shot. The historian's purpose is usually to paint the background against which the events occurred. But in this chapter we are concerned with history, not historiography. Was the state of affairs really there? How long did it last? How far did it extend?

When the historian paints with a broad brush, covering a number of years in one description, this obviously creates an impression rather than an exact representation, for things do not stay the same over a long period. Just as any event may be years long (like the fall of the Roman Empire or the opening up of the American West) yet may be infinitely divided into smaller and smaller sub-events down to a second's duration like an assassin's gun shot, so may a state of affairs be subdivided.[13] Do events really happen, or is there only an unceasing flow of subatomic energy, like the river of Heraclitus? And do things ever stand still long enough to be described as states of affairs? Whether or not events and states are mere creations of the historian's mind, none the less something was there.

What was there relates to the historical agent's assessment of the situation before the action ('Perdidos' was the curt but accurate summary made by the Spanish admiral, who could clearly see the result before Nelson's attack

[11] T. B. Bottomore, *Sociology: a guide to problems and literature*, rev. edn (Allen and Unwin, 1971), p. 99.
[12] E. P. Thompson, *The Making of the English Working Class* (Gollancz, 1963).
[13] For the subdivision of events, see P. Munz, *The Shapes of Time: a new look at the philosophy of history* (Wesleyan University Press, 1977), pp. 26ff. For an attempt to define 'event', see chapter 3, section 4.

at Trafalgar). However, the situation not only shows the agent what can or cannot be done, but also provides the context that gives meaning to the action. (A signature may draw cash from a bank or send a queen to the scaffold.) Is the historian's assessment of the situation the same as the agent's? If not, should it be? If again not, then why not?

Just as the agents may not know they are members of a quasi-group, so they may act in all ignorance that they are part of a trend (declining feudalism) or a movement (the Renaissance). How far can states of affairs be regarded as real elements of the historical field? Should historians describe what they know was there, or should they confine themselves to what the historical agents knew or believed was there and in terms of which they acted? Either attitude comes perilously close to Berkeley's dictum *esse est percipi* – to be is to be perceived. However, the state of affairs is often the context that gives meaning to the action, depending on the extent and duration of that state. As the spatial and temporal dimensions change, so in some cases does the meaning. The shot of Gavrilo Princip on 28 June 1914 alters in its meaning as the dimensions expand spatially from Sarajevo to the rest of Europe and temporally from one day to five years. (The Versailles Treaty was signed on 28 June 1919.) Was its meaning what Princip intended, or what the Austrians thought, or what historians now believe?

Can we now classify the elements of the historical field? To judge by what historians write about, the field contains many elements, often confused and overlapping. They write about men and women, singly and in groups, about institutions (the US presidency), events (the First World War), movements and trends (the Industrial Revolution), ideas and systems of ideas (the sciences), informal sets of beliefs and habits (cultures), art and technology. Can we identify historical particulars to correspond to such titles as 'The Second World War', 'Griff nach der Weltmacht', 'Religion and the Decline of Magic', 'The Frontier in American History'?

I suggest that a historical particular – human or non-human – can be identified by three criteria. First, it has to be named and recognized ('recognition' is 're-cognition', knowing it again). Second, it has to be limited, so that one knows where it stops. Third, it must retain an identity throughout the changes of its existence.

At first sight, there seems little problem with men and women, who clearly satisfy these criteria. But work with prosopography, genealogies and family reconstitution reveals how easily one person can be confused with another of the same name. When names are largely lacking, historians study groups – Romans or peasants. But who was 'Captain Swing'? What was 'magic' or 'civilization'? As to the second requirement (knowing the limits), again it is simple with a man or woman, but what of a people (the Germans), a class (the petty bourgeois) or a war?[14] As for the third, in what sense was the French Revolution in 1794 the same movement as in 1789, or the US presidency in the late eighteenth century the same as in the twentieth? What of artefacts? Material objects – fields, churches, ships – have a place in history, but their importance is secondary to that of the people who built and used them. Other artefacts may be partly material, partly ideal (like a university), or wholly ideal (like a system of law, a religion or a poem). Can we determine their identity, limits and duration?[15]

One way of identifying the elements of the historical field is to seek to discover what the agents (who were indisputably there) saw around them. This would eliminate concepts imposed by later generations like 'peasantry' or 'Renaissance' or 'viral infections', but would raise other problems about such things as demons or phlogiston, in which earlier generations believed but later ones do not. Historical particulars, once identified can be classified according to whether they are dynamic or static. Dynamic particulars can be classified as (1) natural happenings that affect human life; (2) human actions, individual and collective, with their intended and unintended results; (3) the combination of happenings and actions that we call events (in the short term) and trends or movements (in the longer term). Static elements are then classified into (1) the natural environment; (2) human beings, singly and in groups; (3) human artefacts, both physical and mental. The two modes of classification seem unavoidable in a discipline that deals with both change and continuity.

A last question to be asked is whether there are varying degrees of reality among these constituent elements. Was, for example, Oliver Cromwell more real than militant Puritanism? If one conflates the two meanings of history, history becomes equivalent to what historians write, and the past acquires reality in so far as historians write about it. Geoffrey Elton robustly defends the reality of the past against those who 'think that history is what historians write, not what happened'. He asserts that the historian 'knows that what he is studying is real'.[16] But is everything that historians study equally real? Some write of the Great Depression of 1873–96, yet others deny its existence. One critical historian concludes: 'As regards the "Great Depression" itself, surely the major outcome of modern research has been to destroy once and for all the idea of the existence of such a period in any unified sense. . . .But this at least is clear: the sooner the "Great Depression" is banished from the literature, the better.'[17] The fact that writers often impose their concepts on the past (as the epithet 'Gothic' for architecture exemplifies) gives

[14] See, for example, John Lukacs, *The Last European War, September 1939 to December 1941* (Routledge and Kegan Paul, 1976).

[15] For further discussion of identity, see chapter 3, section 5.

[16] G. R. Elton, *The Practice of History* (Fontana, 1969), pp. 76, 112.

[17] See S. B. Saul, *The Myth of the Great Depression, 1873–1896* (Macmillan, 1972), pp. 54–5.

rise to the question whether some historical subjects ever really existed.

If, on the other hand, history is what historians write, then all elements of the historical field are equally real, since the real minds of historians create them. It seems, on the simple Eltonian view, that some of the things that historians write about did occur, and others did not. In the latter case, historians were wrong. If they disagree (as they often do) they cannot all be right. But on the alternative thesis they *could* all be right – though it is not easy to see what 'right' would now mean. I prefer to think that what they study is real, but that there are degrees of reality. This opens up metaphysical questions that cannot, for reasons of space, be explored here.

4 Articulations and Structures of the Field

I now consider whether the historical field is structured by any determinate form of relationships between its constituent elements. By introducing the words 'articulation' and 'structure' I make an analogy with the human body. Its structure is the bony skeleton and musculature, the nervous and circulatory systems, and so on. Its articulation is a matter of how the parts move in relation to each other. Every joint has both a certain freedom and a certain limitation of movement; the body is neither flexible like rubber nor rigid like cast iron. Is history structured and articulated in any comparable way?

I propose to ask four question: (1) whether there are spatial structures and articulations of history, and (2) whether there are temporal ones; (3) what have been the views of historical agents about these; and (4) whether an objective articulation can be discerned in the flow of events.

1 Particular historical events have occurred in different spatial locations, depending largely on their climate, vegetation and fertility. That these have not remained unchanged over the centuries is demonstrated by the term 'the Fertile Crescent'. But settlement has not always been in the most fertile areas. For several thousand years early settlers in Britain preferred the thin and exposed uplands to the rich and sheltered valleys. Changes in method (for example, ploughing), transport (the wagon, the locomotive) and production of wealth (ironworks, ports) have altered the locations, and hence the spatial structures of history, which are both natural and artificial.

2 With regard to the structure provided by time, certain regularities dominate human actions. The earth's rotation on its own axis and around the sun determines day and night and the seasons; the moon's effect on tides and the measurement of time in months is less important. Movements of geological time are, in general, too slow to articulate history. Climatic change, however, had and still has a profound influence on human affairs. Although

it has only recently become the subject of serious historical study, it has a significant effect upon food supply, reproductive rates of humans and animals, death and disease, and probably the optimism or pessimism of cultures.[18]

History is also possibly articulated by great disasters – the Flood, the Black Death, or even the First and Second World Wars. Finally, the basis of Western chronology is the birth of Christ, and if, as Christians believe, this was a divine event then a major chronological articulation of history is caused by God's direct intervention.

3 I now turn to historical agents' views on the apparently objective structures and articulations of space and time in history. It is a well-founded principle of the discipline of history that human actions may be determined as much by false beliefs as by facts, for we can only act on what we *believe* to be true, whether or not it is.

To some extent the more basic spatial articulations have always been recognized: Egyptians never tried to sail their boats on the desert, and Swiss farmers never tried to pasture cattle on a glacier. Yet the limitations of travel were often neither geographical nor technical. The first men who pushed beyond the Pillars of Hercules or circumnavigated Africa or explored the Atlantic were breaking mental as well as physical barriers. Even today our spatial orientations can be grossly distorted by egocentrism.[19] In order to understand fully the actions that make up history, we must grasp how men and women in the past perceived the spatial structure of the world.

It is much easier, one would suppose, to determine the spatial than the temporal shapes and limits of the world. Apart from the regularities already mentioned – the years, seasons, months and days – no natural measures of time are readily observable. Some could be calculated, like the Mayan 'Long Count' of over 5000 years, or the Greek 'Great Year' of some 35,000 years, the former being the basis of a calendar. Usually, however, for periods longer than a year, time has been structured on the basis of kings and dynasties – a method followed by historians from ancient Egypt to the present day, when we still speak of 'Tudor' or 'Victorian' England. We also speak of centuries and millennia – obviously arbitrary divisions, though we persist in characterizing them: 'the eighteenth century' conjures up a picture of wigs, flounced skirts and chamber music.

Sometimes a human event has been chosen as a basis for measuring the years – the first Olympiad, the founding of Rome, the Hijra of Mohammed. Even more arbitrarily, historical time has been divided into ages or epochs, as in the Book of Daniel or the writings of Joachim de Flora, or the divisions of 'ancient', 'medieval' and 'modern' history developed in

---

[18] See E. Le Roy Ladurie, *Times of Feast, Times of Famine* (Allen and Unwin, 1973) and *The Territory of the Historian* (Harvester Press, 1979), and the works cited therein.
[19] See Peter Gould and Rodney White, *Mental Maps* (Penguin, 1974).

the Renaissance.[20] There are, in fact, few natural and objective temporal structures and articulations, most having been made by people themselves in various ways. (Correlating chronologies is still a formidable task for the historian). Thus the framework of the historical field with which people view their actions is, even in respect of time and space, largely of their own devising. Again, it is important to know not only what was the actual structure relating to human actions, but what the agent believed was the structure.

4 The importance of belief is recognized by politicians. Hence in the Second World War the participants were told that they lived in 'their finest hour', or 'the Asian Co-Prosperity Sphere' or 'the Thousand-Year Reich'. This extends to the present the procedure that historians normally apply to the past – dividing it into eras of 'the Crusades', 'the Renaissance', 'Reconstruction', and so on. Yet it is hard to believe that the historical field really was articulated by such movements; first, because of obvious geographical limitations (Russia, for example, knew neither of the first two); second, because not everyone participated in them – perhaps women, children or the lower classes did not; third, because some divisions (like 'Enlightened Despotism', 'the Age of the Democratic Revolution' of R. R. Palmer or the 'Great Depression' of the late nineteenth century) have been disputed and may exist only 'in the eye of the beholder'.[21] Anyone who wishes to argue for genuine, objective divisions of history must establish that the phenomena were not invented by later historians, that 'history' can be restricted to certain classes or groups (for example, that there are 'unhistorical' nations, as Hegel said and Trevor-Roper implied[22]) and, third, that there can be several independent but contemporaneous historical fields.

Something like this was suggested in Toynbee's *A Study of History*, where his schema of the birth and decline of civilizations attempted the most sophisticated articulation of history so far. If Toynbee ultimately failed, as

[20] For Joachim (1145–1202), see Dante, *Paradiso*, xii, 139–41. The traditional view of his three ages or dispensations is modified in Marjorie Reeves, *The Influence of Prophecy in the Late Middle Ages: a study in Joachinism* (Clarendon Press, 1969) and her *Joachim of Fiore and the Prophetic Future* (SPCK Press, 1976). See also Norman Cohn, *The Pursuit of the Millenium* (Secker and Warburg, 1957), chapter 5.

[21] For the Great Depression, see Saul, *The Myth of the Great Depression*, quoted in section 3 above. For the Palmer thesis, see R. R. Palmer, *The Age of the Democratic Revolution: a political history of Europe and America, 1760–1800* 2 vols, (Princeton University Press, 1964), and Peter Amann (ed.), *The Eighteenth-Century Revolution: French or Western?* (Heath, 1963). For enlightened despotism, see M. S. Anderson, *Historians and Eighteenth-Century Europe, 1715–1789* (Clarendon Press, 1979). On the term 'enlightened despotism' Anderson writes: 'The nature of the reality it attempts to describe, its dimensions in space and time, perhaps even its very existence, have all been, and still are questioned by historians' (p. 119).

[22] See G. W. F. Hegel, *The Philosophy of History* (Dover Publications, 1956), pp. 61, 99; Hugh Trevor-Roper, *The Rise of Christian Europe* (Thames and Hudson, 1965), p. 9: 'the unrewarding gyrations of barbarous tribes'.

seems widely agreed – perhaps because the task of finding structure and articulation in history is inherently impossible, or perhaps merely because Toynbee (cleverer, maybe, than his predecessors) was not clever enough – is such an attempt none the less still possible?

5 Rest and Movement in the Historical Field

So far I have sought to identify the historical field, to determine its limits, and to examine its characteristic structure, first by discussing the constituent parts and how they are related. In this section I investigate the driving forces of history.

Perhaps the most characteristic attribute of history is change: as the ancient Greeks said, we live in a world of becoming, between being and not-being. We frequently use metaphors of motion – 'movements', 'forces' – to refer to a series of historical changes. But what sorts of series of changes are the concern of history? Change as a cycle (for example, the hours of the day or the seasons of the year) is distinct from change as a process, which moves steadily away from its beginning and does not return to it, like a life. Further, a series of changes each of which is independent of its predecessor, like the movements of the hands of a clock or a planet, can be distinguished from a series of changes each of which is a consequence of its predecessor, like the stages of a journey or of biological evolution. The examples of apparently independent change (the planet or the minute hand) are not independent of some external controlling force (gravitation or clockwork), yet a series of changes may conceivably be random, quite independent of both predecessor and external force.

Is the course of human life on earth a cycle or a process? The long pastoral tradition of European poetry from the Idylls of Theocritus to the first section of Eliot's 'East Coker' has idealized rural life as closely bound to the rhythm of the seasons. Country life, especially in the long aeons of prehistory, may have seemed just such an endless round, yet some changes were permanent (the working of metals or the domestication of animals), and an apparent cycle became more obviously a process. Human beings have never, perhaps, been so closely a part of nature as to avoid history altogether.

One view of the historical process of human life likens it to the life of an individual, and uses such metaphors as 'the childhood of the human race'. Even so normally hard-headed a thinker as Karl Marx adopted this device to escape the dilemma that, although in his theory art is dependent on the form of the economy, Greek art has appealed to all ages. He adduced the universal appeal of the child, and asked 'Why should the childhood of human society, where it had obtained its most beautiful development, not exert an eternal charm as an age that will never return?'[23] Such an argument is not valid; it is only a picturesque, if unhelpful, metaphor.

Another supposition is that the history of human life is analogous to the evolution of an organism. Certainly a long evolution, from fish to ape, is recapitulated by every child in the womb, but in the 50,000 years of the life of *Homo sapiens sapiens* only slight physiological change has occurred.

Nor can environmental factors account for human change. Since the last Ice Age, the earth's climate has swung through a series of long- and short-term variations, as the science of climatology increasingly reveals. But these waves do not correlate with the fairly steady growth of human intellectual and social development.

The word 'development' implies a series of directed rather than purely random changes. Non-repetitive and apparently undirected change is neither cycle nor process; it is like the unpredictable events of a picaresque novel, or the modifications of the Earth's surface after it began to cool some 5000 million years ago. So far, then, the most promising concept is that of a developmental process, on the analogy of a widening spiral, yet not without the occasional drop or dip as in the ascent of buzzards in a thermal.

This concept of development implies that the changes are connected and, moreover, have consistent direction. One does not have to observe history for long at one of its more 'intense' points, like a revolution or a war, to see that one significant occurrence leads rapidly to another. It is also clear that simultaneous changes of very different kinds affect one another; for example, changes in technology, in social attitudes, in economic theory, in women's dress, in the arts or in morals can occur together with obvious mutual influences. Thus there appear to be what could be crudely described as 'vertical' and 'horizontal' causal links.

To clarify the way in which events are linked, let us consider each of the three types of static elements of the historical field: nature, humanity and artefacts. The natural world undergoes natural changes, both cyclical and processive, the laws of which we believe we understand pretty well. Humanity is also subject to these changes – for example, in being nourished, getting a suntan or growing old. But human change is more often brought about by humanity itself. Some of these changes resemble those due to nature, like killing or curing; other changes operate in the human mode, like ruling or persuading. Human artefacts, both material and ideal, sometimes change through natural processes – for example, the dilapidation of a building through rain, wind and frost – but more often the changes result from human volition, as in the replanning of a city, or from human involuntary action, as in linguistic change. Finally, some changes in nature

---

[23] Introduction to the *Grundrisse*, in *Marx's Grundrisse*, ed. D. McLellan (Paladin, 1973), p. 56.

are due not to natural forces but to human action, like the extinction of the dodo or the destruction of tropical forests.

Natural sequences of change, explicable by the natural sciences, tend to follow fairly predictable lines – winds produce rain, seeds produce plants. But human activities are less predictable. People produce kinship systems, wheels, laws, muskets, symphonies, intercontinental missiles, and so on. The most plausible explanation for this important element of novelty in historical change can be found in what does not change; that is, the element of continuity.

For hundreds of millions of years, our animal ancestors went through a series of natural changes, both cyclical (birth, mating, death) and processive (evolution). Although there was clearly some element of novelty as vertebrates progressed from fishes to apes, such adaptation to environment does not account for the rapid innovations of human history. These came through the development of human language, especially through its capacity to symbolize, and hence to refer to, the not-self. Of course, the development of physical methods of recording thoughts, from hieroglyphics to computers, has powerfully reinforced this capacity. With symbolic language it became possible to communicate and to record facts, not merely (as with animals) warnings, threats and emotions. This ability to give knowledge an objective form, external to the knower, and hence capable of transmission, is crucial to human life and history. Indeed, historiography itself is one form of it. In almost all rational activities (but apparently not in emotional and volitional ones), we can start where our predecessors left off. As Newton said, we may be dwarfs but we stand on the shoulders of giants. Thus it is continuity (of ideas, language and knowledge) that has enabled the human race to bring about increasingly rapid series of changes. Continuity has made it possible for humanity to emerge into history from nature.

What, then, are the driving forces of historical change? All physical energy comes from a few sources: mostly the sun's energy, which nourishes vegetable and animal life and is stored in fossil fuels (coal and oil); partly from gravity; and an increasing amount from intra-atomic forces. If there were no forces other than physical energy, however, the universe would be steadily running down, according to the second law of thermodynamics. Yet so far every manifestation of life contradicts this universal tendency. Some thinkers have postulated a 'life force' which employs physical energies but is not their product. Most scientists deny this; and in any case such a 'life force' would not account for historical change. Something like the concept of volition might explain why a man or a woman should choose to do something rather than nothing. Of course, biological needs (the 'life force' again?) are the cause of some activities, but by no means all. Nor would the satisfaction of merely biological needs account for history, since they would have left us in a state of nature. All civilization, every culture, would seem to be a product of human volition and adaptation, as well as of physical energies. Finally, there is the possibility of spiritual energy. Religious experience in many different ages and cultures seems to have borne witness to a power that rules the universe yet can be found within the individual man or woman.

All this is very difficult. I may well be wrong or confused. Human culture in its infinite variety had been too long established when the curtain of history rose some 5000 years ago for us to understand its causes at all clearly. Yet it seems to me that if we are to account for historical change we have to ask what forces or energies bring it about.

Another issue is the reasons why change is directed in one way rather than another. Nature accounts for some choices, but most human activity results from human intentions, even if many intentions have fossilized into conventions or habits. However, the course of human affairs is often far from what any one individual or group intended. As Hegel puts it, history is 'the slaughter-bench at which the happiness of peoples, the wisdom of States, and the virtue of individuals have been victimized'.[24] Many religions and philosophical theories (of which the Bible or Marxism contain the most familiar) have tried to explain why historical change, apparently brought about by human intentions, has so often been what no one wished. Kant invoked Nature, Hegel the World-Spirit, Marx blind economic forces, de Tocqueville the drive to equality. According to de Tocqueville's view of the French Revolution, 'Chance played no part whatever in the outbreak of the Revolution; though it took the world by surprise, it was the inevitable outcome of a long period of gestation.'[25] Such deterministic language is not unknown in the present century, too, though now we talk of 'functions' and 'laws'.

One may wonder, however, whether any of the concepts invoked to account for these mystifying frustrations and disasters, these 'forces', 'spirits', 'gestations', 'functions', 'contradictions', and so on, are really energies capable of bringing about change and directing it towards an end, or whether they are metaphors, abstract notions, that we use so often as to mistake them for realities.

Is it possible to throw any further light on why historical change has followed the course it has? If we reject the notions of the last paragraph, we are left with the forces of nature and human volition, which seem inadequate. But have we not overlooked something between, something called 'human nature' which, though human rather than animal, lacks the clear rationality of a fully intentional action? It includes our hopes and fears, angers, longings, imaginings and creativities, roughly comprising most of

---

[24] See Hegel, *The Philosophy of History*, p. 21.
[25] Alexis de Tocqueville, *The Ancien Régime and the French Revolution* (Fontana/Collins, 1966), p. 51.

the subject matter of psychology. This area of human behaviour, in which the major part is often played by mental phenomena of which we are not conscious at the time, constitutes much of human action, and hence contributes to the sum of human history. Together with natural forces and human volitions, it imparts direction to the course of change. When several forces act together a physicist may calculate the result (or 'resultant'); but human affairs have a perverse logic of their own. Three forces going south-west, west and north-west will have a resultant in a vaguely westerly direction. But when there is a run on a bank, or when armaments accumulated to preserve the peace actually lead to war, then the result is the opposite of all the volitions; the resultant is, as it were, eastward.

Frequently we have been unable to foresee, or else to forestall, such disasters. But through experience, both in life and in history, we have learnt something of this perverse logic. Thus it may be unnecessary to postulate any unseen force guiding the course of history. These three sources of directed change – physical nature, human nature and rational intention – together with the logic of their interactions may well be enough to explain the processes of change in the historical field. We do not need hypothetical World Spirits or social contradictions; we just need more knowledge.

6 The Historical Field as a Whole

I now turn to the fourth component of a structured entity and consider the historical field as a whole. That it is a whole cannot be taken for granted. Even if it is made up of a number of processes, it does not follow that they form a unity. A unity is distinct from others (external unity), and its parts cohere in some way (internal unity). While the historical field is certainly distinct from the activities of other intelligent creatures, it is not distinct from its predecessor, the field of prehistory, for they overlap at many points. As to internal unity, it has, or appears to have, many divisions.

The subject matter of historiography has conventionally been divided into political history, economic history, religious history, and so on. Today there are two opposing tendencies. One tends towards further division, with existing fields being split up into smaller and smaller plots as specialization increases. The other tends towards a rejoining of the pieces, both by applying concepts and methods across several of the sub-disciplines, and by attempts to tackle the problems of a 'total' or 'global history' – an attempt on a very broad front to restore Maitland's 'seamless web' of history. Since this is a concern of historiography rather than of history-as-events, it belongs to later chapters.

Throughout historic times most men and women have lived within the confines of particular communities – cities, nations, states, empires – and their consciousness of community rarely extended beyond these limits. In so far as they thought about history – whether as chroniclers of history or as agents – they thought of the history of their community. Thus the great majority of works of history have been accounts of a people, a city, a state or an empire; rarely have historians attempted a history of the world. Limitations of knowledge and sympathy have usually kept historical interest, whether of writer or of reader, within much closer bounds. Even today, when both knowledge and interest are far greater and when world history is taught even to schoolchildren, few histories transcend national frontiers. Thus, although here again contemporary historiography differs from its predecessors, the greater part of the historical field arguably consists of a number of histories rather than one; that is, the historical field, at least before this century, was not a unity.

Nevertheless, one must not confuse the nature of history$_1$ with that of history$_2$. The real world of life and action has been divided not by historians but by geography and language. If trade, war, religion or curiosity have brought peoples together, distance and mutual incomprehension have kept them apart. Some separations have been so wide that it is difficult to believe that, even today, Tibet and Patagonia share the same history. On the other hand, although historians have usually separated them, India and Greece have experienced many mutual influences and hence could be said to have a common history.

Although it is therefore an open question whether there is only one 'seamless web' of human affairs stretching over a time-span of about 5000 years and over the whole of the earth, it is still widely assumed today that the historical field is a unity. If this assumption is correct, what sort of unity is it? Has it the oneness of a heap of sand, of a clock, of a mouse or of a man? Is it incremental, mechanical, organic or spiritual? The answer depends on our conclusions about the nature of its articulation and structure (see section 4 above), and about the sort of changes, with their causes, that take place in it (section 5).

Another consideration is whether each part is related differently or in the same way to the whole. In particular, some parts may be more important or fundamental to the whole than others. When dealing with epochs, peoples, regions or topics, historians concentrate on some members rather than others. Is this purely because of greater knowledge and greater interest (characteristics of the historian rather than of the history)? Or are some peoples really more important than others, as Hegel claimed in his theory of 'world-historical peoples'? And what of Ranke's belief that all ages are equally near to God? Is this no more than a historian's axiom or a piece of unworldly piety? The problems of the relationship of the parts to the whole have been explored most thoroughly by the historians of the French

Annales school, though usually they have not seen it quite in the terms that I have stated.[26]

It is the duty of every scholar to try to make sense of the data. This is especially incumbent upon the historian for much of his or her raw material – the events of the recent past – is widely available and challenges each of us. To this end, the historical field as a whole can be portrayed in two ways – by generalization about the many and by characterization of the one. Generalizations about the many are frequently and explicitly used by historians making pronouncements about peasants or Germans or Calvinists. More relevant here are their generalizations about human nature or society or language or war, with historians' implicit assumptions that we can follow their narratives about remote ages or exotic peoples because certain basic human qualities are much the same everywhere. Readers may well succeed in following the narrative – because they comprehend the thinking of the historian who composed it, rather than because they understand the strange people of whom it is told. Yet it is possible that there are certain truths equally applicable to elements in every part of the historical field: for example, that each man or woman had two parents, or that despotism generates resentment. (There is, of course, much more to be said on these lines.) More challenging, however, is the problem of how we may characterize the historical field considered as a whole. I propose six questions.

1 Has it any discernible shape, and is there any discernible pattern within that shape?
2 Has it any structure that may be rationally comprehended, or does it hang untidily together like old cobwebs in a cellar?
3 Since it is not static but consists of series of changes, have these changes any common direction, or any common meeting point if approaching by different routes?

The next three questions, unlike the first three, imply the existence of a mind or minds informing or surveying the whole; otherwise they make little sense.

4 Does the historical field as a whole exhibit any aim or purpose?
5 Does this field manifest any value or values?
6 Does it have any meaning as a whole, and, if so, is that meaning to be apprehended within the field?

Notoriously, it is easier to ask than to answer such questions. Among the obvious difficulties in doing so are the following considerations. First, no one individual can know all that has happened in the past. Second, it is impossible to characterize the whole of something that is not yet completed.

[26] Perhaps the best introduction to their ideas is Traian Stoianovich, *French Historical Method: the 'Annales' paradigm* (Cornell University Press, 1976).

For all we know, we may be still in the first act of a five-act drama. Third, if there is one answer to be given to a question that involves mind (like the last three above), in terms of what mind is it given? Fourth, how can historical creatures like ourselves stand outside history to talk about it at all? Are we not facing a problem similar to that of Archimedes, who said, 'Give me a lever and somewhere to stand, and I will move the world'?

Finally, any answer, if possible at all, would seem to be religious (in the broadest sense) because it relates to what is outside our phenomenal world – and hence, by definition, not perceptible. Yet any answer that makes sense to us must be perceptible *within* this world. More crudely, if the meaning of history is not to be found within history, how can we, being within history, grasp it?[27]

I have not attempted to answer these questions. I have not even explored them. I have only indicated what I believe is the logical place to ask them. With these questions I complete my survey of the four elements required by any structure of the historical field. Each of these elements must be established before anyone can claim to have discerned how that field is structured.

---

[27] I return briefly to the problem of meaning in chapter 12, section 3.

3

From Events to Evidence

Hitherto this book has been concerned with history$_1$, historical events. Now, and for most of the book I shall deal with history$_2$, history-as-account, returning in the last two chapters to the historical field.

1 Consequences

It is easy to say that everything now extant is a result of something in the past, but the statement needs to be analysed if it is to be of any use. First, the concepts 'consequence of' or 'result of' imply both temporal succession and causation. That the present comes after the past is no news, but that the present is caused by the past is strictly incapable of proof. It is rather an assumption made in our thinking, even if not necessarily in our perception, as Kant held. As a modern philosopher of science put it, 'Causes certainly are connected with effects; but this is because our theories connect them, not because the world is held together by cosmic glue.'[1]

It is possible to imagine that the universe, or rather our perception of it, is a series of successive but independent states. (The frames of a film are in independent succession, for no one frame causes another.) In any case, the practical problem is not whether the past caused the present, but (if we accept that it did) which bit of the past caused which bit of the present. If the structural lines of causation can be determined, one sort of thing can be relied upon to cause another sort of thing, thus enabling us to see where we are and how we may proceed. Over the centuries such attempts have contributed to produce science and technology, as well as some parts of religion, philosophy and history. This leads on to the problem of counter-factuals.[2]

The concept 'consequence of' also implies change. To be sure, the state of the Great Wall of China today is, in some respects, a consequence

[1] N. R. Hanson, *Patterns of Discovery: an enquiry into the conceptual foundations of science* (Cambridge University Press, 1972), p. 64.
[2] See chapter 5, section 2; chapter 6, section 4.

of its state yesterday, but since no perceptible change occurred this is not mentioned.

The historical field, as we have seen, contained natural happenings (earthquakes) and human behaviour and actions (loving, building, fighting), which have blended together into the sort of complex entities that historians variously designate as events, states of affairs, trends, movements, and so on. These terms imply change ('events' and 'movements') or continuity ('states of affairs' and 'trends'). I need not here be more specific – not merely because change and continuity, like causation, are assumptions rather than empirical observations, but more cogently because from where we stand in the present we cannot immediately discern one or the other. Whether or not a present object has changed cannot be discovered simply by looking at it. For this, some notion of the past is required. It is this idea that there was a past – moreover, one that was in some respects different from the present – which I shall now examine. In doing so I shall show that the Kantian category of identity is more appropriate than that of causality. Although identity raises many problems, it is more amenable as well as more relevant than causality. It is to questions of sameness and difference, and their relation to past and present, that I now turn.

2   What Comes Through

The most obvious feature of the past is that it requires that some things should have come through to us in the present from former times. It is these, whether the bones of a dinosaur or yesterday's newspaper, that provide the only material evidence of anything that has gone before. These 'things that have come through' may be discussed under four categories: natural, intentional, communicative and processive.

(1) Natural evidence needs little explanation. The earth is old and its rocks contain all that we know of the story of life from pre-Cambrian protozoa to the earliest hominids of the Olduvai Gorge. Simply to visit a place with historic associations – the Mont Ventoux, climbed by Petrarch, beginning, as some say, the Renaissance; or the field of Waterloo – can be very moving. On the Capitol in Rome, said Gibbon, 'the idea of writing the decline and fall of the city first started to my mind'; Dr Johnson, visiting Iona, declared: 'That man is little to be envied, whose patriotism would not gain force upon the plain of Marathon, or whose piety would not grow warmer among the ruins of Iona.'[3] Aside from antiquarianism, though, the modern discipline

[3] Edward Gibbon, *Autobiography*, Everyman edn (Dent, 1911), p. 124; James Boswell, *Journal of a Tour to the Hebrides with Samuel Johnson LLD* (Nelson, n.d.), pp. 298–9, entry of 19 October.

of historical geography is based on a study of past landscapes and how man has altered them. Indeed, many natural objects bear important traces of the past.

(2) Alterations of natural objects lead to the second category – what I have called 'intentional'. When nature and its products have been worked on by humans for their own purposes, they become artefacts. A tilled field, a cleared forest, a bridged river, a goose-quill pen, a house, a bottle of wine or a laser are all artefacts whose continuance into a later age bears witness of the earlier times from which they came. Particularly interesting are artefacts that reveal changes in customary behaviour. Sometimes old tools, houses, furniture, pens, bicycles, and so on, appear strange or inadequate to present needs, and this makes us realize that things were once rather different. When visitors are shown round an English 'stately home', they are often less interested in the elegant drawing- and dining-rooms than in the kitchens, sculleries and stables exhibiting the implements used by servants in their daily work. Such everyday utensils bring home to us most vividly the difference between past and present.

(3) One particular class of artefacts forms the basis of almost all our knowledge of history. I have made this a category of its own – 'communicative', because the intention embodied in these objects is to convey some sort of message, emotional or rational. They include songs, cave and rock paintings, statues and pictures in churches and temples, and many other (though not all) forms of art. Most 'communicative' artefacts, however, bear some sort of writing – from Sumerian cuneiforms to the miles of government papers that load the shelves and racks of our record offices, and now including electronic tapes, floppy disks and microchips. Historians no longer believe (as was the fashion at the turn of the century) that history must be based entirely on documents, but these still form by far the greater part of source material, as a glance at the sources listed in any scholarly book confirms.

In these communicative objects, however, there is a distinction between those whose message was intended for contemporaries or near-contemporaries only, and those intended for the eyes of future generations. Most writing is aimed at communicating immediately; but some people write even their letters and diaries with a view to their future reputation. Inscriptions on stone or metal were usually designed for posterity. Most are humble tombstones, but one also thinks of the young Lieutenant Rawlinson laying the foundations of Assyriology as he climbed the Rock of Behistun in 1835, or the Emperor Asoka, whose pillars and rocks proclaimed his justice and humanity throughout India.[4] In the late seventeenth and eighteenth

[4] See Seton Lloyd, *Foundations in the Dust: a story of Mesopotamian exploration* (Penguin, 1955), p. 93; A. L. Basham, *The Wonder that was India* 3rd edn (Sidgwick and Jackson, 1967), pp. 53–5.

centuries the study of non-literary evidence (coins, medals, inscriptions) played
a critical part in the developing science of history.[5] Theodor Mommsen's
massive labours to produce the *Corpus Inscriptionum Latinarum* were a landmark
in Roman history.[6] With an eye to fame, Louis XIV established a special
Academy of Inscriptions in 1663; his anger at a Dutch medal of 1668 was
allegedly one of the causes of the Franco-Dutch war of 1672–8.[7] It is not
only inscriptions but books that aim to shape future reputations. The
memoirs of politicians and generals, from Richelieu and Bismarck to
Goebbels and Churchill, Eisenhower and Patton, all bear witness to this.
Historians are rightly more cautious in using material that is deliberately
aimed at them; they prefer the direct and unsophisticated letter.

(4) The fourth category, the 'processive', presents more difficulties. In
many cases, however, the revealing continuity that leads from the past to
the present is enshrined in a process rather than an object. If we understand
the process we can infer the earlier stage in the past from the later stage
present to us. For example, natural processes explain the growth of crops
or the fall of rain, and social processes account for the inheritance of a title,
or education; a familiarity with Greek and Latin literature indicates an
old-fashioned schooling. Such deduction is by no means infallible, but an
understanding of such processes helps historians to make their constructions
from objects of the past.[8]

3 Awareness of Difference

So far I have considered things that survive from the past and thus, by their
continuity, give us evidence of the past. Yet these alone would not tell
us that there was a past. Animals and very young children can be well
acquainted with old objects without regarding them as being other than
contemporary. What gives us an idea of 'pastness'? A. J. Ayer says it is
merely our experience of temporal succession.[9] Any answer requires a
consideration of the immaterial.

The most important element, I think, is memory. Although primitive
peoples, like the very young and very old, often confuse memories and
dreams, most of us believe that we can usually distinguish them. The

[5] See A. Momigliano, 'Ancient history and the antiquarian', in *Studies in Historiography*
(Weidenfeld and Nicolson, 1969), p. 16.
[6] See U. von Wilamowitz-Moellendorf, *History of Classical Scholarship*, ed. H. Lloyd-Jones
(Duckworth, 1982), pp. 156–8.
[7] See P. Goubert, *Louis XIV and Twenty Million Frenchmen* (Allen Lane, 1970), p. 112; also
P. Geyl, *The Netherlands in the Seventeenth Century*, part II, *1648–1715* (Ernest Benn, 1964), p. 100.
[8] See chapter 1, section 4; chapter 4, sections 1 and 3.3.
[9] See *The Problem of Knowledge* (Penguin, 1956), p. 152.

importance of memory is that it gives a knowledge of when things were different; yet there is at least one factor, one's own self, that links the strange past to the familiar present. Hence there is an awareness of change; and change always implies the continuity of something.

What we may call 'hearsay' also contributes to our sense of the past. Hearsay consists of what people say about the past, based on memory, imagination, reading or more hearsay. Most children listen with curiosity to parents and, more especially, grandparents relating tales of 'When I was a girl (or boy)'. Much in this line are the more public forms of myth, legends and folklore. In all these cases, the truth is hardly at issue. What strikes our imagination and makes the tales memorable is the contrast between the observable present and the described world of the past.

Folklore leads on to other components of our cultural environment, including customs, morals, habits, religious rituals and other 'forms of life'. The richest part of our cultural environment is our native language.[10] It is commonly found that some customary forms, though still in use, do not quite square with present reality. Certain words and phrases may appear outmoded; perhaps certain moral attitudes or fashions in clothes seem out of date. When we perceive that forms of life we have inherited or grown up with do not quite fit current reality, we are made aware of the past and how different it was.

4   What does not Survive

I have discussed the things that have survived from the past because they furnish our only evidence, not formally that there was a past, but substantially of what the past was like. Logically, I should also look at the sort of things that do *not* survive.

First, men and women do not survive, except most of those born in the past hundred years or so.

Secondly, events do not survive. Life is an unbroken stream of happenings, none so brief that it cannot be divided into even smaller parts. The great majority of these are too trivial to notice. But occasionally something happens that seems worthy of note; this is an incident, an occurrence or, more significant, an event. The *Shorter Oxford English Dictionary* defines 'event' as: 'An incident, occurrence; especially (in modern use) an occurrence of some importance.' Its importance is, of course, not inherent but a judgement by observers. Equally arbitrary is the composition and duration of the event. It may be anything from a split-second explosion to a war of several years'

---

[10] For language and forms of life, see Ludwig Wittgenstein's *Philosophical Investigations*, 3rd edn (Basil Blackwell, 1968), *passim*, and the voluminous literature flowing from it.

duration; one might say that the Civil War was the most disastrous *event* in American history. However, any past occurrence or string of occurrences designated as an event will, almost *ipso facto*, not have survived into the present. Similar considerations apply to states of affairs, trends, movements, and so on.

Again, most phenomena of nature do not survive for long. 'Où sont les neiges d'antan?' asked the poet Villon. The brief life of insects of the genus *Ephemeridae* gives them their name. Tortoises and elephants may outlive humans, and some trees live several thousand years, the oldest being the bristle-cone pine, now so important for prehistoric knowledge.[11] Inorganic objects, especially rocks, however, do survive – often with little change throughout the short course of history – and the reconstruction of the prehistoric past depends on these.

As for artefacts, most do not survive, though, as shown in the previous section, many of those that happen to do so are very informative. Even more tantalizing, perhaps, are the non-material losses of the past – concepts, beliefs, customs, *mentalités*, religions and even languages. Several thousand languages have been lost, more than the four or five thousand that are still spoken.[12]

Although in general these things have not survived, the historian's duty and pleasure is to recover as many as possible. Much of human progress may depend on a growing understanding of past ways of thought. It has often been observed (if too often forgotten) that one of the historian's duties is to restore some of our losses. Sir Maurice Powicke wrote:

> I do not think that the most valuable function of the historian is to trace back the institutions and ways of thought which have survived, as though we were at the end and climax of history. It is at least as important to retrieve the treasures that have been dropped on the way and lost, which, if restored, would enrich our civilization.[13]

This comment is especially apt from a medievalist.

Of course, among such treasures may be lost manuscripts (the missing books of Tacitus), lost scores (Schubert's Tenth Symphony or Bach's *St Mark Passion*) or lost paintings (Leonardo's *Battle of Anghiari*). Precious as these objects are, it is hardly the work of historians to recover them. It is the immaterial treaures that they can try to restore to us – lost beliefs, lost values, lost outlooks on life, and perhaps lost insights and understandings. Some

[11] Colin Renfrew, *Before Civilization: the radiocarbon revolution and prehistoric Europe* (Penguin, 1976), chapter 4.

[12] See George Steiner, *After Babel: aspects of language and translation* (Oxford University Press, 1976), p. 51.

[13] F. M. Powicke, *Modern Historians and the Study of History: essays and papers* (Odhams, 1955), p. 95.

grasp of these is, indeed, essential to their work, for they can have little hope of correctly interpreting the relics our forebears left behind, or of understanding their actions, unless they know how they thought. But the history of ideas is now advancing rapidly as a discipline in its own right. M. S. Anderson wrote of the eighteenth century:

> the mind of the age in its broadest sense, the way in which ordinary people thought and felt, is now at least in some parts of the continent, the object of scholarly analysis with very exciting results. History as an academic discipline advances less dramatically than the physical sciences, with fewer 'great discoveries' and less obvious discontinuities. But it does advance none the less; and the advances are solid and permanent ones.[14]

5 Identity

Sir Karl Popper remarked of change that it 'still remains the fundamental problem of Natural Philosophy'.[15] One question, especially for the historian, is how much change something may undergo before it becomes something else. It is crudely illustrated by the story of George Washington's axe, which was exhibited as the very same tool with which he had cut down his father's cherry tree, though it had had five new handles and three new heads. Behind this joke is the ontological question whether at least some things should be considered as existing in four dimensions rather than three. Does a stone, a tree or a person occupy time as well as space?

A second problem arises from the social context. Materially, it was no longer Washington's axe; socially it fulfilled the same role as the original axe. Thus there was both succession (not change) and continuity; the succession was material, but the continuity was social. It was in some ways like the succession of men who followed Washington as President of the United States, while the role was continuous. Or perhaps it was more like successive actors taking over the same part in a long-running play.

Why should working historians raise their heads from their notes and card indexes to ponder these problems? The reason is that the problems are inherent in historians' attempts to understand and reconstruct the past. They must decide whether an object of their enquiry has remained the same over a span of time and therefore whether what they have said about it is likely to remain true. Again, they must decide whether any change or continuity

[14] M. S. Anderson, *Historians and Eighteenth Century Europe, 1715–89* (Clarendon Press, 1979), p. vi.
[15] See *Conjectures and Refutations: the growth of scientific knowledge*, 5th edn (Routledge and Kegan Paul, 1974), p. 79.

they may have observed is substantive or social. For example, the House of Commons that gave power to Churchill in May 1940, yet had supported appeasement in 1938, was substantially the same; but politically or socially . . . ? How far were the 'isolationist' Americans of the 1930s the 'interventionalist' Americans of the 1940s or 1980s?

Here one may be misled by language. As Wittgenstein remarked, philosophy is, among other things a battle against the bewitchment of one's intelligence by language.[16] Once a name is given to something – for example, an office, a body of men or an institution – that name tends to stick long after the function has changed so much that the name is no longer appropriate.[17] Should our queen still be called a monarch? We can also be misled by verbs in the indicative mood, as in such statements as 'Caesar was ambitious', 'Bismarck was a statesman', 'Hitler was a megalomaniac', 'the USA desires peace', 'China is a superpower'. Since such statements are usually made without time limitation, we tend to assume that they are, or were, true throughout the existence of the person or body concerned. Strictly we should say 'Caesar was ambitious', or 'the USA desired peace', 'at such and such times'.

In all these ways we are led to assume that things remained the same when often they underwent considerable change. What, then, gave them sufficient continuity for the same name to be appropriate and for the attribution of certain qualities to be, on the whole, justified?

I now look more closely at the sort of subjects the historian is examining. The elements of the historical field can be placed under three headings – natural objects, human beings and artefacts, both physical and mental.[18] In considering identity, however, one may conveniently group them differently: (1) visible and material objects, whether natural or artificial; (2) human beings; (3) ideas and idea-systems (the remaining component of the category of artefacts); (4) institutions. Though not elementary but complex because they are a mixture of human beings, ideas and material objects, these are significant components in history.

There are, however, other things whose existence in the historical field is at least debatable – events, trends, states of affairs, quasi-groups, movements, and so on. As I have argued, there is strong reason to doubt whether these are not the inventions of later ages. Since they are not themselves material and visible, and were not objects of belief of people at the time, it is difficult to argue that they existed *as distinct and unmistakable entities* in the historical field.

Visible and material objects, on the other hand, exist as long as they are

---

[16] Wittgenstein, *Philosophical Investigations*, part I, no. 109.
[17] See chapter 2, section 3.
[18] See chapter 2, section 3.

physically there, and when they have gone they no longer exist. Yet lakes do not disappear overnight; they dwindle into strings of ponds, then into marshes, finally into fertile grazing or wasteland. At what point does the lake cease to be? Brunel's ship the *Great Britain* lay for many years as a rotting, rusty hulk in the Falklands. In 1971 it was brought back to Bristol and is now being built in its original form. Did it cease to be a ship? Will it be a ship again – even though it may not sail the oceans? Having lost its function, has it changed, or partly lost, its entity? Is a retired general still a general without his function?

What of human beings? Although they seem to last from birth to death, are they always the same person throughout? By adulthood not only have they changed their physical constituents three times already; their personalities sometimes seem so radically different from what they were at earlier stages that one wonders in what sense they can be the same people. Of course, there are numerous physiological and psychological factors, which change or are replaced at different rates. But could it be that in the course of a varied lifetime we exhibit complex cases of George Washington's axe? Is each person like a long rope, made up entirely of short strands, with no one fibre common to the whole length? What is the 'I' that continues for seventy or eighty years? What does continue? The packet of genes? The memory? Or perhaps only the social niches in which we fit? Like the axe, people may be sustained only by a social continuity.

Ideas and idea-systems, which are neither material nor visible, present different but just as many problems. Thanks to R. G. Collingwood, it is much debated whether, or how far, it is possible for a historian to rethink the thoughts of a historical agent. 'All history is the history of thought,' he wrote. 'The history of thought, and therefore all history, is the re-enactment of past thought in the historian's own mind.'[19] Many people have argued against Collingwood that it is not possible for someone else, in a different age and situation, to think the same thought; it can be only a similar thought. For, if it is actually the *same* thought, does this not imply that thoughts can have an existence independent of the minds that think them? This supposition leads on to something like Karl Popper's theory of a third world (or 'World Three') of objective ideas and idea-systems.[20]

Popper distinguishes between, on the one hand, statements in themselves (or thought contents), which can stand in logical relations to other statements, and, on the other, thought processes, whose relation to other thought processes is psychological, not logical. Thus your thought process of fear cannot contradict either my thought process of courage or even your thought

[19] R. G. Collingwood, *The Idea of History* (Oxford University Press, 1961), p. 215.
[20] See K. R. Popper, *Objective Knowledge: an evolutionary approach* (Oxford University Press, 1972), chapters 3 and 4; also his *Unended Quest: an intellectual autobiography* (Fontana/Collins, 1976).

process of courage at a different time. However, a thought content 'that is a bull' can and does contradict the thought content 'that is a cow' if they refer to the same animal. As Popper puts it, 'thoughts in the sense of contents or statements in themselves and thoughts in the sense of thought processes belong to two entirely different "worlds".'[21] This leads him to postulate the existence of a 'third world' in addition to the 'first world' of physical objects and the 'second world' of subjective experiences including thought processes. This 'third world' or 'World Three' is a world of statements in themselves, of thought contents, of problems, theories and critical arguments. It is the world of objective mind, where epistemology is possible without a knowing subject.[22]

A critical discussion of the theories of Collingwood and Popper would take too long – though we may note Popper's own criticism of Collingwood.[23] The relevant questions here are how far, and in what ways, historians can possess themselves of the thoughts of an earlier age: in short, what survives? A possible answer is that, if statements in themselves have an objective existence outside time and space, this enables them to be thought at any period by anyone. This seems to be the case with idea-systems even more than with single ideas or statements – for example, systems like Euclid's geometry or Roman law. Subjective experiences, on the other hand, which have no such independent existence, cannot come through to us from the past and therefore must be reconstructed as accurately as possible by the historian's imagination.

Finally, institutions are even less helpful to the historian. Although they survive easily into the present, institutions, more than the other three components of history are social products. Indeed, they are not only produced but also sustained by society, and they are therefore far more susceptible to social change than the others. Hence, though they survive in great numbers from the past to the present, in doing so they have undergone considerable alteration. Therefore they are of less use to one who wants to know about the past than are survivors of the other three categories.

Certainly, considerable efforts are often made to preserve them from change. Hence the insistence on ritual, ceremony and tradition, which is so marked in military and religious establishments. Nevertheless even these undergo reforms and modernizations. Sometimes institutions are capable of generating emotions, and thus of influencing actions, out of all proportion to their contemporary significance. This was true, for example, of the Holy Roman Emperor, who in the Thirty Years War was able to attract loyalty (or even hostility) quite disproportionate to his power as emperor (as

[21] See Popper, *Unended Quest*, p. 181.
[22] See the titles of chapters 3 and 4 of Popper, *Objective Knowledge*.
[23] See Popper, *Objective Knowledge*, pp. 186–190.

distinct from his power as a Habsburg prince). Even as late as the nineteenth century the unification of Germany was complicated by German loyalties to the name of emperor, even though the title was of the Austrian, not of the Holy Roman Empire.

But of all the things that have come through from the past the most significant is the written word. Voluminous as are the documents for certain aspects of recent public affairs, for most of history, even for this century, there is not nearly enough. More will be said about this later. Here it is appropriate to stress that what survives is just the written word or, more exactly, a piece of writing. Words, language, meanings, message and significance are still, at this stage, problematic. They are not to be taken for granted. Indeed, in a few cases, like the marks on the seals of the Indus Valley civilization from Harappa and Mohenjo-Daro, it is not even certain that the object is, in fact, a piece of writing.

Now, having considered the survivors of the past, we look to what may be their significance for the historian in the present.

4

The Evidence of History

1 Arguing from Evidence

Evidence is crucial to history. By this I do not mean merely that historians, unlike other imaginative writers, must have evidence for their assertions, but that evidence is literally 'crucial', for it is the point where two realms intersect. The historical field (history$_1$) produced evidence, which in turn forms the basis of historical knowledge (history$_2$). Without evidence there can be no historical knowledge, though there can be historical guesswork. (Not the least valuable part of an education in history is that it enables the student to discriminate between the two.)

In the last chapter I looked at the present as a consequence of the past and considered what sort of things 'come through' from the past, making a transition to the present. Here and in a number of subsequent chapters I shall consider present activity, leaving past activity to one side. It is a sobering thought that all we can know about the past must be derived from the present; and it is even more strange to realize that *all* the present constitutes evidence, in one way or another, for the past. But to say this is as trivial as to say (as in chapter 3) that the past caused the present. In both cases one must be more precise. What part of the present is evidence for what bit of the past? Historians' skills are needed to trace the intimate connections between one and the other. Sometimes spectacular advances in historical knowledge are made by the discovery of new material evidence – like the tomb of Tutankhamun, the Dead Sea Scrolls or the Paston Letters. Often, however, great progress is made by new insights into the significance of existing evidence; for example, A. J. P. Taylor's *The Origins of the Second World War*, T. K. Rabb's *The Struggle for Stability in Early Modern Europe* or Lawrence Stone's *The Family, Sex and Marriage in England, 1500–1800*.

Historical evidence can never be conclusive. Sherlock Holmes talked about 'deduction', but in fact his conclusions could not have been deduced from his evidence. Here he is explaining his 'science of deduction and analysis' to Dr Watson:

The train of reasoning ran, 'Here is a gentleman of a medical type, but with the air of a military man. Clearly an army doctor, then. He has just come from the tropics, for his face is dark, and that is not the natural tint of his skin, for his wrists are fair. He has undergone hardship and sickness, as his haggard face says clearly. His left arm has been injured. He holds it in a stiff and unnatural manner. Where in the tropics could an English army doctor have seen much hardship and got his arm wounded? Clearly in Afghanistan.' The whole train of thought did not occupy a second. I then remarked that you came from Afghanistan, and you were astonished.[1]

Another conversation with Watson runs like this:

'Yes, I've had a busy day,' I answered, '. . . but really I don't know how you deduced it.'

Holmes then explains that his conclusion derived from the state of Watson's boots.

'Excellent!' I cried.
'Elementary,' said he. 'It is one of those instances where the reasoner can produce an effect which seems remarkable to his neighbour, because the latter has missed one little point which is the basis of the deduction.'[2]

Holmes's mode of arguing (though not, as he claims, deductive) is similar to the historian's mode in two respects. The first is that Holmes is not deducing, but making guesses of greater or lesser probability. This becomes evident if one considers the distinction between necessary and sufficient conditions. The account that follows is a great simplification, but it should suffice here.

A condition (C) is said to be a *necessary* for the event (E) if E never occurs without C. For example, we may say that fire (E) never occurs in the absence of oxygen (C) (whether the statement is true is beside the point). Stated formally, a necessary condition is

$$\text{If not C, then not E}$$

from which we may deduce

$$\text{If E, then C}$$

We may not, however, deduce either

$$\text{If C, then E}$$

---

[1] A. Conan Doyle, *A Study in Scarlet*, chapter 2.
[2] A. Conan Doyle, 'The Crooked Man', in *The Memoirs of Sherlock Holmes*.

(for example, if oxygen, then a fire) or

If not E, then not C

(for example, if no fire, then no oxygen).

A condition (C) is said to be *sufficient* for the event (E) if whenever C occurs then E occurs. For example, whenever a car runs out of petrol (C), the engine stops (E). The lack of petrol is a sufficient condition for the engine to stop. Put formally

If C, then E

and equally

If not E, then not C

(if the engine has not stopped, then it has not run out of petrol). But we may not deduce from these *either*

If not C, then not E

(for example, if the car has not run out of petrol, then the engine has not stopped) *or*

If E, then C

(for example, if the engine has stopped, then the car has run out of petrol). Driving a car would be a lot simpler if these last two statements were true. Yet it is such logically inadmissible conclusions that Holmes draws. (That Afghanistan is not in the tropics is irrelevant.)

It is the same with history. It is correct that a papist murder of Sir Edmund Berry Godfrey in 1678 would be a sufficient condition of his corpse with signs of violence. But from the existence of such a corpse one should not conclude a papist murder. (Formally 'If C, then E' does *not* imply 'If E, then C'.) People did, however, jump to this conclusion. The Commons petitioned King Charles to banish all papists from a radius of twenty miles round London, while the City placed chains across the streets. As the City Chamberlain said, 'He did not know but the next morning they might all rise with their throats cut.'[3]

Again, the emperor's grant of Italy to the papacy would be a sufficient condition of the Pope's possession of it. However, the Popes knew that their possession did not imply an imperial grant and they forged the 'Donation of Constantine'. The forgery was exposed by Lorenzo Valla in 1440. The issue is the same with all suspect documents. Their plausibility rests on an argument like this:

[3] See J. P. Kenyon, *The Popish Plot* (Penguin, 1974), p. 92.

If A wrote a certain document, then that is a sufficient condition for
    the existence of the document at some point in time   (True)
But the document does exist at this point in time   (True)
Therefore A wrote it   (False)

This argument is manifestly invalid. The mere existence of the letter does
not prove that A wrote it. All we can say is that, *if* A had written it, then
such a letter would have existed. It is the same with all historical evidence;
it can never be conclusive. It can at best achieve a very high degree of
probability.

This question of probability is a second link between historians and
Sherlock Holmes. Holmes used one probability to support another, as when
he informed Watson at their first meeting that the latter had been in the
Afghanistan campaign. Not all the inferences taken together could be said
to prove it, but the probabilities multiplied together give such a high
probability that Holmes had no hesitation in telling the astonished Watson
where he (Watson) had been. And Holmes was right.

Similarly, historians draw a number of probable conclusions whose
probabilities reinforce each other. Thus on many points their conclusion
is correct beyond any reasonable doubt. Unfortunately, unlike Holmes, they
can never confront the subjects of their speculations to receive confirmation
from their own mouths. History$_2$ at best can be no more than a tissue of
mutually supporting probabilities.

2   The Concept of Evidence

If, as I have said, all our knowledge of the past rests on present evidence,
what are we to understand by this key concept? Under 'evidence' the *Shorter
Oxford English Dictionary* gives '1. The quality or condition of being evident. . . .
3. That which makes evident. . . . 5. Ground for belief; that which tends
to prove or disprove any conclusion.' 'Evident' is defined as '1. . . . Obvious
to the sight. 2. Clear to the understanding or the judgement.' (In these
definitions I have omitted meanings marked as obsolete.) There are two
related concepts here: that of being directly apparent, and that of being
ground for a belief. For that which is apparent (A), there is a corresponding
belief (B) which is grounded on (A). Such a grounding is a matter of
judgement.

To illustrate my points from the second Sherlock Holmes story, the clean
state of Watson's boots (A) was apparent to Holmes and afforded him ground
for his belief (B) that Watson had made his rounds in a cab, not on foot.
Similarly, the body of Sir Edmund Berry Godfrey was directly evident (A)
and provided grounds (or was thought to do) for the belief (B) that there

was a Popish plot to kill the king. Since this belief is now held to be false, it appears that the reasoning from (A) to (B) was fallacious. These two examples show the importance of the act of judgement that connects (A) with (B), which may be correct or incorrect.

However, the notion of 'being ground for' may be taken strictly and logically, or loosely and psychologically. If the judgement was rationally made, then we may say that the clean boots were indeed grounds for the conclusion. In the second, looser, usage we may say that Godfrey's murder was ground for belief in a Popish plot. Since such a conclusion was invalid, since the murder did not afford a rational basis for such a belief, then we may say that the Protestants *took* the murder as ground for their belief. This is a psychological statement, and is quite consistent with saying that the murder did not afford ground for their belief, which is a logical statement. I prefer the stricter usage.

From the point of view of historians, when they draw a conclusion from the documents before them, those documents will have led them to that conclusion. Whether documents afford rational grounds for such a conclusion is, however, another matter. History, unlike mathematics, is not a science of certainties, and only rarely are a historian's reasonings empirically confirmed – unlike those of Sherlock Holmes. For example, historians have debated in a number of books and articles whether or not Adolf Hitler aimed at world power. Their evidence consists largely of three books: *Mein Kampf*, written in 1924–6, *Hitler's Secret Book* (*Hitlers Zweitesbuch*), written in 1928, and *Hitler's Table Talk* (*Hitlers Tischgespräche im Führerhauptquartier*) of 1941–4.[4] Very different conclusions have been drawn from this evidence, so it is at present impossible to say for what belief it provides rational grounds. At the moment we are in the uncomfortable situation of having to admit that the evidence doubtless provides grounds either for the belief that Hitler did aim at world power or for the belief that he did not, but that the existing evidence is inadequate for either. (See section 3.3.) Thus the relationship between apparent evidence (A) and correct belief (B) is not so simple in fact as in logic.

---

[4] See Adolf Hitler, *Mein Kampf* (*My Struggle*), 3rd edn (Hurst and Blackett, 1938), *Hitler's Secret Book*, ed. Telford Taylor (Grove Press, 1983); *Hitler's Table-Talk, 1941–1944*, intro. H. R. Trevor-Roper, 2nd edn (Weidenfeld and Nicolson, 1973). See also Eberhard Jäckel, *Hitler's World View: a blueprint for power* (Harvard University Press, 1981); Milan Hauner, 'Did Hitler want a world dominion?', *Journal of Contemporary History*, 13, 1 (January 1978). The debate continues.

3   The Structure of Evidence

3.1   *Recognition*

In the use of evidence, three factors are important: the facts, the connecting processes and the judgement. I consider each of these in turn.

First, the evidence should be 'obvious to the sight': it should be clear what the evidence is, even if there is doubt about what it is evidence for. In short, we must first get our facts right; otherwise any conclusion grounded upon them is likely to be wrong. If Dr Watson's apparent suntan was, in fact, theatrical make-up, or his stiff arm was due not to a bullet in the shoulder but to a stick he was concealing in his sleeve, then Holmes would either have been misled or have been right for the wrong reason. Similarly a historian using a medieval document must be sure that it is written in handmade ink on parchment, and not a clever forgery.

Of course the historian always has a duty to ensure that any evidence used is what it purports to be. At this stage I am concerned not with its significance in the past, but only with its present nature. If it is a material object – a letter, a stone, a building – the historian must check that its apparent qualities are genuine. Such qualities include its size, shape and construction, its material make-up, colour, texture and smell; in particular, the exact form of any letters, signs, symbols, etc., that it bears. Thus a historian may use a magnifying glass not to see into the past but to see the present correctly. He or she must also ensure that any human witness is not an imposter. Before present evidence can be used as the first link in a chain that leads into the past, an accurate description of that first link is essential. (In this respect, as in others, we cannot hope to be right about the past if we are wrong about the present.)

A simple example is that of two hunters – a tourist and a local guide following a wild animal. The guide can see signs on the ground – slight indentations, disturbed vegetation, small pieces of dung – and can interpret these as evidence that a leopard went that way. In this interpretation the hunter uses a mutually supportive set of reasonings similar to those of Sherlock Holmes. The tourist, however, cannot even see the signs on the ground. He or she can see the ground but not that it has been indented, can see the grasses but not that the blades are bent, and can see the dung but cannot distinguish it from mud. In short, the tourist cannot see what the evidence is; while the guide can both see the evidence correctly and know what it is evidence for.

The guide's ability to do this is probably the result of an education in which traditional skills are handed down. The historian also has to acquire such skills, though not usually as part of a formal education. These are known as the auxiliary sciences of history (see section 4).

3.2   Processes

The use of evidence requires a correct understanding of the processes – that is, the temporal series of changes – that have produced the evidence. Processes are the chains along which the historian's thinking can move from the present to the past.

Over time, a building will decay under the elements, it may be looted for building materials, and may be damaged for military, religious or other reasons. After ages of destruction and decay it may be restored by a nineteenth-century architect, reconstructed in the twentieth century, and given various provisions for tourists. Present-day visitors may believe that what they see – for example, a temple in the Roman Forum or an English cathedral or a French fortified town – is how the building originally was. A glance at eighteenth-century drawings of these same buildings as picturesque ruins (for example, by Piranesi) should remove any impression of that kind. Scholars wishing to use the building as historical evidence must make a careful study of the processes of destruction, decay, restoration and reconstruction before they can comprehend the building as it originally was. Art historians, like art dealers, should know the provenance of a picture – that is, through whose hands it has passed – but they should also know the chemical qualities of the inks, paints, colours, chalks, pastels, etc., as well as of the canvas, wood, linen, paper, etc., on which the picture has been made. Sometimes the skill of the restorer reveals alterations or even totally different pictures under the surface pigment. However, if restorers go too far, the picture in the gallery can be more a reconstruction than a restoration.

Archaeology has in this century made valuable contributions to history by supplementing written sources. Archaeologists can not only examine an object to see how it has changed. When an object has disappeared altogether, as in the case of a wooden structure, they can identify the post-holes and so form a good idea of the size, shape and nature of the building that stood there. The royal estate at Yeavering of the seventh-century kings of Northumbria is a good example of the co-operation of historian and archaeologist.[5] A knowledge of the processes both of timber construction and of natural decay enables the historian to work backwards from present evidence (in this case, little more than topsoil intrusion into the subsoil) to past reality (in this case, a royal court).

Moreover, scholars of place-names can support both historians and archaeologists. The processes to be unravelled are those of linguistic

[5] P. H. Blair, *An Introduction to Anglo-Saxon England* (Cambridge University Press, 1962), p. 209.

change and development interacting with social and political change. This is exemplified by two fortresses near Stirling (Dumyat and Myot Hill) which incorporate the name of the local Pictish tribe, the Maeatae, and thus indicate the proximity of their tribal boundary. It is argued that the name 'fortress of the Maeatae' would be given by a neighbouring people, not by the Maeatae themselves.[6]

Other examples may be taken from the history of land use and landscape, from the history of industry and the use of memorized genealogies, myths and legends, in the study of unwritten or preliterate history.[7]

These examples indicate something of the wide variety of processes that the historian needs to understand before grasping what the present evidence was in the past. Similar questions of provenance and process apply to written evidence, as Kitson Clark explained:

> The questions 'through whose hands has this evidence passed and what have they done to it' cannot be confined to those who have had documents in their charge. They must be asked of everyone else who has transmitted the evidence upon which the history which men and women are going to use is based.[8]

3.3   Judgement

After having accurately assessed the present facts and understood the processes that have brought the evidence to its present condition, historians must make a judgement; that is, they must answer the question, for what is this evidence adequate? Is it adequate for the conclusion they will draw from it? The concept of 'adequate evidence' merits closer attention.

Judgement should not be merely subjective; evidence should not be just 'adequate for me'. In a criminal trial great care is expected to be taken to establish the objective reliability and relevance of the evidence. Evidence should not be 'adequate for us' – that is, for the court or for our social group. A higher standard is required.

However, even if 'adequate evidence' is not subjective, it lacks the objectivity

---

[6] See F. T. Wainwright, *Archaeology and Place-Names and History: an essay on problems of co-ordination* (Routledge and Kegan Paul, 1962), pp. 72–4. This book is a revealing essay on the mutual support of the three disciplines.

[7] For the first, see the pioneering works of Marc Bloch, *Les Caractères originaux de l'histoire rurale française* (Oslo, H. Aschehoug 1931), in English as *French Rural History: an essay on its basic characteristics* (Routledge and Kegan Paul, 1966), and W. G. Hoskins, *The Making of the English Landscape* (Hodder and Stoughton, 1955). For the history of industry, see R. A. Buchanan, *Industrial Archaeology in Britain* (Penguin, 1972) and Jennifer Tann, *Gloucestershire Woollen Mills* (David and Charles, 1967). For unwritten history, see Jan Vansina, *Oral Tradition: a study in historical methodology* (Routledge and Kegan Paul, 1965); David Henige, *Oral Historiography* (Longmans, 1982); Paul Thompson, *The Voice of the Past: oral history* (Oxford University Press, 1978).

[8] G. Kitson Clark, *The Critical Historian* (Heinemann, 1967), p. 82.

of a natural phenomenon. Clearly it is a concept, and therefore depends for its existence upon minds. When or where there are no minds, there can be no evidence. The footprints of a dinosaur preserved in rock are evidence for us that a dinosaur walked there, but in the dinosaur's world they were not evidence. There could be evidence only when minds evolved capable of the concept.

One may conclude, then, that 'adequate evidence' is a rational concept, appealing to reason. Such an appeal to reason cannot be empirically justified – though it may be exemplified. For example, the mathematical proposition that $(x^3 + y^3) = (x + y)(x^2 - xy + y^2)$ is exemplified but not proved by the fact that $(3^3 + 2^3) = (3 + 2)(3^2 - 3.2 + 2^2)$. Nor are there any first principles from which we may deduce the concept of adequate evidence. Like other rational concepts – such as responsibility, probability (in the non-mathematical sense), verisimilitude, justice – the concept of adequate evidence must depend in practice upon the consensus of rational minds. For it is, as I have shown, both mind-dependent and rational.

It is now becoming clear that evidence does not exist in and for itself. It is not some sort of recognizable object, like a flower, a stone or water. Virtually anything in the world may be evidence for something else if a rational mind so judges it.[9] It is also becoming clear that adequate evidence, like truth and justice, is a rational ideal at which we aim but to which we can never fully attain. In practice, however, decisions have to be made. No court of law achieves perfect justice, but cases have to be settled. Similarly, though we weigh evidence as carefully as we can, in the end we have to decide whether or not to rely upon it. So we appeal to a rational consensus.

What sort of people do we appeal to? If the evidence is holes in the ground we ask an archaeologist; if it is the spoor of a lion we ask an African hunter; if an ancient document we ask a historian; but if it is the statements of witnesses to a crime we ask a jury of ordinary people.

What sort of qualities do these people possess who are called in to assess the adequacy of the evidence? According to what I have argued above (in sections 3.1 and 3.2), they should not only be able to appreciate what the evidence actually is, but also have enough relevant knowledge to follow the processes by which what is evident in the present may be connected to alleged happenings in the past. Sometimes this requires specialized knowledge, as of archaeology or tracking, but in the case of trials by jury it is considered more important to understand the everyday life of the society in which that court is held. They should also make their decisions rationally, so that any other reasonable person possessing the same knowledge would reach the same conclusion. Often this informed rational judgement is as far as one can go. In other cases, as in detective stories, subsequent events confirm or refute the conclusions

---

[9] Cf. R. G. Collingwood, *The Idea of History* (Oxford University Press, 1961), p. 280: 'In scientific history anything is evidence which is used as evidence.'

drawn from the evidence. If Dr Watson were to conclude his narratives a few pages from the end, we should not know whether Holmes was correct in his boasted 'deductions'. Since historians' conclusions concern the past, they can never know, by empirical confirmation, whether they are correct. The best they can hope for is more evidence, evidence perhaps so overwhelming that it puts their case beyond all reasonable, even imaginable, doubt. It is, for example, hardly imaginable that the battle of Waterloo was not fought in 1815. Yet it can never be proved, if proof means something more than a set of mutually supporting high probabilities. If a sceptic demands as proof either a logically tight deductive argument or empirical verification, these demands cannot be met.

4 Documentary Evidence

In the previous section I indicated some of the diverse kinds of evidence that historians use. All of the present can be evidence for the past; indeed, much progress has been made in this century by using quite unexpected kinds of evidence – as in industrial archaeology or demography.

Nevertheless, most historical evidence still consists of written documents – usually, writings on paper, parchment, papyrus or clay. Writing is, however, to a small extent, also found on metal (coins and medals) and on stone (monumental inscriptions). Documentary evidence is strictly only primary sources, documents originating in the period under study. Every historian must, however, also use the work of earlier historians of the same subject, even if only to disagree with them. Such secondary sources certainly provide evidence for the past, but for most of the nineteenth and twentieth centuries, in fact since the days of Ranke and the beginning of the opening of the great archives, it has been *de rigueur* for the historian to prefer and to   concentrate upon primary sources. (Few historians would not feel they were risking their professional reputation if they published a history resting entirely on secondary sources.) However, the use of primary sources requires not only a lot of time and patience but also a special training. Unless one is a scholar proficient in the period, one would probably learn more about Tudor government from reading Geoffrey Elton and more about the political and religious thought of the English Revolution from Christopher Hill than from reading the primary sources.

I shall now take a closer look at this unprocessed raw material. While not describing all the techniques of the critical historian (Kitson Clark's book does that very well[10]), I shall mention a few of them.

[10] Kitson Clark, *The Critical Historian*.

4.1   Use of the document

First, the document as a physical object may have to be examined to establish that the paper or parchment, ink, watermark, seals, and so on have been correctly identified. This calls for similar chemical skills as an art restorer possesses. Next, there has to be an accurate reading, which may require the skills of a palaeographer. An old document may be quite illegible in certain places. Infra-red rays may help, but if some of the paper or parchment is missing (owing to the action of fire, rodents, damp or ants) then a guess has to be made about what was there. Abbreviations, elisions and the use of symbols often add to the difficulty. Errors quite commonly made by the scribe, copyist, typist or printer make a reliable reading more difficult to establish; one must not merely discern the letters and the words but also make sense of the whole document.

As any archivist knows, old documents contain many forms and conventions which may mislead the uninstructed reader. Such is the purely fictitious lawsuit and its final agreement ('fine') used in English medieval and early modern conveyancing in the Court of Common Pleas.[11] In addition, if the document is not in the historian's own language it has to be translated – with all the attendant problems. (Most documents of English history well into the sixteenth century were in Latin.) After all this work has been done, the scholar is probably not reading the original musty deed in the record office, but a fair copy or translation in typescript or, perhaps, in print in a volume of printed documents. Before this stage has been reached it will have been copied several times. A collection of printed documents must have an editor, who may not have been absolutely scrupulous.[12] At all these stages errors and distortions can creep in.

A document is chiefly looked to for evidence either about the writer's state of mind or about the state of affairs that he or she intentionally or unintentionally reveals. The pitfall here, of course, is that the writer is usually writing for his own purposes, not to provide future historians with what *they* want to know. If, however, the writer is writing for the benefit of future generations rather than contemporaries, he may be trying to mislead them. (Think of the memoirs of Cardinal Richelieu, Cardinal Retz or Bismarck.) Hence one should always try to establish the original purpose of the document before putting it to one's own purposes. Often the writer does not intend to reveal his purposes to the recipient; thus the historian, some centuries later, may also be deceived. Again, if one looks to the writer for facts, one may be

[11] See C. A. F. Meekings's introduction to *Abstracts of Surrey Feet of Fines, 1509–1558*, Surrey Record Society, vol. XIX (1946).
[12] See Kitson Clark, *The Critical Historian*, pp. 117–18.

misled, since the writer not only may be mistaken about the facts but may also give them a bias in order to persuade or mislead the recipient, or may even be lying.

I have indicated the caution that is needed in using documentary evidence. So many are the possible pitfalls that some historians, especially in France, make use of a number of auxiliary historical sciences – such as diplomatic, palaeography, heraldry, chronology or numismatics. The English tradition tends to favour historians doing all this work for themselves. Which method is better must be judged by the results.

4.2 Availability of documents

While keeping alert for new sources, working historians usually have a shrewd idea where most of their evidence will be found. Probably starting with their own personal library (small, select but relevant), they then move on to a university or other large library like the Bibliothèque Nationale, the British Library or the Library of Congress, which contain the required printed sources and perhaps others on microfilm. At some point they will go to the archives for their primary sources, sometimes also consulting private collections, although these are increasingly being placed in public archives.

Both in private and in public hands the documents may have undergone changes – either damage caused by careless storing or handling, or improvements resulting from mending, or restoring. In the majority of cases such changes may be negligible, but the scholar must always be aware of their possibility.

A more important problem is that of availability. In view of the vast amount of historical evidence contained in the numerous repositories, both great and small, it frequently comes as an unpleasant surprise to researchers to find how little of it is relevant to their immediate purpose. It is even more dispiriting when they suspect, or even know, that valuable evidence exists which for some reason is not available. Most researchers have encountered various frustrations even in the best of archive offices. Some accounts of these have been published – as, for example, R. C. Cobb's remarks on French archives, or the series of articles on national libraries that appeared in *The Times Literary Supplement*.[13] A number of guides to the major sources of evidence have been written. G. R. Elton has edited a series, *The Sources of History: Studies in the Use of Historical Evidence*;[14] other examples are Geoffrey Parker's *Guide to the Archives of the Spanish Institutions in or concerned with the*

---

[13] R. C. Cobb, *A Second Identity: essays on France and French history* (Oxford University Press, 1969), pp. 53–63; *The Times Literary Supplement*, 7 September 1984 and 5 October 1984, pp. 994, 1007, 1126.
[14] Published by the Cambridge University Press. See also his *Modern Historians on British History, 1485–1945* (Methuen, 1970).

Netherlands, 1556–1706[15] and Daniel H. Thomas and Lynn M. Case's *The New Guide to the Diplomatic Archives of Western Europe*.[16] Nevertheless, a large part of the working historian's skills have to be acquired by personal experience. Where frustrations are encountered, however, they are likely to be due more to lack of resources than to incompetence on the part of archivists, and the best of archivists cannot produce documents that do not exist – not to mention those under government ban.

It is often largely a matter of chance which documents survive what Bacon called 'the shipwreck of Time'. For example, when India was partitioned, the muniments of government offices were also divided; those relating to the struggle for a separate Muslim state (Pakistan) were dispatched to Karachi, while those relating to the new state of India remained where they were. Large quantities of the Pakistan records failed to arrive. In 1947 the railways were overburdened with refugees and devastated by violence. Some time later the Pakistan archives turned up in sacks in warehouses on railway sidings. Some were lost; many were damaged by rats, termites or damp. Thus for any history of the partition of India the sources for one side will be much fuller than for the other.[17]

It is true that a great deal of what we should like to know about the past lacks documentation, and so is largely, though not entirely, beyond our knowledge., However, a great many existing documents have not yet been thoroughly researched and will therefore keep historians busy for many years yet. Moreover, new and unexpected material is always coming to light. Most hopeful, perhaps, are the fresh insights given by new techniques such as aerial photography, computer-based analyses, etc., and by new understanding of what known but neglected documents can tell us – as in the work of Pierre Goubert on Beauvais and the Beauvaisis or Emmanuel Le Roy Ladurie on the peasants of Languedoc.[18] Some times new areas are

---

[15] See his account of Dutch archives in Geoffrey Parker, *The Dutch Revolt* (Penguin, 1979), pp. 277–8.

[16] University of Pennsylvania Press, 1975.

[17] I have no reference for this. I repeat in good faith what was told me by a historian of modern India. But, for similar examples, see Cobb, *A Second Identity*, p. 62.

[18] Pierre Goubert, *Cent Mille Provinciaux au XVII*e *siècle: Beauvais et le Beauvaisis de 1600 à 1730* (Flammarion, 1968); Emmanuel Le Roy Ladurie, *Les Paysans de Languedoc* (Flammarion, 1969). Some indications of the way history is moving are given by the following books, among others: Geoffrey Barraclough, *Main Trends in History* (Holmes and Meier, 1979); Charles F. Delzell (ed.), *The Future of History* (Vanderbilt University Press, 1977); Roderick Floud (ed.), *Essays in Quantitative Economic History* (Clarendon Press, 1974); Felix Gilbert and Stephen R. Graubard (eds), *Historical Studies Today* (W. W. Norton, 1972); Georg G. Iggers, *New Directions in European Historiography* (Wesleyan University Press, 1975); Emmanuel Le Roy Ladurie, *The Territory of the Historian* (Harvester Press, 1979); Emmanuel Le Roy Ladurie, *The Mind and Method of the Historian* (Harvester Press, 1981); Theodore K. Rabb and Robert I. Rotberg (eds), *The New History: the 1980s and beyond: studies in interdisciplinary history* (Princeton University Press, 1982); Lawrence Stone, *The Past and the Present* (Routledge and Kegan Paul, 1981).

opened up, as in E. D. Genovese's *Roll, Jordan, Roll: the world the slaves made.*[19]

5 Evidence as Communication

Since historical documents are not collections of facts deposited in the archives for the historian's enlightenment, their nature and purpose must be ascertained. In most cases, they are communications between contemporaries. Linguistic communication is used for a variety of purposes, rarely with the intention solely to inform. The following summary attempts to simplify something of J. L. Austin's theory of speech acts in *How to do Things with Words*. When we say (or, by extension, write) something, we perform two or sometimes three acts. In all cases we perform a locutionary act, which is 'roughly equivalent to uttering a certain sentence with a certain sense and reference, which again is roughly equivalent to "meaning" in the traditional sense.'[20] What we utter has meaning, but it may also warn, inform, order, ask, and so on. Such utterances, Austin says, 'have a certain (conventional) force' and perform 'illocutionary acts'. Thirdly, 'perlocutionary acts', are performed by utterances that bring about or achieve something, such as to convince, persuade, surprise, deter or mislead. Thus what is said can have a deliberate and marked effect on someone else's beliefs or behaviour. In short, an utterance always has a meaning, usually embodies an intention, and often achieves an effect; most of this applies to written communication too.

Historians should remember that they are not (except rarely) the intended recipients of the written communications being used as evidence. They are eavesdropping on conversations between men and women remote from and perhaps unlike themselves, with different language, assumptions, norms and values. Usually they hear only one side of the conversation, and often not all of that. Bearing in mind what Austin shows can be done with words, historians may ask themselves what acts the writer of a document was performing. The locutionary act may seem fairly clear (though there are many well-known pitfalls in sense and reference). What illocutionary and perlocutionary acts may also be performed by the writer is more difficult to establish, but historians should make every effort to find out. Many historians have been far too careless in attributing intention and effect. We read, for example, that 'A persuaded B' to do something. The evidence for this is a letter from A to B. A's letter may reveal A's intention to persuade B; that is, the illocutionary force is clear. The perlocutionary effect, however,

[19] Deutsch, 1975.
[20] J. L. Austin, *How to do Things with Words* (Oxford University Press, 1962), p. 108.

is not to be taken for granted. We require more than A's letter to know whether A did persuade B. We need to know B's consequent (not merely subsequent) state of mind and consequent (not merely subsequent) actions, which cannot be learned from A's letter.

Another aspect of language is that of coding. Documents can, in most cases, be regarded as communication in the code of a written language. Apart from all the other considerations proper to the decoding of an encoded message, two points are worth noticing. One is that the message often contains no more information than is consonant with intelligibility. This is known in linguistics as 'the principle of least effort'. The consequence is that much relevant information and many agreed attitudes, values, feelings, and so on, are assumed ('taken as read') by both senders and recipients. What is well understood by the participants, however, may not be well understood by historians, who tend to be left either in frustrated ignorance because the message does not tell *them* all they want to know, or, worse, in a state of delusion because they have made incorrect assumptions about what is not stated.

Reduplication, the other important characteristic of coding, is, in a way, opposite to the principle of least effort. Since in speech, and to a lesser extent in writing, some important part of the message is liable to be missed, it is often repeated in a different form. In a medieval charter, for example, when the legal draftsman was not sure how to describe something he would often put in two or more definitions. 'One messuage, one toft, two orchards, two gardens' would refer to three things not six; an example of misleading reduplication.

I hope I have indicated how some acquaintance with linguistics and the philosophy of language may be of practical use to historians working with written sources. Even parts of the theory relating to speech rather than writing may well be relevant, for many documents claim to be reporting what was said. An example is the letter from Cavour, dated at Baden-Baden, 24 July 1858, to King Victor Emmanuel, reporting his conversation with the Emperor Napoleon at Plombières. The editor's note to the English edition adds, 'Almost nothing is known from the French about the meeting at Plombières, and Cavour's letter to the king is therefore the most direct evidence we have.'[21] This indicates both the importance and the vulnerability of the piece of evidence, for one may well wonder whether the conversation went exactly as Cavour recollected or reported. Hansard's parliamentary reports offer a more familiar and probably more accurate example of speech in writing.

[21] In Denis Mack Smith (ed.), *The Making of Italy, 1796–1870* (Macmillan, 1968), pp. 238–47, 248.

6 Facts

What is History? by E. H. Carr is perhaps the best short book to deal with the question of facts. In the first chapter, 'The Historian and his Facts', Carr makes a number of rather strange remarks. He distinguishes 'the facts of history from other facts about the past', and denies that there is a 'hard core of historical facts existing objectively and independently of the interpretation of the historian'. Instead he insists that some interpretation 'enters into every fact of history'. He quotes Geoffrey Barraclough as saying that 'the history we read, though based on facts, is, strictly speaking, not factual at all, but a series of accepted judgements.' 'The facts,' he goes on, '. . . have still to be processed by the historian.' Yet the historian must 'respect his facts'. He must seek 'to bring into the picture all known or knowable facts relevant . . . to the theme.' Finally, the historian starts with 'a provisional selection of facts, and a provisional interpretation in the light of which that selection has been made'. In the process they work upon each other, so that, he concludes, history is 'a continuous process of interaction between the historian and his facts, an unending dialogue betwen the present and the past.'[22]

What, then, is a fact? Carr seems to be unclear whether a fact exists in the world of things or the world of ideas. Again, he sometimes speaks as if a fact is hard, unalterable and self-contained (like a pre-Rutherford atom); but sometimes speaks as if it is at the mercy of people who can alter or even construct it. Many others are little clearer than Carr seems to be. Although the problem is too big to be properly dealt with here, it is worth trying to clarify it, for few concepts are commoner in talk about history than that of 'the facts'. (Again I am trying to simplify a difficult issue.)

I start with the provocative statement that 'the historian has no facts to begin with, only evidence.' This is usually met by some such objection as 'But the battle of Waterloo was fought in 1815. Isn't that a fact?' To which one can reply, 'Yes, it is a fact. But it was created in part by historians and other people.' 'What!' comes the indignant response. 'Do you mean to say that there *was* no battle of Waterloo?' 'No, I do not. There was indeed such a battle. It is not the battle that is our problem; it is the concept of fact.'

What, precisely, is the mode of existence of a fact? If the battle of Waterloo is (or was) a fact, and the cat sitting on the mat is a fact, then surely a fact is part of the world – of that objective, physical world that also contains cats and mats and soldiers and guns. But is it? How big is a fact? What is it made of? Can you put it in a bag? Can you spill your coffee on it?

Or do facts, perhaps, belong to the ideal world? Are they ideas, notions,

[22] See E. H. Carr, *What is History?* (Penguin, 1964), pp. 10–30.

suspicions, hopes, fears, doubts, guesses, theories? Not at all; indeed, we use facts to measure the adequacy or correctness of our ideas, guesses, theories, and so on. 'Are they in accordance with the facts?' we ask. So it seems that facts are hard, objective, reliable. They have neither the subjectivity nor the malleability of an idea. 'You can change your ideas but you can't alter the facts' seems obviously true. It implies that the world is as it is. We must, as Carr says, 'respect the facts'.

Facts may, however, be objective without being material. Mathematics has the same no-nonsense qualities, yet it is not material. One cannot change it to suit oneself; like facts, it can be used to check one's ideas. But do facts constitute an independent system, like logic or geometry? Clearly not; they seem to have something to do with the state of the world. They change with it. When the cat comes off the mat the facts change but not the mathematics. (Cat plus mat still make two things. The diagonals of the rectangular mat still bisect each other.) In order to get nearer to an answer, I shall ask some more questions about facts:

1 Can you see a fact? Yes, if you know what to look for.
2 Can you point to a fact? Not unless the gesture is accompanied by words.
3 Can you dream about a fact – as distinct from dreaming about people, things and states of affairs? No, unless you also dream the appropriate words.

It seems, then, that words form an indispensable part of the fact.

Where do we find facts? Not in the world – one is not likely to trip over a fact. We find them, especially (though not only), in books. Books do not contain battles and shipwrecks; they contain words. Are facts the same as words or sentences? Clearly not; but sentences (often, not always) make statements, and statements can be true or false, according to whether they state the facts. 'Facts,' it has been said, 'are what statements (when true) state; they are not what statements are about.'[23] How do we know whether a statement is true? Not because 'it fits the facts', for that is almost tautologous. Rather, one may say that we find out whether a statement is true by checking whether it corresponds with the state of affairs in the world. (I ignore the special difficulty that this presents for statements about the past. It will do for cats on mats. I also assume the correspondence theory of truth in preference to any other theory.)

To recapitulate, facts seem not to belong at all to the world of ideas. As for the world of things, which consists of nature, people and artefacts, facts seem not to be among these things, yet somehow closely connected. The

[23] See P. F. Strawson, 'Truth', in *Truth*, ed. G. Pitcher (Prentice Hall, 1964), p. 38. Cf. D. Emmet, 'What makes a true proposition true is something other than another proposition to which reference may be made'; and 'to call a proposition true is to refer it in some sense to something beyond itself': *The Nature of Metaphysical Thinking* (Macmillan, 1966), pp. 15–17.

same goes for the world of words – of speech and writing, conversation and books. Facts are not identical with any part of this world – sentences, paragraphs, chapters – yet again they seem to be closely and mysteriously linked. By such considerations as these I am led to conclude as follows:

1 Facts are not ideas, though we may think about them as well as about anything else.
2 Facts are indissolubly connected with both the world of things and the world of words. They are not, however, fully and properly members of either world.
3 A fact is, therefore, a sort of hybrid that belongs partly to the world of words and partly to the world of things. It cannot be separated from either world, yet neither world can contain it.

What, one may ask, connects the two parts of a fact? It is the same as that which connects words to the world – human beings. It is by human practice and human judgement that words (sounds or symbols) have reference to the world. Words cannot so refer in a world without humans – neither in the pre-human world of dinosaurs and pterodactyls nor in the non-human world of animals. (I assume that all animals are incapable of language, something that is not quite true.) *Within* such worlds there can be no facts, though of course one can state facts *about* those worlds.

Facts are not identical with statements, since more than one true statement can state the same fact as in the two sentences 'Sources of rivers are higher than their mouths' and 'Rivers flow downhill.' Such statements are not tautologous. One cannot deduce one from the other. To know that they both state the same fact, one must be acquainted with the world of things. There is nothing in the first sentence to indicate that rivers do not flow uphill from mouth to source. Thus what links the two is human judgement. Facts belong to both worlds, but they are correctly formulated only when a human mind judges that there is a fit between the word-part and the world-part of the fact.

If, then, the very existence of facts depends upon human judgement, it is clear that historical facts are not historical events or historical statements; they are products of human judgements both about events or states of affairs and about statements appropriate to them.[24] When (as in the case of the battle of Waterloo) these judgements have always more or less coincided, we agree that a fact has been established. However, if we disagree about either the events (for example, was the *Belgrano* on course for the Falklands fleet when its sinking was ordered in May 1982?) or the appropriate words (for example, was the battle of Asculum a victory for Pyrrhus?), the 'facts' are in dispute.

---

[24] Cf. what Barraclough said about history being 'a series of accepted judgements', quoted above by Carr, *What is History?*

The chief task of the historian is therefore to do two things: to establish as firmly as possible events and states of affairs in the past; and to find the most appropriate words in which to relate and describe – that is, to communicate – these findings to other people. Facts need not be mentioned, for 'fact' is a slippery concept and, unless carefully handled, may only obscure the issue.

7   Structures of Evidence

To conclude this chapter, I examine whether historical evidence yields any discernible structures, whether there are any relationships which determine the nature of the whole. By 'the whole' I do not mean all that exists in the present. Rather, the question 'what is the structure of the evidence?' can only be asked in relation to a particular matter. Hence the phrase 'structure of the evidence' could mean at least three things.

(1) It might mean the structure of what is available, compared to what is not. This would reflect no more than the chances of time – fires, damp, neglect, etc., against preservation, intended or unintended. There can be little significant structure here.

(2) It might mean the structure of how the evidence is preserved in various repositories and how it is arranged according to their filing systems. This, again, though useful, would tell us little about evidence as such. It could hardly be the informing or shaping structure.

(3) It might mean how the evidence relevant to a particular problem comes together to suggest a solution. This view would appeal especially to R. G. Collingwood or Sherlock Holmes. But this tells us more about a particular problem than about evidence in general.

At this point it becomes clear that what is meant here is not the structure of the material things that are evident, but the structure of the concept of evidence itself. As I have argued in this chapter, it seems that nothing is evidence *per se*. It is an abstract idea which only takes on meaning (like 'meaning' itself, or 'truth', 'intention', 'responsibility' or 'significance') in relation to minds.

I have discerned three important relationships between human minds and that which is evident: (1) the ability correctly to recognize what the evidence is; (2) the grasp of those processes by which past existents have come to be what they now are – that is, present evidence; (3) the judgement that understands the significance of these past existents for the problem with which the historian is concerned.

To illustrate this, I take an example from Collingwood's work on Roman

Britain, described in his autobiography.[25] When Collingwood realized the significance of Hadrian's Wall, he expected watch-towers to be found along the coast of the Solway Firth. A search of old archaeological publications revealed that some had been found, and Collingwood proceeded to look for others. What I have designated as relationship (1) – the ability to recognize what exists in the present – offered little problem to an archaeologist, since cut stones were arranged purposefully in the ground. Relationship (2) – to grasp that these were the remains of a tower of the Roman period – required (as explained in section 3.2 above) the ability to unravel the processes of deterioration, to work back from what there is to what there was. The third relationship – the judgement about the significance of these towers – did not occur until Collingwood made his study.

Such I believe, is the threefold structure of historical evidence.

In conclusion, I should like to suggest that rather more philosophical and critical thought be given to the concept of evidence. Historians recognize evidence as central to their enterprise, and they rightly give it a great deal of attention, both in relation to particular problems and in its material form. For example, the critical historian on picking up a new work of history looks at the back to discover the sources used for it. Nevertheless, the concept might well be explored in a more general and philosophical sense, not only to benefit working historians but also because it is (as I hope I have indicated) a concept interesting in its own right.

---

[25] R. G. Collingwood, *An Autobiography* (Penguin, 1944), p. 88.

5

From Evidence to Construction

1   The Fusion of Mind with Evidence

The discussion of evidence in the last chapter emphasized that 'evidence' is not a material thing but a concept involving a threefold relationship between (1) that which *is* evident, (2) that *of* which it is evidence and (3) the mind that makes the judgemental link between them; that the written evidence is quite distinct from 'the facts'; and that the historian, when using written evidence, is usually in the position of an eavesdropper upon an incomplete set of coded communications.

We are now approaching the kernel of the problem of historical knowledge, the problem of just what happens when historical evidence is metamorphosed into a construction of the past. In what ways is the historian prepared for this fusion of mind and matter – the historian's mind and the historian's matter? For it is this coming together of two very different things that creates historical knowledge. I shall then consider how the evidence is prepared for such a fusion.

At this point I should explain that in discussing historical knowledge I am referring primarily to that of the historian. He or she is, after all, the pioneer in establishing sound knowledge of history. But I do not wish to suggest that only historians can contribute to historical knowledge – still less that such knowledge matters only to them. The importance of historical knowledge for the non-specialist (and vice versa) will also have its place in this book.

2   The Function of the Historian in Relation to Evidence

The function of the historian in relation to the evidence can be viewed in three different ways, which I distinguish as the archaic, the positivistic or limited, and the imaginative or extended.[1] I shall discuss each in turn.

[1] I may be too optimistic in using the term 'archaic'. Collingwood believed that this mode still flourished in 1936, and it is not certainly extinct today: R. G. Collingwood, *The Idea of History* (Oxford University Press, 1961), p. 258.

2.1 The archaic or scissors-and-paste type

The archaic mode is that described so scornfully by Collingwood as 'scissors and paste'.

> The method by which it proceeds is first to decide what we want to know about, and then to go in search of statements about it, oral or written...Having found in such a statement something relevant to his purpose, the historian excerpts it and incorporates it, translated if necessary and recast into what he considers a suitable style, in his own history.[2]

Such a method makes few calls upon historians' intelligence, still less their imagination. The most they have to do is to consider the relative trustworthiness of their authorities if they conflict on a particular point, or to cast out what they find unacceptable because it conflicts with the views of their own (supposedly more enlightened) age. One can hardly speak here of a fusion of evidence and intelligence, that fusion which in the work of a great historian releases impulses of light and energy. The scissors-and-paste school of historiography has little to recommend it, unlike the other two approaches.

2.2 The positivistic or limited type

The second view rests less on established works of history; it makes use of the concept of 'sources' rather than of 'authorities'. Collingwood makes the distinction thus: 'The document hitherto called an authority now acquired a new status, properly described by calling it a "source", a word indicating that it contains the statement, without any implications as to its value.' The real distinction, however, is made when people enquire of a statement contained in a source not whether it is true or false but *what it means*.[3] This step forward leads to Vico's more sophisticated approach to history and on to the long (largely German) story of historicism, as well as the modern concern with hermeneutics.

It may be questioned, however, whether Collingwood was correct in saying that 'the first person to make this point (about meaning) was Vico'.[4] Great as was the achievement of this eighteenth-century Neapolitan lawyer, he may have been anticipated in this respect by English scholars, especially the physician Dr Robert Brady. In his *Introduction to the Old English History*, published in 1694, Brady writes of his texts: 'Before the use of them I

[2] Ibid., p. 257.
[3] Ibid., pp. 259, 260.
[4] Ibid., p. 259.

considered again and again whether I might not be mistaken in their true meaning and like wise considered all Circumstances and compared them with other relations of the same Times and Things.'[5] David Douglas, from whose book on English historians of the late seventeenth and early eighteenth century this extract is taken, comments: 'This was no idle claim.' Thus the importance of grasping the original and contemporary meaning of documents was already appreciated by at least one Englishman before the end of the seventeenth century. 'In that he treated his texts as the product of the medieval past', says Douglas, 'and sought to discover their meaning to the men who wrote them, his work has remained of permanent importance after its polemical significance has evaporated.'[6]

The crucial point, however, is the question of meaning. As Collingwood says, 'To ask what it means is to step right outside the world of scissors-and-paste history into a world where history is not written by copying out the testimony of the best sources, but by coming to your own conclusions.'[7]

The concept of meaning is notoriously difficult. Certainly it is nowadays generally agreed that the historian must establish the original meaning of the documents. But is this, as Brady said, 'their true meaning'? Is there only one possible meaning? To the nineteenth-century scholar Magna Carta was a foundation of the English Constitution, to an eighteenth-century American it was a charter of republican liberties, to a seventeenth-century parliamentarian it was a triumph of Saxon over Norman principles, while to its thirteenth-century contemporaries it meant a triumph of the baronial party over the king's party – not necessarily a good thing. Can it be that only the last of these is the true meaning of Magna Carta? It is even more difficult to argue that there is only one meaning for a whole passage of history. (What was the meaning of the Thirty Years War?)

There are, broadly, two defensible positions on this – what I have called the positivistic (not positivist) or limited, and the imaginative or extended (which is not to deny the use of imagination to those of the positivistic preference).

Nowadays nobody, I suppose, claims to write history as it actually happened – 'wie es eigentlich gewesen'.[8] Even Ranke was at the beginning of a very long career when in 1824 he made this claim, which he probably would not have made in his later years. More modestly, Bury, in his

---

[5] D. C. Douglas, *English Scholars* (Jonathan Cape, 1943), p. 158.
[6] Ibid., p. 155.
[7] Collingwood, *The Idea of History*, p. 260.
[8] It is not quite certain what Ranke meant by this. The normal translation of *eigentlich* is 'actually' or 'really'. However, at least one modern version reads 'how, essentially, things happened'. See Leopold von Ranke, *The Theory and Practice of History*, ed. G. G. Iggers and K. von Moltke (Bobbs-Merrill, 1973), p. 137. The translator of this passage was Wilma A. Iggers.

inaugural of 1902, argued that history is a cumulative science based on the amassing of facts – rather like pre-Darwinian natural history. He speaks of 'the faith that a complete assemblage of the smallest facts of human history will tell in the end', insisting that 'the only way to true history lies through scientific research.'[9]

A similar faith in the objectivity of history, if adequately based on research materials, was propounded by Lord Acton in his editorial letter of 12 March 1898 to the contributors to the *Cambridge Modern History*. 'In critical places', he wrote, 'we must indicate minutely the sources we follow, and must refer not only to the important books, but to articles in periodical works, and even to original documents, and to transcripts in libraries.' This would be 'history, original and authentic', and written so impartially that 'our Waterloo... satisfies French and English, Germans and Dutch alike; that no one can tell, without examining the list of authors, where the Bishop of Oxford laid down the pen, and whether Fairbairn or Gasquet, Liebermann or Harrison took it up.'[10] This is the 'voice of history' with a vengeance. One recalls Fustel de Coulanges, the historian of *The Ancient City* (1864), telling his applauding students: 'It is not I who speak. It is history that speaks through me.' Needless to say, he too believed that 'history is and should be a science.'[11]

Such faith has been much moderated since Bury; indeed, it is by no means certain that Bury remained as positivist as this.[12] Nevertheless, some of our best historians today believe that historical facts are both firm and knowable, and that there is only one correct interpretation of these facts. As against E. H. Carr, G. R. Elton argues firmly for 'the independent and real existence of historical events', which implies that 'a very large number of somewhat basic facts' can, in theory, be 'observed absolutely'. Hence 'of these simple facts an enormous number are precisely known.' He goes on to assert that 'all the facts of history are theoretically in this knowable category', though, of course, many are not, and some never will be.[13] Elton here confuses 'events' with 'facts' and I have already argued that they are not equivalent.[14] Thus, although I agree with Elton that the historian must try both to know and make known as far as possible 'the independent and real' historical events, this is not the same as accumulating facts. Elton speaks of 'the mass of

---

[9] See 'The science of history' in J. B. Bury, *Selected Essays*, ed. Harold Temperley (Cambridge University Press, 1930), pp. 17 and 19. The lecture is also printed in F. Stern (ed.), *The Varieties of History: from Voltaire to the present*, 2nd edn (Macmillan, 1970), pp. 209–23.

[10] See Lord Acton, *Lectures on Modern History* (Macmillan, 1906), appendix I, pp. 317–18. See also Stern (ed.), *The Varieties of History*, p. 249.

[11] Stern (ed.), *The Varieties of History*, p. 179.

[12] See C. J. W. Parker, 'English historians and the opposition to positivism', *History and Theory*, 22, 2 (1983), p. 121.

[13] G. R. Elton, *The Practice of History* (Fontana/Collins, 1969), p. 80.

[14] See chapter 4, section 6.

historical facts' and advocates 'the cumulative building up of assured
knowledge of both fact and interpretation.'[15] However, since I believe it is
occurrences that are known, not facts, I should deny that facts can be
accumulated, and I doubt whether history is strictly a cumulative discipline.
Facts are, at least in part, the products of judgement. I think Elton would
maintain that the facts, once established, point to one correct interpretation
– even though in practice we may not always know enough firmly to establish
any interpretation. He would probably deny that a passage of history could
be interpreted in several equally legitimate ways; that a series of occurrences
may have more than one meaning. Nevertheless, Elton is surely right to
stress the 'problem of the relationship between the genuine truth of the
historical event and the discovery of that truth from the evidence left behind'.
Nor is it to be doubted 'that the truth can be extracted from the evidence
by the application of proper principles of criticism.'[16]

The problem of capturing the truth in our net of concepts, and expressing
it in our linguistic and literary apparatus, is, I think, underestimated by
positivistic historians. Like Acton, they tend to put too much trust in the
original source. Many historians have been perhaps too profuse in the
quotations that interlard their writings (especially when they are descriptive
rather than narrative or analytic), and have been too ready to introduce
readers and students to primary sources. Many of these sources are direct,
vivid and pithy in a way that the historian often is not. Yet I doubt whether
primary sources (especially in selected extracts) do speak unequivocally; they
can, to the uninitiated, be dangerously deceptive. To use them in this way
is almost to go back to the scissors-and-paste stage and to treat original
sources as authorities.

On the other hand, the positivistic view does have the great merits of
stressing the necessity of adequate evidence, of asserting the reality of the
past, of reminding historians of their duty to know and to make known this
reality, and thus of denying relativism.

2.3   The imaginative or extended type

The distinction between the positivistic and imaginative view of the historian's
function was partly indicated by Sir George Clark, who in his 1957 General
Introduction to the *New Cambridge Modern History* wrote of the great historical
scholars of the nineteenth century: 'They came to think of facts as the
indestructible atoms by the adding of which together true history could be
composed. With something of this sort in mind they looked forward to a
future when it would be possible to write "definitive history".' This view

[15] Elton, *The Practice of History*, pp. 84–5.
[16] Ibid., pp. 78, 97.

was clearly expressed in the quotations from Bury and Acton above. Clark goes on to mark the divide: 'Historians of a later generation do not look forward to any such prospect. They expect their work to be superseded again and again.'[17] He points out that knowledge of the past has come through one or more minds, has been thereby 'processed', 'and therefore cannot consist of elemental and impersonal atoms which nothing can alter.' However, he does not explain any further than this why modern historians expect to be superseded, and while commenting that 'few of the historians were speculative enough to inquire what facts are' he himself does not attempt such an enquiry.[18]

As to the question why historians nowadays expect to be superseded, this surely has nothing to do with whether facts are atomic or not. One explanation is the growth of historical knowledge, which, as I have already remarked, is due both to the increase of available evidence and to the more effective interpretation of evidence. Interpretation often draws on developments in other sciences, such as medicine, statistics and anthropology. All this alone would make the supersession of history books inevitable. However, questions of context, significance and meaning are also relevant here. Knowledge of a historical event (not 'fact') may take on a very different significance according to the context in which it is placed. The occurrence itself, of course, remains the same. Even the statement of it, though subject to the vagaries of changing language and implication, may remain the same. (At least, I allow it for the sake of argument.) But the context can make all the difference. Dabs of red paint may be identical in size, shape, tone and shade, but their significance is quite different in different pictures – by a Breughel, a Rembrandt, a Picasso, a Mondrian. So with history.

For example, the evacuation of the British Expeditionary Force from Dunkirk in May 1940 acquired immediately its almost legendary status in the British history of the war, and in British memories that status is even now hardly diminished. It seemed a manifestation of Britain's long, proud maritime tradition. Yet in the context of German history it seems very small, and it hardly occurs at all in French history (except, perhaps, as an act of desertion by an ally), though soldiers of all three nations were involved. It is salutary to see any well-known passage from an unfamiliar point of view: the Russian history of the Second World War, the Indian history of the mutiny of 1857, an Arab history of the Crusades, for example. The same events are related, but in their different context they take on different values and different degrees of significance.

Historical events also change in their significance from different viewpoints

[17] In *New Cambridge Modern History*, vol. I: *The Renaissance 1493–1520*, ed. G. R. Potter (Cambridge University Press, 1957), p. xxiv.
[18] Ibid., p. xxv.

in time. English historians in the eighteenth and nineteenth centuries were much impressed by the Glorious Revolution of 1688–9 and its settlement; yet in this century attention has been focused on the Civil War and Interregnum – sometimes called the 'English Revolution' *tout court*, as if 1688 had been forgotten. Again, consider how a German of 1898 would have viewed 1848, and then how a German of 1948 did so. Americans have seen their Civil War as a moral crusade, a triumph of greed or a sad national necessity, each view in turn predominating in historical thought.

Thus, with the appearance of fresh evidence, new interpretations of old evidence, and changes of context and viewpoint, it is not surprising that the works of historians are continually being superseded. Any one period of the past may be seen by successive ages in a variety of different lights and from many different perspectives. History, it is often remarked, needs to be rewritten in each generation. Although this does not imply a relativist view of historical truth, it may be that no generation sees all the truth, while different ones fail to see different parts of the truth.

Nevertheless solid foundations for future progress can be laid; sound scholarship yields results that do not need to be repeated. The progress that Elton believes in and Anderson celebrates does indeed occur in historical studies.[19] All this involves the imagination. Indeed, as Elton points out, any good historian must be able to make 'an imaginative reconstruction of how things must have happened': 'Imagination, controlled by learning and scholarship, learning and scholarship rendered meaningful by imagination – those are the tools of enquiry possessed by the historian.'[20]

Yet some historians allow their imagination to suggest not only what must have happened, but what might have happened. One example is Gibbon's passage on the Moors' rapid advance from Spain into France in AD 731–2:

> A victorious line of march had been prolonged above a thousand miles from the Rock of Gibraltar to the banks of the Loire; the repetition of an equal space would have carried the Saracens to the confines of Poland and the Highlands of Scotland: the Rhine is not more impassable than the Nile or Euphrates, and the Arabian fleet might have sailed without a naval combat into the mouth of the Thames. Perhaps the interpretation of the Koran would now be taught in the schools of Oxford, and her pulpits might demonstrate to a circumcised people the sanctity and truth of the revelation of Mahomet.[21]

Aided by the splendour of the prose, these two sentences arouse the

[19] For Elton, see *The Practice of History*, p. 85 and *passim*. For Anderson, see chapter 3, section 4.

[20] Elton, *The Practice of History*, p. 112.

[21] Edward Gibbon, *The History of the Decline and Fall of the Roman Empire*, chapter 52.

imagination by placing the events upon a colossal stage – a setting that stretches a thousand miles in each direction and looks ahead over a thousand years. Not only is such a flight an effective device; it is also a justified piece of historical thinking. When we select a particular event and attempt to determine its historical significance, one of the criteria we use is the consideration of what might have happened without it. Gibbon's next sentence is: 'From such calamities was Christendom delivered by the genius and fortune of one man.' His purpose, of course, is to show the historical importance of Charles Martel and the battle of Poitiers. To return to my earlier example, the British, rightly or wrongly, attached great importance to the successful evacuation of their army from Dunkirk, believing that otherwise they would soon have fallen to the *Wehrmacht*. To the Germans the event was only a slight and, as it seemed, temporary setback in an otherwise successful conquest of western Europe. For the French, since the cause and their country were already lost, the additional loss of the British army may not have made things any worse. No one will know the truth of these suppositions. With such counter-factual reasoning, the hypothesis cannot be verified. Nevertheless, that is how people judge the significance of events. Clearly it is possible to take two views about this. However, the function of the imagination is to provide historians with a more creative attitude to their evidence. Lord Dacre took up this theme in his valedictory lecture at Oxford on 20 May 1980: 'Freewill, the choice of alternatives, is in the actor: the historian's function is to discern those alternatives, and that, surely, is the function of imagination. Therefore I have entitled my lecture "History and Imagination".'[22] He concludes: 'For in the end, it is the imagination of the historian, not his scholarship or his method (necessary though these are), which will discern the hidden forces of change.' To which one can only add 'and the hidden forces of non-change'. David Ogg, summing up the reforms of Maria Theresa and Joseph II, remarked: 'these were among the objects of the new cameralist school. The success of their application may account for the delay of revolution in the Austrian lands until 1848.'[23] As Lord Dacre implies, there are no rules whereby one may attain this sort of insight, but to penetrate to the deep currents that move the course of events is perhaps the greatest task of the historian.

3 The Stages of the Transformation

Before concluding this chapter on the transformation of evidence into historical construction, it may be useful to suggest the stages involved. I

[22] *The Times Literary Supplement*, 25 July 1980, pp. 833–5. The lecture is reprinted in H. Lloyd-Jones, V. Pearl and B. Worden (eds), *History and Imagination: essays in honour of H. R. Trevor-Roper* (Duckworth, 1981).
[23] D. Ogg, *Europe of the Ancien Régime, 1715–83* (Fontana/Collins, 1965), p. 207.

set them out in what I take to be the logical rather than the chronological order, both because they do not always occur strictly chronologically, and because historians in their work may keep returning to earlier stages. The stages are, I think, as follows:

1   Imagination or speculation, when the historian considers what he or she might study.
2   Selection, and perhaps preparation, of the evidence.
3   An attentive reading of the sources.
4   The embryonic or tentative metamorphosis of the evidence into a coherent construct or mental picture.
5   The recognition that, on the one hand, everyone must do this for himself, but, on the other, in so doing he is guided and controlled in many ways.

I shall enlarge a little on each stage.

First, how historians choose a piece of work, and how long they take to do so, vary enormously. Gibbon described how, from early youth, he 'aspired to the character of an historian'. 'While I served in the militia,' he continued (which he did between the ages of twenty-three and twenty-five) '. . . this idea ripened in my mind.' He chose, then rejected, a variety of subjects, from the Italian expedition of Charles VIII or a comparison of Henry V with the Emperor Titus, to a life of Sir Philip Sidney or Sir Walter Ralegh, and a number of others. It was not until he was in Rome at the age of twenty-seven that 'the idea of writing the decline and fall of the city first started to my mind.'[24]

Historians do not always begin with their theme; sometimes they begin with the evidence. (In my own case, it was so frequently encountering the name of Ralegh in the records of the High Court of Admiralty that turned me to writing the history of his family.) The origins of two pioneering works of the *Annales* school furnish interesting contrasts.

In his introduction to *Les Paysans de Languedoc* Emmanuel Le Roy Ladurie recounts how his attention was drawn, by a geographer friend, to the cadastral survey of Languedoc, which dated back to the fourteenth century and described in detail the surface, nature and value of all the landholdings. This sort of Domesday Book of southern France (it covered only the area of the *taille réelle*) would, he thought, make possible a long history of property. His initial presupposition about the origins of capitalism was challenged, and gradually, his concerns with a history of landholding broadened through population, products, prices, taxes, dues, revenues and wages to the peasants themselves. Although he had obtained the evidence in order to find confirmation of existing views, before long the evidence got hold of him ('C'était

---

[24] Edward Gibbon, *Autobiography*, Everyman edn (Dent, 1911), pp. 108, 124.

le document qui s'était emparé de moi'). In the end, he embarked on the adventure of writing total history.[25]

A decade earlier another Frenchman, Pierre Goubert, having been forced to spend some years in the Beauvaisis, decided to attempt a total history of this small region to the north of Paris. He was curious to discover the reality of life for all the people of this region during the seventeenth century, but he soon found it necessary to retreat from such a broad objective, and so he left on one side institutional, military, religious, juridical, moral, intellectual and even agrarian history.[26] The archives were so abundant, however, that, in spite of the usual difficulties of access, dispersal and lacunae, he was able to build up an original and inspiring demographic, social and economic reconstruction of a small but complex area of some two hundred parishes. The work was done almost entirely from uncatalogued and often unsorted documentary sources.[27] But, if Goubert's aim narrowed, his sympathies did not; he believed that the struggles of these seventeenth-century people deserved the social historian's attempts to understand them.[28]

With regard to the second stage in my suggested schema – the selection and treatment of the evidence – to a large extent the evidence selects itself. For most periods of history, the greater part of the written evidence has now been lost. Even for recent years, where yards of files are added to the archives each year, survival is very patchy. Anyone who tries to write a history of his or her own family or locality over the last hundred years, for example, soon discovers that the odd survivals – concert programmes, holiday snaps, affectionate letters, bus tickets, and so on – serve as reminders of how much has been lost. In addition, historians can never be as methodical as they would wish in selecting from the evidence that remains. Even if time and resources allow them to examine every relevant document, they are often allowed only one reading. Although historians will make notes and transcripts, their thoughts will range back and forth in a creative interplay between the evidence and the construction. Carr has described history as 'a continuous process of interaction between the historian and his facts, an unending dialogue between the present and the past' (I prefer the word 'evidence' to 'facts').[29] However unless historians have all the evidence to hand, in their study or library, this interaction is handicapped, since they

---

[25] Emmanuel Le Roy Ladurie, *Les Paysans de Languedoc* (Flammarian, 1969), pp. 5–10.

[26] Pierre Goubert, *Cent Mille Provinciaux au XVIIᵉ siècle: Beauvais et le Beauvaisis de 1600 à 1730* (Flammarion, 1968), pp. 10, 15.

[27] Ibid., pp. 14, 15–22. For inspiration, see, for example, Kenneth A. Lockridge, 'Historical demography', in *The Future of History: essays in the Vanderbilt University Centurial Symposium*, ed. C. F. Delzell (Vanderbilt University Press, 1977), p. 53.

[28] 'Tous ont droit à ce grand effort de sympathie et, si possible, d'intelligence': Goubert, *Cent Mille Provinciaux au XVIIᵉ siècle*, p. 415.

[29] E. H. Carr, *What is History?* (Penguin, 1964), p. 30.

cannot visit the library in California or the archives in Rome every time
a fresh inspiration or a sudden doubt strikes them. Moreover, because there
is often not enough time to read the masses of available documents, historians
must follow their hunches.

Again, languages act as a selecting agent. Any major passage of European
history such as the Renaissance, the Reformation or the twentieth-century
wars involves most European peoples. One cannot hope to understand much
of the history of a nation unless one can read its language. Even the most
objective of French or German histories have different overtones when read in
the original. In any case only the most important primary sources are available in translation. Even if a European historian can read English, French,
German, Italian and Spanish, this still leaves at least a dozen other languages.
Such sources must be either ignored or translated – an unsatisfactory or even
impossible solution. For the history of Asia or Africa the problem is worse.

Sometimes historians require the services of one of the so-called auxiliary
sciences: palaeography, epigraphy and diplomatic; iconography (the arts of
the book and of the picture); chronology and genealogy, heraldry, sigillography
and numismatics; linguistics and toponymy (the study of place-names);
historical geography and topography, and other sciences.[30] Such studies are
so specialized, not to say arcane, that historians cannot hope to master them
and have time for their chosen occupation. Their task is, therefore, not so
much to read seals or blazons as to know how to evaluate the result of the
experts' researches upon the evidence. Since in all these matters, from translation to iconography, the evidence reaches historians at second hand, they
are not full in control, and must rely on judgement, experience and luck.

The third stage of the process involves a careful reading of the sources.
As has often been said, one should read and reread the sources until one
can almost hear the voices. When one feels one is really 'getting inside' the
subject, it is a profoundly satisfying experience, both because and in spite
of the fact that it goes beyond cold logic, which points out that one is merely
looking in on a distant, coded communication. The process of communication begins with the mental content of the writer, which is first reduced to
a code; then the coded message (the text) is transmitted to the receiver; the
message is decoded by this recipient; and finally this understanding is
incorporated into the mental content of the recipient. It is into the middle
of this process that the historian intervenes, swooping down and carrying
off the message like a skilfully intercepted pass in football. Not surprisingly,
any initial feeling of triumph is often replaced by doubt whether one can
understand or decode the message as correctly as its original recipient did.
The historian must read and think and read again.

---

[30] See, for example, Centre Nationale de la Recherche Scientifique, *La Recherche Historique
en France de 1940 à 1965* (Paris, 1965).

This gradual absorption of the evidence, the interplay that Carr describes, leads to the metamorphosis, the fourth stage. From the evidence the historian now builds up an intellectual construction of the past. The historian's subjective experience is to create in the present a picture of the past. However, this experience must vary according to the mind of the historian.[31] It may be colourful and picturesque, as with G. M. Trevelyan; it may be drawn in firmly moral blacks and whites by Macaulay; or it may be a rather abstract framework of girders constructed by an economic historian out of models and statistics. No two historians have exactly similar experiences, because no two historians have exactly similar minds.

This leads to the fifth and final stage (in logical sequence, as I have said, not in actual practice). The creative but subjective experience of the historian is highly important, not only because it is by this means alone that we can (as Holborn says) obtain any objective knowledge of the past, but because everyone's beliefs about the past constitute some similar sort of subjective experience; the historian's creative experience differs only in degree, not in kind, from that of any man, woman or child. History is not governed by rules, laws or theories according to which data must be marshalled. The correct 'placing' of a piece of evidence, however banal, depends on the subjective imaginative judgement of the individual, and even the best historical knowledge is no more than the concurrence of such judgements. What sort of considerations bear upon judgements, how they are inspired, guided and controlled, will be the subject of the next chapter. Here I wish only to stress that, in an important sense, every man must be his own historian.

[31] See above, chapter 2, section A.

6

The Historian's Mind and the Historical Construction

One of the key questions in the study of history is how far the structures of the historian's construction correspond to the structures of the past that is so described. This is more than simply asking whether the historian's ideas correspond to reality. The question concerns the structures of a complex account of an important part of history.

As I have explained, the historian makes a construction of the past in a creative mental effort based on the available evidence. It is comparable, but not necessarily very similar, to the creation of a poem, a symphony or a scientific theory. In the last chapter I examined one of the two elements in this creative fusion: the evidence. I now turn to the other element: the historian's mind.

The Historian

I recall again that (as pointed out by Holborn) our objective knowledge of the past is necessarily gained through the subjective experiences of the historian.[1] The word 'experiences' does not, however, imply that historians are merely passive transcribers of the records. On the contrary, the study and the writing of history clearly demonstrate that these highly individual activities are essentially creative. We should expect no less distinctiveness in writing history than in making poetry. Each activity has its forms and traditions; each explores the limits of the possible; each transforms subjective thought into objective reality; each is the product of a unique individual mind. Properly to understand the nature of a work of history we need to understand its author. E. H. Carr's dictum, 'When you read a work of history, always listen out for the buzzing',[2] is true to some extent, but the implication is derogatory. What is called for, I suggest, is something along

[1] See chapter 2, section 1.
[2] E. H. Carr, *What is History?* (Penguin, 1964), p. 23.

the lines of John Livingston Lowes's study of the making of one poem in *The Road to Xanadu*.[3]

It may be objected that this would do too much honour to Professor Dry-as-Dust and the other toilers in the historiographical industry. In reply I would urge that it is not merely a question of literary merit. Since Aristotle's day the poet and the historian have exchanged roles as public educators. In ancient times it may well be that Homer did more than Thucydides, Virgil than Livy, to shape the world that people saw. But in modern times what poet can match the influence of historians in portraying the modern world, and hence, by implication, increasing our understanding of our societies and our own positions in them? A number of historiographical studies have acclaimed the importance of Macaulay, Ranke, Michelet, Burckhardt and Treitschke in the development of their craft. Yet more might be said of the extent of their readership. It would be even more worth while to attempt to estimate how much a modern Englishman's perception of the Tudors is due to G. R. Elton, of the English Revolution to Christopher Hill, of the diplomacy of the Great Powers to A. J. P. Taylor, or of the Bolshevik Revolution to E. H. Carr.

As I have observed, no two minds are alike, not even in historical scholarship. Merely to 'listen out for the buzzing' is not enough. What should we look at?

One well-tried method is to examine someone's 'life and times'. I shall attempt this in a more precise and orderly way, dividing the task into six parts, three for 'the times' and three for 'the life'.

1.1 The historian's age

E. H. Carr has remarked that the historian is not apart from but a part of history – 'just another dim figure trudging along in another part of the procession'.[4] The point has been well taken, and now most students know that it is not enough to grasp what the historian says; they must also be aware of when he said it. Perhaps too much has been made of this, especially by those non-historians who claim to regard historians as so much the product of their age, so *zeitgebunden*, that what they say is hardly worth reading in another age. (Is it partly because of this prejudice that works of history grow so quickly out-of-date and are relegated to the dim recesses of secondhand bookshops?) Herbert Butterfield, on the contrary, argued that, just because historians *are* a product of their age, one must study the full historiography of a topic before embarking on a fresh study. He demonstrated that the latest work is by no means always the most reliable. In a study of the historiography

---

[3] J. L. Lowes, *The Road to Xanadu: a study in the ways of the imagination* (Pan Books, 1978).
[4] Carr, *What is History?*, p. 36.

of the origins of the Seven Years War, he showed that scholars followed Frederick the Great's errors for over a century, that the crucial role of Russian actions was not suspected before German scholarship of the 1860s and 1890s, and that the facts became clear only when the Russian papers were published in 1912. Then, however, he had to admit that 'on our particular subject, everything that has been written since [i.e. 1896] seems to represent a decline in scholarship. Some of our twentieth-century writing would have been better if it had even shown a knowledge of the work of nearly sixty years ago.' Again, 'Since 1900 historians have even shown a tendency to revert to routine and slip the story back into the traditional grooves.'[5]

A closer examination of the historian might explain such practices. In this section I refer to three characteristics of the historian's age, suggested by the notions of posterity, *Zeitgeist* and propinquity.

A historian's understanding of his chosen period is affected by the fact that he comes after that period, and, to a lessser extent, by how much time has elapsed since that period. For example, we in the twentieth century must, perhaps, remain invincibly ignorant of much that was apparent to our ancestors in, say, the thirteenth, but we do have some idea of what came after the thirteenth. We do know that in Europe there was to be a Renaissance, a Reformation and a scientific revolution, even though the effect of these great events may render much of the medieval mind opaque to us.

The *Zeitgeist* is more questionable. But if we grant that there is some sense in which each age has its own individual flavour – evoked perhaps most vividly by popular music, dress fashions, photographs or interior decoration – then these differences in spirit are likely to influence historians' views of their subject. One must not forget, however, that the greatest historians often have a knack of surmounting these obstacles of time and spirit, of *Zeit* and *Geist*. Butterfield remarked of Ranke: 'His "hunches" are one of the interesting features of the story. In the last resort, sheer insight is the greatest asset of all.'[6]

With regard to propinquity, we may take up Carr's point that history does not proceed in a straight line but winds about, 'sometimes doubling back on itself'.[7] The nineteenth century, though more remote from the Middle Ages than the eighteenth, found that period easier to understand. Nor is it just superior scholarship that so clearly marks Sir Ronald Syme's *The Roman Revolution* as a work of the twentieth century. One age may be distant in time yet close in spirit to another, and a later period may well be at a historiographical advantage.

[5] Herbert Butterfield, *Man on his Past* (Cambridge University Press, 1969), chapter 5, pp. 153, 160.
[6] Ibid., p. 170.
[7] Carr, *What is History?*, p. 36.

1.2   The historical knowledge of the age

If we turn from these general considerations of the age to what is particularly relevant to the historian, the most important would seem to be the extent and accuracy of the historical knowledge of the age. As Butterfield points out, the growth of such knowledge is not along a steady line of ascent, and later periods may be more ignorant than earlier ones. To a considerable extent, however, historical knowledge is cumulative; at least the evidence is. One can hardly expect the same exacting standards of scholarship before the famous 'opening of the archives' in the nineteenth century as after it. So, when trying to explore the mind of any historian, one must discover what was the 'state of the art', what was actually known at the time of writing, what data and techniques were available. If the growth of knowledge and its dissemination, despite a general progress, diminish at certain times (as almost certainly happens in totalitarian states), this must be taken into account when one studies the mind of a particular historian.

1.3   The basic suppositions of the age

It is not enough to investigate the extent of historical knowledge in this rather positivistic form. The 'times' contribute more than historical information to the formation of the historian's mind. Among these contributions are some of which he or she is probably unaware and therefore never makes them explicit. Collingwood calls them 'absolute presuppositions': 'Whenever anybody states a thought in words, there are a great many more thoughts in his mind than are expressed in his statement. Among these there are some which stand in a peculiar relation to the thought he has stated: they are not merely its context, they are its presuppositions.' He points out that 'Every question involves a presupposition', and that a presupposition is either relative or absolute.[8] For example, the accuracy of a yardstick is presupposed when used for measuring, but the presupposition of its accuracy may on occasion be questioned. Thus the presupposition 'This is a yard long' is relative to one set of questions (for example, how long is this room, this lawn?) but is itself the answer to another – 'Precisely how long is this yardstick?' Although most presuppositions are of this relative kind, some are more fundamental. Collingwood defines an 'absolute presupposition' as 'one which stands, relatively to all questions to which it is related, as a presupposition, never as an answer'. Examples of absolute presuppositions are 'Every event has a cause' or 'God created the universe' or 'Monarchs are endowed with divine authority' or 'Every injustice calls for revenge.' 'Absolute presuppositions

[8] R. G. Collingwood, *An Essay on Metaphysics* (Clarendon Press, 1940), pp. 21, 25, 29.

are not verifiable,' says Collingwood, only relative ones. However, the importance of an absolute presupposition is not its truth but it logical efficacy, which depends not on the supposition's being true but on its being supposed.[9]

Collingwood goes on to argue that metaphysics consists purely of the study of absolute suppositions: 'Metaphysics is the attempt to find out what absolute presuppositions have been made by this or that person or group of persons, on this or that occasion or group of occasions, in the course of this or that piece of thinking.'[10] Collingwood's definition of metaphysics as simply the study of absolute presuppositions is both too narrow and too wide. As Körner has shown, it is too narrow because it excludes metaphysical speculation, and it is too wide because, on Collingwood's account, 'any kind of principle could conceivably be accepted as an ultimate presupposition.'[11] But Collingwood is surely right that such a study – though not under the name of metaphysics (Körner suggests 'historical dogmatics') – would be highly profitable.

Anthropologists have demonstrated that different cultures each have their own sets of absolute presuppositions. Some societies differ in these respects so much from our own that we have been forced to admit that the suppositions taken for granted in the modern Western world are far from being universal. This is true even of what was once held to be the distinguishing mark of humanity, the faculty of reason. The consequence has been many lengthy and unconcluded debates in sociology and philosophy.[12] If presuppositions of rationality are not common to all, it is less surprising to find even greater differences in presuppositions of morality, politics and cosmology.

That societies can differ so fundamentally has been clear from the work of anthropologists since at least the beginning of this century. The Bolshevik Revolution, the growth of fascism, and the super-power rivalry that has followed the Second World War have all demonstrated that what was one civilization can be divided into two hostile and almost mutually incomprehensible societies. One may ask whether in these cases the differences in absolute presuppositions are not as great as those between, say, Bronislaw Malinowski and the Trobriand Islanders or Evans-Pritchard and the Nuer. The fate of Western civilization in the twentieth century demonstrates that sets of absolute presuppositions are changeable. No society is condemned to continue with the same set upon pain of dissolution. The logic of such basic changes, how and why they may be

[9] Ibid., pp. 31, 32.
[10] Ibid., p. 47.
[11] Stephan Körner, *Fundamental Questions in Philosophy* (Penguin, 1971), pp. 190, 191.
[12] See, for example, Bryan R. Wilson (ed.), *Rationality* (Basil Blackwell, 1974).

validly made, has been demonstrated by Körner, especially in *Categorial Frameworks*.[13]

All this affects historians in two ways. It affects their studies, because (as the more alert now realize) they must grasp the absolute presuppositions, the unspoken assumptions, of the society under review, in order to understand what has occurred. It equally affects their own productions; of this they may be less aware. The world in which the historian lives has its own presuppositions, no less than others. Nevertheless he has a better chance than most of recognizing (through comparisons with other ages) at least some of the suppositions of his world. The historian's thinking may be clarified by studying some philosophical aspects of this problem variously discussed by, for example, Collingwood, Körner and Toulmin. In particular, of course, the current assumptions of any age about scientific and historiographical methods must be taken into account.[14]

1.4   The historian as individual

For lack of space I have been able to do no more than indicate this fascinating topic of 'historical dogmatics' (to use Körner's phrase). Now, however, I turn from the society to the individual, from 'the times' of the historian to 'the life'. The characteristics of the age, which I have discussed under three headings, are all in principle open to historians; consciously or unconsciously, they may draw on any of them and make them relevant to their work. In practice, however, historians select from the whole range of possibilities, which are thereby limited even as they are realized. For example, current prejudices and enthusiasms about the Middle Ages acted powerfully upon the author of *Past and Present*, but little upon the historian of the French Revolution or the biographer of Frederick II and of Cromwell. Not all historians were as flexible as Carlyle, however. One cannot imagine Macaulay writing like Ranke, his contemporary, or Burckhardt like Buckle, or Acton like Bury. The differences, of course, lie not so much in the age as in the individual, whom I now consider.

First, I examine the individual simply as a person, not as a historian. His mind, that creative instrument which I am trying to assess, is in some part a product of his psychology, physiology and neurology. To determine

[13] Stephan Körner, *Categorial Frameworks* (Basil Blackwell, 1970). Stephen Toulmin, in *Human Understanding* (Clarendon Press, 1972), vol. I, has begun a similar exploration from a slightly different angle. For a good discussion of Collingwood's position, see Rex Martin, 'Collingwood's doctrine of absolute presuppositions and the possibility of historical knowledge', in *Substance and Form in History: A collection of essays in philosophy of history*, ed. L. Pompa and W. H. Dray (University of Edinburgh Press, 1981), p. 89. For a different view, see Lionel Rubinoff, *Collingwood and the Reform of Metaphysics: a study in the philosophy of mind* (University of Toronto Press, 1970).
[14] See, for example, Butterfield, *Man on his Past, passim*.

the nature of these in any particular individual and to discover how they affect his thinking and working is difficult, yet impossible to neglect. Relevant questions should not be ignored because they are difficult to answer. Explicitly to state a problem and to acknowledge that one does not know the answer is not only the first step to wisdom, as Socrates taught; it is often the beginning of the solution, as the history of science amply demonstrates.

The next set of relevant considerations – the individual's experiences – presents fewer problems. For reasons of space, discretion or sheer ignorance, the biographies, even the autobiographies, of historians usually omit many experiences that have affected the mature working mind. None the less, the autobiographies of Gibbon and Collingwood, the letters of Macaulay and Acton, the recollections of de Tocqueville or Meinecke (to name but a few) do tell us much about the nature, both the excellence and the shortcomings, of their histories.

One must also consider the possibly quite restricted social milieu of the historian. Some have been great travellers, like Ibn Khaldoun; some have been well acquainted at first hand with European culture, like Gibbon or Acton; some, like Stubbs or Creighton, have led comparatively secluded lives in a vicarage, rectory or college; some have exercised political power, like Thucydides, Macaulay or Churchill; some have been competent linguists, others restricted virtually to one language. Social class is relevant too. Perhaps the most common origin is the professional middle class, but Thomas Carlyle and A. L. Rowse, Alexis de Tocqueville and Lord Acton had other backgrounds. Social milieu and, in particular, its *mentalité* are a matter not only of origins but of everyday life. In this century, as historians have become professionals, most are attached to an institution of learning or, less often, government, and this has tended to limit and homogenize their environments. It is a matter for debate whether the resultant increase in sheer technical ability has, in many cases, been bought at the expense of that knowledge of the wider world enjoyed by historians of earlier centuries.

Lastly, the contemporary world of learning is likely to have an effect on the historian's mind. Issues of government, of national pride or of theological controversy would have affected nineteenth-century historians. In this century the greatest external influence on historians has probably been the rapid development of the social sciences. It is, perhaps, to be regretted that an intellectual upheaval of great importance, that of modern art, has had little effect upon historians in general, despite its relevance to their work. The distinction between reproducing what is seen and revealing what is unseen is surely relevant; so is the relationship between perception and expression, or the many different ways of perceiving the world. They might profitably consider why Cézanne rebelled against impressionism. But of the impact of economics and sociology (and, to a lesser extent, anthropology, political science, demography and linguistics) there is no doubt.

1.5   *The historian as professional*

I now move from intellectual but non-historical influences to those of the historian's own profession. These influences are usually most fully described in the biographies and autobiographies of historians, where we learn about their education, and the two or three scholars who most helped them to set out on the right path. We read rather less, however, of the day-to-day influences of professional colleagues upon working scholars. Nevertheless conversations in studies, pubs, common rooms, conferences and committees probably take up several hours a day. Because of their informality they leave little record, but no one who has lived this life can doubt its importance. Indeed, one may hazard a guess that these conversations play a larger part in moulding their outlook and understanding than most academics are prepared to admit.

More formal influences, which are more easily recognized, are those of the historical profession worldwide, exercised mainly through books, the articles and reviews in learned journals, and conferences and seminars. These enable – indeed, subtly compel – scholars to maintain an awareness of other work being done in their field. Since they are usually very sensitive to the opinion of this public, they are almost imperceptibly nudged away from some topics, approaches, methods or theories, and towards others. For it is here that academic fashions are set. Easy as it is to make fun of the academic world (profitably demonstrated by several bestselling novelists), one must also recognize that this worldwide network of scholarship performs fairly effectively the function of maintaining standards.

Lastly, historiographical traditions provide the context in which historians choose what they should work on and how they should do so. Such traditions may inhere in a university; those of Cambridge or the London School of Economics or Chicago or (two centuries ago) Göttingen are not difficult to recognize. The tradition may belong to a political position (like that of left-wing writing on the French Revolution) or to a nation, like that of mid-nineteenth-century Prussia. In addition, the subject itself has its own tradition, like the pre-eminence of landownership in English or of demography in French local studies. In these, and perhaps in other ways too, the profession of the historian helps to form the individual mind.[15]

---

[15] Three interesting studies of French historiographical traditions are Charles-Olivier Carbonell, *Histoire et historiens: une mutation idéologique des historiens français, 1865–1885* (Toulouse, Privat, 1976); William R. Keylor, *Academy and Community: the foundations of the French historical profession* (Harvard University Press, 1975); T. Stoianovich, *French Historical Method: the 'Annales' paradigm* (Cornell University Press, 1976).

1.6   *The historian 'qua' historian*

When a historian works *qua* historian, his or her mind has an individuality which is, almost certainly, more than the sum or the resultant of all the influences I have mentioned. Historians have their personal predilections, their own *idées fixes*, their own curiosities. These personal idiosyncrasies provide a considerable part of the mental energies indispensable to their task; they largely determine how their minds work. They are, in some yet to be discovered way, closely connected with the powers of imagination and creativity.

Before contemplating the shape of the final historiographical product, historians must ask themselves how they see their subject. Do they see it as a vertical arrangement, a narrative that follows a direct but narrow path through time, ignoring most of the contemporary or concomitant happenings? Do they see a society or an age spread horizontally, unfolded in all its fullness and richness? Their task then will be to describe it rather as one might a stage-set or a landscape. Do they attempt to combine the two and describe everything in motion – of necessity only over a short time or in a restricted space? This is *histoire globale* or total history. If their view is more selective and abstractive, they may decide to pursue a theme – attitudes to death or methods of agriculture or the formation of bureaucracies, perhaps. Then they will seek, identify and abstract examples relative to their thesis. They will also probably (1) compare them with similar examples from other ages or societies; (2) relate them to some social scientific theory; and (3) resort to some use of quantitative methods. In short, this work will draw from, and tend to fade into, a social science. Such methods are particularly favoured by French historians of the *Annales* school.

In all these approaches, historians employ their intentions, their hopes and fears, their beliefs, their methodological, even metaphysical, principles, their grasp and use of language and of languages, their hermeneutic capacities, and so on. All these are all relevant to the major task of seeing and understanding the past, and hence making a reasonably accurate and functioning mental model of it. It is not merely a question of how they will tell their story; it is, first and foremost, a question of how they see the past and the material it has supplied.

How a historian sees the past is only a part of how he or she sees the world. The final colour and shape of a historian's construction is bestowed by his or her own *Weltanschauung* (assuming that this world-view is not merely a copy of someone else's). Dominating all technical considerations of evidence, method, interpretation and construction is the individual human being. The German critic, Erich Heller, writing of Oswald Spengler's massive work on civilizations, *The Decline of the West*, insisted Spengler must be rejected 'not because his history is incorrect, but because it is untrue. . . . Spengler's history is untrue because the mind which has conceived it is, despite its learning and seeming subtlety, a crude and wicked mind. The image of man which lurks behind Spengler's vast historical canvas is perverted.' Heller goes on to say that Spengler has no ideas of freedom, love, pity or pathos. 'It is a worthless and deeply untruthful sort of history which lacks these qualities, for they are the proper tools of human understanding.'[16]

I think Heller is right to judge historical work in these terms. If history is no more than the handling of data, then it can be done by a copying clerk or a machine. But surely it is a very human activity. Historical work is done *by* men and women, *about* men and women, *for* men and women. If history is a science, then it is one of the most human of sciences.

2 What the Mind Brings

The essential task of the historian is, then, to effect a creative fusion between his or her mind and the evidence. Oakeshott puts it like this: 'The activity of the historian is pre-eminently that of understanding present events – the things that are before him – as evidence for past happenings.'[17] Having considered the formation of that mind, I now turn from its general characteristics and faculties to its operations upon a particular subject.

People have an almost intuitive understanding of human life and society which, for example, enables the reader of a novel or the spectator of a drama to enter in thought and feeling into the world portrayed. Since we know how human beings generally live, with a little practice we can make the necessary adjustments to the social milieu of a class, country or age other than our own. Readers and spectators are assisted by descriptive passages in novels, by costumes and settings on the stage, and by the words and actions of the characters. Similarly historians must grasp not only what is said and done but the social context in which this occurs.

As a historian approaches the evidence, his or her mind is by no means a *tabula rasa*. As well as possessing a universal, quasi-intuitive understanding of life and society, he or she also brings to the topic some picture, however vague or inaccurate, of that past society – whether it be ancient Egypt, medieval Provence or Nazi Germany.

A similar process was described by Popper in a 1948 paper on the aims of science, entitled 'The Bucket and the Searchlight: Two Theories of

---

[16] Erich Heller, *The Disinherited Mind* (Penguin, 1961), p. 169.
[17] Michael Oakeshott, 'The activity of being an historian', in *Rationalism in Politics and Other Essays* (Methuen, 1967), p. 150.

Knowledge'. He begins by attacking 'the bucket theory of the mind', the view 'that before we can know or say anything about the world, we must first have had perceptions – sense experiences.' Accordingly, 'our mind resembles a container – a kind of bucket – in which perceptions and knowledge accumulate.'[18] Although Popper is talking of knowledge in general, one can recognize here a common attitude to historical knowledge as a mere accumulation of facts – perhaps a view encouraged at school by bad textbooks and lazy teachers.

Such is the 'bucket theory of knowledge' which Popper rejects, preferring instead the 'searchlight theory'. Pointing out that all organisms react to stimuli, and that many can, within limits, learn from experience, he suggests: 'We shall regard the process by which the organism learns as a certain kind of change, or modification, in its dispositions to react, and not, as would the bucket theory, as an (ordered or classified or associated) accumulation of memory traces, left over by perceptions that are past.' In this process, if one holds a series of expectations about the world and then finds one or more disappointed (as when one is made aware of a missing step by placing one's foot where one expected it to be), one must then correct that system of expectations.[19] Again there is a parallel with learning history. Anyone who started to study the Tudors holding expectations of 'Bluff King Hal' and 'Good Queen Bess' would, after careful attention to the teacher or a good textbook, be compelled to change those images.

Popper points out that 'it is observation rather than perception which plays the decisive part.' It is not so much a matter of passively receiving impression as knowing what to look for – hence the 'searchlight'. On this theory, 'observations are secondary to hypotheses.'[20]

I shall not pursue further Popper's development of this theory of knowledge. (Indeed, when he comes to apply it to history I think he gets it wrong[21]), but these aspects are relevant to the work of historians. As they begin their task, they leave behind the school-engendered view that knowing history consists of memorizing a bucketful of facts, since that view cannot survive the impact of researching in primary sources. They may not, however, see that the way to gain knowledge is to make carefully directed observations in the light of a specific, but loosely held, hypothesis. Furthermore, as Popper emphasizes, progress is made not so much by accumulating data that support the hypothesis as by being alert to those data that do not. Paradoxical as it may seem, good historians, like good scientists, should actually seek to have their expectations disappointed.

[18] Karl R. Popper, *Objective Knowledge: an evolutionary approach* (Clarendon Press, 1973), p. 341.
[19] Ibid., pp. 343–4.
[20] Ibid., pp. 342, 346.
[21] Ibid., p. 355.

In a section called 'The Fallacies of the Historian' in his book on the historiography of the Seven Years War, Butterfield castigates the frequent failure of historians to view the evidence without prejudice – what he calls 'the historian's blind eye'. Although Russia was the key to the problem, and 'there could be a number of patent facts definitely pointing to Russia', many a historian would recapitulate them 'like a man in a day-dream', totally missing their significance because he 'had his attention focused elsewhere'. Again, Butterfield points out 'the common defect of historians to poke the new evidence into the old structure of the story'. This, he says, is because 'the old story has dug itself deep and made grooves in our minds.'[22] A similar process was described by Thomas Kuhn in *The Structure of Scientific Revolutions*, in which he explains that the paradigms of 'normal sciences' have to be replaced when incompatible data can no longer be forced into the old structure, but demand a radically new paradigm.[23]

In the light of what Popper and Kuhn have said, it is easy to understand why historians fall into the trap of following what Butterfield calls the grooves of the old story. They have to bring *some* expectation to the topic, and this expectation is often derived from their first encounter with the subject. In the case of the Seven Years War, Frederick the Great, unwittingly, 'set future historiography on the wrong track'.[24] Butterfield's solution consists 'of reducing the whole narrative to its primary materials and then putting the pieces together again in a genuine work of reconstruction', but he does not explain what model is to be used for this. He says, 'a child of seven, fresh from the bosom of nature, would hardly fall into the error'.[25] But a child of seven would have no model at all, however incorrect, of the origins of the Seven Years War. Historians must begin somewhere; they must have some notion of what they are dealing with. Although Butterfield has identified the fault, his remedy seems to be based on an untenable ideal of empiricism.

> Sometimes, we might feel, it would even be better if the historian could actually go to work with a mind unloaded of all hypotheses – could collect his facts and amass his microscopic details, and place everything in chronological order, until the moment comes when he can brood over the whole without any *parti pris*. It might be better if he could. . . wait until the pattern begins to stare at him from a multiplicity of facts, as his mind mixes itself into the assembled data.'[26]

---

[22] Butterfield, *Man on his Past*, pp. 158–62.

[23] Thomas S. Kuhn, *The Structure of Scientific Revolutions*, 2nd edn (University of Chicago Press, 1970).

[24] Butterfield, *Man on his Past*, p. 144.

[25] Ibid., p. 159.

[26] Ibid., p. 160.

This is surely the old heresy that all a scientist has to do is to collect the data; then their significances, perhaps a new law of science, will be immediately apparent. Scientific theories are not so constructed, as is now well accepted. So, in opposition to Butterfield, I would argue that the searchlight must be directed – directed especially upon evidence that does not fit the old hypothesis. Truth may live at the bottom of a well, but she will not leap out of the bucket, fully formed, like Athene from the head of Zeus.

In the very act of collecting the facts, historians make the judgements of relevance that betray them into the old error. Accordingly, both scientists and historians must be alert for what disconfirms their hypothesis and not be lulled into security by finding many things that confirm it. Like liberty, scientific progress can only be bought at the price of eternal vigilance. Recently, however, historians have increasingly shown themselves ready to discard old hypotheses. In avoiding rigidity, however, some writers also avoid rigour, so that hypotheses are both accepted and jettisoned on insufficient grounds.

3   How the Mind Works

Whether they are writing a restricted narrative (as of diplomatic negotiations or of a parliamentary campaign), or making a comparative or analytical study of types of complex phenomena (as of revolutions or of trade cycles), or attempting some sort of all-embracing history, all historians require some grasp of the society in which these events occur. As I have argued, they begin with a picture or model, however inadequate, and proceed to modify it as they learn more. For example, a historian might regard the opening of the Seven Years War as a 'diplomatic revolution', a change of partners among the four powers – England, France, Austria and Prussia. After discovering that Russia, Saxony, North America and India must also be taken into consideration, not to mention the Dutch, the Swedes and the Spaniards, he then has a picture of eight or ten powers with common or conflicting interests spread over an area extending roughly from the Urals and the Hooghly to the Mississippi. Although it might be supposed that they operated like the great powers of today, further study would reveal that speed of transport and communication, the nature and effectiveness of armies and navies, the degree of governmental control, and the methods and tacit assumptions of diplomacy all differed very considerably from the world of the late twentieth century. Allowances have to be made for all these. By adjusting, altering, extending, diversifying and deepening the historian modifies the first crude model along the lines suggested by the evidence, until he feels that his understanding of the whole story is much closer to what actually occurred. (If historians feel, though, that their understanding is still inadequate and much remains to be done, they are surely correct.)

The good historian will also try to understand how men and women of that time saw their own world. It is a common practice for historians to intersperse their narratives or descriptions with direct quotations from primary sources, to give directness, vividness and accuracy. It is often forgotten, however, that the historian is addressing a contemporary public, with all the presuppositions of its own age, while the words of the witness, the historical agent, were spoken or written perhaps centuries earlier in another age that was different physically, socially and (most important to stress because least apparent) ideologically. The historian's view and the witness's experience of the events may not coincide as neatly as the text might suggest. Not only should historians be well aware that the agents' view may differ; they should keep this distinction in the forefront of their mind, and ensure that readers do likewise.[27]

In order to understand how and why changes occurred in past society, one must remember that neither the historian's nor the agent's view can be static. Whether or not the historical agents (the Newcastles and Kaunitzes, for example) gave much thought to how and why their world was changing, the historical observer (the student of history) must certainly be aware of these changes, however imperceptible to the contemporary eye. With the benefit of hindsight and the long view, one can discern the deep and invisible currents that were sweeping men and women on to another and stranger world than the one they thought they knew. Historians rightly enjoy plumbing and charting these currents, but they are sometimes too ready to account for them. Because of the subtleties of political and social analysis, the grasp of economic theory, the metaphysical and even theological assumptions that may be involved in accounting for *why* (as distinct from *how*) things change, explanations are not to be made lightly and glibly. Moreover, historical modes of explanation of change have themselves been subject to wide swings of fashion – which demands even greater humility in offering explanations.[28] The good historian therefore needs a flexible and corrigible model of the past age to allow for all those changes, however they are to be interpreted.

Before leaving the subject of what historians bring to their evidence, I shall note some rather more extraneous considerations which affect the work of metamorphosis, of imaginative historical construction.

Since the quantity of historical data is far beyond the combined capacities of all existing historians, students must have some idea of the limits of their researches; for example, the history of a regiment, not of a whole army, or of the economy between 1919 and 1939, not throughout the age of capitalism. They must also have some preliminary idea of the approach,

---

[27] See also chapter 7, section 3.
[28] See chapter 7, section 5; chapter 9, section 2.

the proposed methods and the form (narrative, analytical, comparative, etc.) of the finished work, although these can be subsequently modified. A further necessity is a practical notion of how much time, money, energy and evidence is required and how much is available. Like the king in the gospels, one must count one's soldiers before deciding whether and how far to go ahead.[29] Finally, historians need to be aware of the demand for their work and the encouragement or discouragement they are likely to receive. Apart from inner drives of curiosity or ambition, the work may be supported by the profession and by a publisher. If a piece of work is recognized as desirable by their colleagues or their educational institution, they will receive verbal, intellectual and even financial assistance. If they seek (as they usually do) the larger rewards of fame and fortune, they will look to a publisher, who may well suggest considerations of the market and of production costs which do not exactly coincide with their ambitions or their colleagues' wishes, but which cannot be ignored.

4   What the Mind Achieves: the Historian's Construction

I have likened the blending of the evidence and the historian's mind to nuclear fusion, or to the creation of a work of art. The analogy of a work of art is appropriate partly because the past is a vision. The past does not live in potsherds and documents; it lives in the human imagination. Artefacts are dead things; what once gave them life was the part they played in the lives of men and women, in their loves and hates, their hopes and fears. As these men and women have gone down into the dark so the documents and tools have lost the purpose and meaning with which their users once endowed them. These objects never had so much life even as Lesbia's sparrow,

> Qui nunc it per iter tenebricosum
> Illuc, unde negant redire quemquam.[30]

What life they had was not theirs; they could never go down to Orcus. Only the human life around them gave them resonance, and from that they drew a spurious vitality.

If, unlike Lesbia and her sparrow, these artefacts had no life to lose, some could prolong their physical existence to the fascination and puzzlement of a later age – a child's toy in an Egyptian tomb, a crackling deed of sale in a lawyer's office, a faded Victorian photograph. From such artefacts the

[29] Luke 14: 31–2.
[30] Catullus, 'Lugete, O Veneres Cupidinesque...' A rough rendering would be:
That now goes down the shadowy road
To the place whence none, they say, ever returns.

historian has to rebuild that world whose purposes gave them what secondhand life they had, and must envisage that society whose hopes and fears gave meaning to these dead things. The complexity of human society, with its geographical, physical, biological and cultural components, can be grasped only by a human mind, which alone has the imaginative power to re-create it. But a further paradox of history is that a vision cannot be shared; it is created by one mind, and the structure and contents of that mind help to shape the vision. Yet, as with painting or poetry, that private vision is intended to be shared. Directly, this would be impossible – without telepathy; indirectly, it may be shared through the medium of words, of colours, of musical notes, and so on. How such a medium is employed by the historian will be discussed in the next two chapters. Here I wish first to look at the form and content of the vision, that is, of the historian's creation of a past world.

In the best works of history (such as Burckhardt's *The Civilization of the Renaissance in Italy*, de Tocqueville's *The Ancien Régime and the French Revolution*, Marc Bloch's *Feudal Society*) there is unity and completeness. The work appears complete, not in the sense that it can never be improved upon but because all important constituents have been dealt with; the work has unity because it demonstrates how the constituents hold together, how they react on one another, and how they are subordinated to dominant and unifying principles. An inferior work of history is inadequate in one or more of these respects. It may lack completeness by omitting topics equally as important as those included; it may lack unity becasuse there is no obvious coherence among the constituents, or because no clear chronological, geographical or material limits are established, or because no dominant or unifying principle is discerned. Such a work has no real conclusion; it merely stops, and may be resumed at that point if the author or the publisher decides that more of the same would be desirable.

Works of this kind are not wholes as a work of art is a whole. One would not improve Beethoven's Ninth Symphony by tacking a few more tunes and a couple of movements on to the end. In such a case the end is foreseen from the beginning; the work is planned (even if loosely) from the start. Its internal relations, if not altogether foreseen at the start, are perceived as the work progresses and in retrospect are seen to have been there all along.

Inferior historians may defend their works' lack of unity by claiming that, because of 'the seamless web of history', there are no self-evident starting or stopping places. They may defend the lack of completeness by complaining that, since they cannot put everything in, they are free to choose what to omit. The answer in both cases is to point out that the works lack structure.

Here I am not talking about the events, the evidence or the resulting printed and published book. I am talking about the understanding of a portion of the past (often in answer to a set of problems) that is achieved by the working of the historian's mind. As an instance of this I discussed Fischer's hypothesis about German aims in the First World War.[31] The Burckhardt thesis, the Pirenne thesis, and others more or less rigorously worked out, are familiar to historians. Such embracing and explanatory sets of ideas are neither historical events, nor historical evidence, nor historical books; they are intellectual constructions comparable (though of course not identical) to works of art or to scientific theories. Like the latter they may not be final, but like the former they have a unity. Such a construction is made logically, though not necessarily chronologically, after the historian's mind has combined with the evidence – Carr's 'continuous process of interaction between the historian and the facts'[32] – and usually before publication.

In science, it would perhaps be possible to run a number of experiments, apply a slide rule to the results and claim that one had arrived at a scientific theory. This claim would be false. Someone who, like the young Hitler, copies postcards and lithographs is not thereby an artist. Someone who writes a scissors-and-paste history is not a historian. The diligent student who faithfully copies down every word of the lecture is not a scholar. In each of these cases the essential element is missing: there has been no thinking. The material has passed from earlier to later stages without ever going through a mind; the processes have been merely mechanical.

A *superior* mental construction has, I have argued, a recognizable wholeness and completeness – qualities that indicate the presence of a structure. A structure admits of, or results from, both analysis and synthesis; that is to say, something is broken down so that the constituent parts can be recognized, and then the whole is examined to discover how the parts come together. This relationship of parts to parts and parts to whole is what gives the entity its essential nature and so constitutes its structure.[33]

How is this process of analysis performed by the historian? There are two approaches – the historical and the non-historical. The non-historical approach uses a type of analysis derived from some other discipline, such as law or economics. For example, to describe an economic event like the recovery of the British economy from the depression of the early 1930s, the historian examines demand, interest rates, capital, labour costs and labour supply, technology, population changes, and so on.[34] Unemployment in the same period is analysed into frictional, structural, cyclical and seasonal types

[31] See Prologue, section 2.
[32] Carr, *What is History?*, p. 30.
[33] See chapter 1, section 1.
[34] See R. S. Sayers, A History of Economic Change in England (Oxford University Press, 1967), pp. 55–6.

of unemployment, each with its distinct nature and causes.[35] This type of analysis belongs to economics rather than to history.

Of more interest here is the historical mode of analysis, developed by the practice of historians. At its simplest, a survey of the past is like a memory or a chronicle; it consists of a record of a sequence of events. But this is not history; history begins when events are not merely recorded but to some extent explained. *The Anglo-Saxon Chronicle* in its earlier stages consists of entries like these:

699 In this year the Picts slew Beorht the ealdorman
702 In this year Coenrad succeeded to the Mercian kingdom[36]

In its later stages the chroniclers have some idea of historical narrative:

1090...the king was considering how he could take vengeance on his brother Robert, pay him out most effectively, and conquer Normandy from him. However, whether by reason of his astuteness, or by means of costly gifts, he took the castle and the harbour of St. Valéry....

While these events were taking place, this country was utterly ruined by unjust taxation and by many other misfortunes.[37]

Three things in particular go beyond the mere record of events. One is the record (by implication, an explanation) of a mind planning events – 'the king was considering how'. Another is the clear recognition of the need for a satisfactory explanation – 'whether by reason of his astuteness, or by means of costly gifts'. The third is the identification of cause and effect that does not invoke the will either of man or of God – 'utterly ruined by unjust taxation and by many other misfortunes'. Such a recognition of impersonal causes is rather rare in the writing of history at that time.

These examples do not show a full historical analysis, but they do indicate the direction of development. The key to this development, I believe, is the imagination. On the one hand, the imagination can perceive a relation of cause and effect between two events such that if one occurs the other must follow. (Whether such a relation actually exists, and whether it is correctly apprehended in any particular instance, is a matter of philosophical debate. The perception must, in any case, precede any logical justification.) On the other hand, the imagination can conceive that things might have been otherwise, and wonder why they happened as they did. Some explanation is called for – often in terms of a strict sequence of cause and effect. Here one begins to siolate the elements of the situation: if this had been different,

---

[35] See Alan E. Booth and Sean Glynn, 'Unemployment in the interwar period: a multiple problem', *Journal of Contemporary History*, 10, 4 (October 1975), pp. 611–36.
[36] *The Anglo-Saxon Chronicle*, trans. G. N. Garmonsway (Dent, 1953), p. 41.
[37] Ibid., p. 225.

then perhaps that would have been different. If Harold had not been fighting Norse invaders in Yorkshire, he would have prevented William landing at Pevensey, if Lincoln had not gone to Booth's theatre that evening. . ., and so on. This kind of reasoning involves both counter-factuals and causes, and leads to increasingly scrupulous historical analysis. When the situation has been resolved into all its constituent parts, when the relative weight and influence of these parts has been estimated, then one can gauge how they combine to form the whole. This is the structure of the historian's understanding which is correct just in so far as it corresponds to the structure of events.

Such is the underlying logic of a historical construction. In practice, however, most people, whether historians or not, proceed rather differently; that is, not by analysis, but by modifiying an existing picture or model. This, I suggest, is what happens: we begin with a crude initial notion of the case (such as the making of the constitution of the United States, the French Revolution or imperial Germany); when the evidence is examined in the light of these expectations (to use Popper's terms), some of them are disappointed – France did not undergo fundamental change at the Revolution; Germany was not the victim of aggression; the American Constitution was not a democratic triumph. These 'disappointments' should lead, not to an awkward fiddling with the model (what Butterfield calls 'poking new evidence into the old structure'), but to the creation of a new and more comprehensive whole, often providing an entirely fresh perspective – and achieved, as Collingwood says, by asking a new set of questions.

A fresh perspective, with new questions, may come from the application of ideas from some other discipline, frequently a social science; from a remarkable piece of new evidence (Ladurie's Montaillou); from an unusual opportunity (Goubert's Beauvais); or from a striking experience (Gibbon on the Capitol). Finally, and largely inexplicably, it may come from the recesses of the historian's psyche, so that even he or she cannot identify the source. In every case, however, if this new vision is to be intellectually satisfactory, it must be well structured – that is, capable of analysis and synthesis – and the structure of the construction must match the structure of the past.

Having recalled what structure involves, I shall look briefly at some of the other relevant structures.

First, there is the structure of the events (discussed in chapter 2). Correctly to discern and identify these is, I repeat, the primary object of the historian's enquiry, yet this may be diverted by other structures. As I explained above, the structure of the evidence may be distorted by any of a multitude of factors so that it by no means accurately represents the structure of the actual events.[38] Historians can also be misled by the structure of existing historical

[38] See chapter 3, section 6; chapter 4, section 4.

accounts. Until they can examine all the evidence themselves, historians should probably make a thorough historiographical survey of their topic, as Butterfield suggests.[39] All existing works may be wrong (there will be little point in new researches if they are not), but unless they are identical they cannot all be right. By observing their differences, historians will not only realize that the question is still open but be inclined to regard their own eventual conclusions with more humility.

Next, there are the structures of the historian's mind, formed in the various ways discussed in section 1. Anyone who works in isolation cannot hope to transcend these but must always be their prisoner and perhaps their dupe. But usually historians submit their ideas to their colleagues and often to a wider public, and criticism can help to overcome personal peculiarities and limitations. Unfortunately, since critics are occupied with their own different concerns, they may be committed to those very beliefs that the historian seeks to replace. Yet he or she must also remain true to his or her own vision.

Lastly, the historical construction may be affected by the structures of future publications and the practical limits of the work – limits of access, time, energy, money and material. A future book or article must certainly have a structure, but it cannot possibly be exactly the structure of events.[40] This, too, is a distraction to be avoided, for the historian's sole endeavour must be to make the structure of his or her (mental) construction faithfully match the structure of events.

5 Relevant Structures: a Checklist

In the last section I outlined the structure of the historian's construction, as well as some of the other structures that might distort it. Now it is perhaps worth while to recapitulate some of the points made about structure in general in chapter 1, and see how they may relate to this construction and to the mind that fashions it – that is, to the task of historical understanding.

My central aim is to suggest that the concept of structure can be used to achieve a better understanding of history (see section 1). The aspect of this concept that I have emphasized is the relation of the constituents that determines the peculiar character of the whole.[41] Since it is clear that in this relationship some constituents and relations are more important than others, we have the practical advantage of knowing where to concentrate our attention.

[39] See chapter 6, section 1. Also R. G. Collingwood, *An Autobiography* (Penguin, 1944), pp. 89–90.

[40] I think that Hayden White's definition oversimplifies the matter. See above, section 3.

[41] See chapter 1, section 1.

History, it may also be recalled, has many structures, and it is worth identifying, classifying and evaluating these structures. An initial attempt at identifying and classifying has been made in suggesting six types of structure under the two headings of 'inherent' and 'imposed'.[42]

First of the inherent structures are logical, mathematical and, less certainly, epistemological and semantic structures that seem to be basic to the universe; second are the physiological and neurological structures of the human organism; and third are the structures of 'the world' – that objective reality with which science purports to deal – which are cosmological, metaphysical and perhaps historical structures; All these types, though often relating to humanity, seem to lie beyond the human will. They confront us.

The second trio of structural types are created by the human mind and imposed upon the world in attempts to understand and change it. In a world without human life they would not exist. Thus, fourth, there are social structures – how we perceive, represent and organize our environment both natural and human. Built from experience rather than conscious design, these are, in an important respect, constituted and reinforced by language. Hence arise the cognitive structures, the almost intuitive understanding of social life (described in section 2) that is basic to historical understanding. Fifth are theoretical structures, based on a conscious and explicit schema or theory often derived from another discipline (law, theology, economics, sociology) and then applied to history. Sixth, there is historians' own structuring of history by dynasty, geographical proximity, institutions or social groups, or abstract notions of subject matter – local, military, political, even sexual or 'gender' histories. There are also the more esoteric structures of philosophers or theologians – various 'ages', cultures, civilizations or epochs, sometimes under a tutelary spirit or 'idea'.

I now deal with how each of these applies to the historian's construction. Although historians are unlikely to be explicitly concerned with the first type, it will be characteristic of their age and mental background to make certain assumptions of this kind. For example, orthodox historiography in the Soviet Union is supposed to conform with Engels's theories of the dialectic. While it is not the task of historians to determine the nature of the universe at this metaphysical level, all should recognize that they do make certain assumptions about it. If they disagree, the difference may be at this deep level rather than over matters of fact. In any case, it is good for all of us to be aware of the metaphysical presuppositions that underlie our thinking.

Similar considerations apply to the second type. Again, although historians do not investigate neurological and psychological structures, such mental structures, expecially those concerning speech and language, are deeply involved in their work. Current controversies about artificial intelligence,

---

[42] See chapter 1, sections 2 and 4.

for example, or the roots of speech may be relevant to historians' work. Again they may produce better work if they are aware of the issues and know their own view of them.[43]

The third type of structure is more obviously relevant, since the nature of both the natural and the social world is part of historical knowledge. Again, historians make certain assumptions about the world during the course of their work, and they must therefore both be aware of their assumptions and ensure they are up to date.

The second group of structure types demands even greater caution, for these are not *within* the universe but are imposed *upon* it by the human mind. Although they may be unavoidable, they are also suspect. For why should the world be exactly as people say it is, or (more rashly) say it must be?

Structures of the fourth category – roughly, social and cultural structures – are basic to living, thinking and speaking. They are nowadays the field of enquiry of the social or, preferably, human sciences. The degree of speculation and the wide range of theorizing found there bear witness to the difficulty of the problems. For example, sociology often distinguishes between 'groups' and 'quasi-groups'.[44] Groups belong to structures of the fourth category, quasi-groups to those of the fifth.

For the fifth group are not *socially* constituted structures like those of a market, a football team or a political party, but *theoretically* constructed structures, which produce hypothetical entities, like the British Constitution, the worldwide proletariat ('Workers of the world. . .'), the petty bourgeoisie or M3 (as in money supply).

The sixth group, historians' own inventions, are such obvious snares that no one need be caught. They include movements like the fall of the Roman Empire, the Crusades, the Renaissance, the Counter-Reformation, and so on. Trends and transformations are also traced or invented. To give one example: during the course of the eighteenth century in Europe there was a marked change in attitudes to the poor, the mad, the sick and the criminal, as well as towards children, women, savages, slaves and animals. The hard evidence is changes of behaviour, the soft evidence is the expression of opinions. By putting these together, historians have argued customarily for a growth in rationality and sensitivity, associated with the Enlightenment and early romanticism. More recently, a number of works have challenged these conclusions on the grounds that such changes of behaviour could be better accounted for in other ways.[45] Thus, some argue, it was not that greater humaneness and sensitivity led to the changes, but that the changes,

[43] See also chapter 7, section 3.
[44] See chapter 2, section 3.
[45] For example, Pieter Spierenburg, *The Spectacle of Suffering* (Cambridge University Press, 1984); David Brion Davis, *Slavery and Human Progress* (Oxford University Press, 1984).

brought about for other reasons, permitted a humanitarian and rational attitude to appear that already existed. If the changes had less reputable causes, perhaps the desire for wealth or power, humanitarianism (for example, the anti-slavery movement) might afford a convenient cover.[46] One is therefore led to ask whether there was a genuine independent humanitarian movement in the eighteenth century, one that brought about significant changes in human behaviour, or whether the changes occurred for quite other reasons, so that any new humanitarianism resulted from rather than caused these changes.

Since most of these challenges to accepted ideas are made by historians themselves, there is less need to fear that they are mistaking imposed structures for inherent ones. The highly critical attitudes that predominate in historiography in the West today cannot, however, be taken for granted. They were not always present in other ages, nor are they found in many other parts of the world today. Indeed, even late twentieth-century Western thought is not entirely free, whether from subtle external pressures or hidden prejudices. None the less, historians today are perhaps less guilty of dogmatically imposing their own ideas upon the past.[47] Rather, like good Popperian scientists, they (as a profession rather than as individuals) are trying a series of models in turn to see which best fit the evidence as interpreted by the latest and fullest understanding of human affairs.

Since there are many ways in which historians can be misled, I have thought it worth while to differentiate these six types of structure so that they may have a clearer notion of the pitfalls to look out for. These are, perhaps, a set of controls or tests to be run on the historical construction.

6   Modes of Construction: a Checklist

We are now at the pivot of this book. At the very heart of historical activity is the point where the historian, in completing the construction of the past, begins to look to the present and the future and to consider how this new-found knowledge can be shared with other people. I have examined in turn the historical field (chapter 2); how some elements of the historical field survive from the past to the present (chapter 3); how these elements constitute the evidence of history (chapter 4); the various attitudes of historians to the evidence (chapter 5); and (in this chapter) how the historian's mind works upon the evidence to produce the historical construction. So far,

[46] See David Brion Davis, *Slavery and Human Progress.*
[47] I believe that the worldwide network of mutually critical scholars does, in the end, make for genuine progress. See also M. S. Anderson, quoted in chapter 3, section 4, and G. R. Elton, *The Practice of History* (Fontana/Collins, 1969), p. 85.

then, our attention has been concentrated solely upon the past. From now on we shall be looking more to the present and the future; for the historian's construction from the past takes on a life of its own in the present.

It would doubtless be neater to end this chapter here and proceed at once to the discussion of the subsequent life of the historian's brainchild. However, as I suggested in section 2, in bringing this child to birth the historian is not concerned solely with the past but cannot refrain from wondering how the work will relate to other people – that present and future public, both professional and general, with whom the work is to be shared.

There are, then, a number of considerations to be noted here. Although to some extent they look forward in the sense that I have just explained, they chiefly belong to the historian's construction and therefore should be mentioned in this chapter. There are, I believe, ten different ways of working that may be involved in this construction. It is unlikely that any one piece of work will contain all ten, but they provide a useful checklist for the historian and his or her public, enabling them both to be more aware of the process. Each of the ten has its own particular skills, methods, attitudes, norms, and so on, which some thoughtful writers explicitly discuss from time to time.

(1) Narrative is the most familiar historical mode – some say the only true one.[48] This consists of identifying some entity – perhaps a person, a family, an institution, a mental attitude, a set of ideas – and then following this single thread over the course of a number of years.

(2) Descriptive history, by contrast, tends to ignore the passage of time and to give an account of a (supposedly) contemporaneous state of affairs.

(3) Global history, not often attempted, tries to combine the two by giving a full account of the whole of a society or 'world' (like the Mediterranean world of Philip II) *and* moving forward over a limited period of time.

The next three methods delve rather deeper below the surface of events.

(4) The analytical approach breaks down its subject (say, the Reformation in Germany) into its constituent parts – for example, the state of the German church: new ideas and opportunities; political pressures upon the German emperor and the princes; the fortunes and misfortunes of the papacy.

(5) The comparative approach selects some of these parts or, less often, the whole, and sets them beside one or more similar situations or occurrences at another time or place. Comparison yields many fresh insights, but it tends

[48] See chapter 1, section 4, for narrative. Also Herbert Butterfield, 'Narrative history and the spade-work behind it', in *History*, 53, 178 (1968).

to blur the fine definition that many historians labour after, as well as obscuring the importance of the unique.[49]

(6) The interpretative, often following close upon the other two, offers a coherent acount of 'what really happened', by contrast with what seems to have happened. This 'makes more sense', being more familiar or more logical than the apparently meaningless or misleading jumble of facts.

The next four methods are more integrative, and therefore require even deeper levels of thinking.

(7) The empathetic approach is an attempt to forget oneself and one's own age, and think oneself into the world and even the minds of the historical agents being studied. Some philosophers of history (Dilthey or Collingwood, for example) regard this as the only valid way of working. Other philosophers – Comte, Hegel, Marx – tended to look at history from an exterior perspective. Max Weber (not strictly a historian) gave *Verstehen* a more clearly defined role in the social sciences. This concept, as used by Dilthey, Weber and others, has given rise to almost a separate discipline of hermeneutics. How far a historian is prepared to go along these lines is a matter of choice, but a work threatens to be very dull if it has no insight into what it was like to be, for example, a citizen of Pericles' Athens, Shakespeare's London or Samuel Adams's Boston.[50]

(8) A historian can use the constructive approach in two ways. The first way, largely employing insight, creates a world of the past big enough for our thoughts to move in (as Eileen Power did in *Medieval People*). However, apart from creating, or re-creating, a world, historians also use their material to construct an argument or thesis (examples of this were given in section 4). In doing this they are, of course, no longer concentrating solely upon the past but are also looking to the effect their work may have upon the present.

(9) At this point I consider the explanatory mode. Although it is often closely bound up with interpretation (my sixth item), the essence of explanation is, I take it, to clarify the minds of other people.[51] Today, perhaps more than at any previous period, explanation, at whatever level, is considered an essential part of the historian's work. Indeed, we tend to reject works of earlier historians less for the unreliability of their facts than for the inadequacy of their explanations.

---

[49] See Peter Clarke, 'Political history in the 1980s: ideas and interests', in *The New History: the 1980s and beyond*, ed. T. K. Rabb and R. I. Rotberg (Princeton University Press, 1982), p. 45. For further discussion of comparison, see chapter 10, section 5.
[50] Some idea of recent thinking in this direction may be found in William J. Bouwsma, 'Intellectual history in the 1980s: from history of ideas to history of meaning', in *The New History*, ed. Rabb and Rotberg.
[51] See chapter 4, section 5. In J. L. Austin's terminology, explanation is an illocutionary use of speech.

(10) My final item is the evaluative approach. Historians have long disagreed about how far it is their function to incorporate value judgements in their thinking and writing. The Acton-Creighton correspondence furnishes a well-known example.[52] It has often been pointed out that our very vocabulary is morally loaded – for example, the 'September Massacres' of 1792 – so that a 'value-free' language is virtually impossible. Moreover, it is very difficult for historians to keep their own personality and *Weltanschauung* out of their work. The central point, however, is that historical work done for a non-historical or extra-historical purpose is, *qua* history, immediately suspect. If it is written to justify a certain kind of religious belief or attitude to the universe, some moral position, some political cause, it will tend to evaluate history accordingly. This does not necessarily make it either bad history or a bad book; think of R. H. Tawney's *Religion and the Rise of Capitalism* or Charles A. Beard's *An Economic Interpretation of the Constitution*. On the contrary, enthusiasm for a cause may give the intellectual fire to produce great works. But, here again, both writer and reader, both historian and audience, should be aware of what is going on.

In offering this checklist of historical approaches I wish to emphasize that historians normally use several (though rarely all) of these at the same time. In any individual work, however, one approach is likely to be dominant and thus to flavour the whole. When one examines a historical construction (at this pre-publication stage, it is usually one's own work or that of a friend), therefore, it would be helpful to differentiate these activities, to be aware of which one is taking place at any particular point, and to establish which is dominant. There is, of course, much more to be said on each of these ten points, which have been discussed in detail elsewhere. Working historians may well wish to follow up such discussion.

[52] It is printed in L. Creighton, *Life and Letters of Mandell Creighton* (Longmans, 1904), vol. I, pp. 368–75.

7

From Construction to Historiography

1 The Matching of Structures

The last chapter was devoted to what I take to be the essential historical task of bringing one's mind to bear upon the evidence, and from that contact creating a mental construction of some portion of the past. I am suggesting that the validity of such a construction largely depends upon how well its own structure matches the structure of the past. Of course, at this point we come up against the central paradox, the 'Catch 22' of historical knowledge. From what position can we impartially view both the past and our present construction of it to see how well they match? Like Archimedes, we say 'Give me somewhere to stand'.[1] The problem is not peculiar to history: neither the natural world nor the universe as a whole would present so many difficulties if scientists, philosophers or theologians could stand outside and gain a clear perspective of the whole. But in history, science and metaphysics, as well as in personal relations, we have to stand where we are – in the world, not outside it.[2]

Scientists can improve scientific knowledge only by being better scientists; there are no short cuts. The same applies to history. My hope in writing this book is that by paying more attention to the various structures we shall become better historians.

With the second half of the book, I take up the major problem for the historian and his or her mental construction: how can this best be conveyed to the minds of the audience? Seen more closely, the problem is: how can the structures of the one match the structures of the other? The answer to the first part of the question is: through the medium of historical work in verbal form. Yet this medium must itself be structured, and the problem is that the two sets of structures involved must be incorporated into the medium. In considering the problem of matching the structure of the mental

[1] Cf. chapter 2, section 6.
[2] In religion I am less sure; see chapter 12, section 3.

construction to the structure of the past, the historian had a task that was at least conceptually simple. With the second problem, that of conveying the construction to the mind of the audience, the task is more complex. For the medium that effects this conveyance must itself be structured in a way that simultaneously matches *two* other structures – namely that of the mental construction and that of the minds of the audience. It is not easy to write good history.

2   The Verbal Construction

This medium with the Janus-like form is a verbal construction. It is a set of words that constitutes a book, a lecture, an article, and so on. The historian's private vision is enshrined in words for the purpose of communicating it to others. When considering the importance for the historian of verbal communication, one should not forget the host of linguistic, semantic and literary problems that arise whenever one uses words.

I begin with a few simple points about verbal communication – words, ideas, things, people. Here again a structural approach may be employed.

Popper observed that even the simplest of organisms can modify their behaviour in response to stimuli.[3] This is the basic relation of organism-environment. In the highest organisms, the relation is between mind and world – perhaps a crude I-it relation.

At a certain point in the evolutionary ladder (certainly no higher than the anthropoid apes) some organisms recognize common interests with their fellows and act deliberately in co-operation. They increase this co-operation when they make noises (signals) to each other. At some point early in human prehistory, symbols replaced signals – that is a particular sound made a particular reference. Words appeared and language began.

For most purposes it is essential for language to have meaning. This concept was illustrated by a triangle in a pioneering work, *The Meaning of Meaning*, by C. K. Ogden and I. A. Richards in 1923. A simplified form of the diagram appears in figure 2.

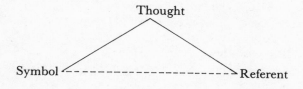

Figure 2   The three-term relation in a statement

[3] See chapter 6, section 2.

As they explain it: 'the three factors involved whenever any statement is made, or understood, are placed at the corners of the triangle, the relations which hold between them being represented by the sides.'[4] Thus, to pursue my explanation, the mind-world relation (of two terms only) has become a three-term relation: mind-symbol-world. The role of the mind here is crucial. It is mind that both recognizes and chooses to employ the symbol, in the relation at the left-hand side of the triangle; it is mind that makes the reference to the world (or that part which is relevant), in the relation at the right-hand side of the triangle. As for the base of the triangle, Ogden and Richards insist that this represents no direct relation: 'Between the symbol and the referent there is no relevant relation other than the indirect one, which consists in its being used by someone to stand for a referent.[5] In other words, the symbol's meaning is not *inherent* but derives only from its use. (This, I believe, is something the historian should bear in mind.) This three-term relation, 'involved whenever any statement is made, or understood', is crucial to both thought and language, for in both we employ symbols – and usually, but not always, these symbols are words.

If language arises from the need to communicate with creatures not unlike oneself, a second person is implicated. So far I have explored meaning as if only one mind were involved, but, of course, communication implies two (or more) minds. When two people communicate (let us call them A and B), they both employ Ogden and Richards's triangle of meaning, and they must use a common set of symbols. (We *can* think of more complex situations, such as two people carrying on a conversation in two languages both of which they understood, but the basic situation calls for common symbols or there would be little point in the existence of symbols at all.) Their conversation, then, might be represented by the triangle in figure 3, which shows two people (A and B) conversing by means of a common set of symbols (S). But, since the symbols must have referents, both A and B are employing the Ogden-Richards triangle (in obverse and reverse), as in figure 4.

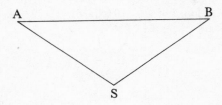

Figure 3   A conversation using a common set of symbols

[4] C. K Ogden and I. A. Richards, *The Meaning of Meaning*, 8th ed (Kegan Paul, Trench, Trubner, 1946), p. 10.
[5] Ibid., p. 11.

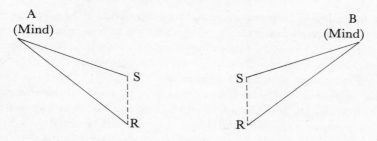

Figure 4   A conversation using three-term relations

It must be recalled that there is no direct relation between S and R, between symbol and referent, between word and thing. The relation between S and R is indirect, for it must pass through the mind – that is, both of A and of B. The symbolism will not work unless roughly identical relations between S and R are made by A and B; that is, unless they understand roughly the same thing by the words they use. For successful communication it is necessary, first, that A and B use the same symbols (in the diagram, AS = BS) and, second, that A and B make the same reference (in the diagram, AR = BR). Since SR is not determined (that is, symbols have no fixed referent), then SR depends on the combination of AR with AS and of BR with BS. Hence, if SR in A's triangle is equivalent to SR in B's triangle, then AS is identical with BS and AR with BR.

As Wittgenstein stated: 'If language is to be a means of communication there must be agreement not only in definitions but also (queer as this may sound) in judgments.'[6] In other words, if people are to talk to one another they must agree not only about words but about how they see the world. When they do so agree we may put our three triangles together to make a tetrahedron whose four points are the two communicants (A and B), language or a set of symbols (S) and their common referent in the world (R), as in figure 5.

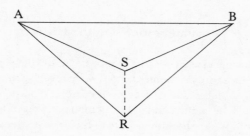

Figure 5   The four-term relation in a communication

[6] Ludwig Wittgenstein, *Philosophical Investigations*, part no. I, 242 (Basil Blackwell, 1968), p. 88.

The diagram illustrates that successful communication involves a four-term relation. Communication fails if the two minds in communication *either* use the symbols differently *or* make different references. In J. L. Austin's words: 'If our usages disagree, then you use "X" where I use "Y", or . . . your conceptual system is different from mine.'[7]

The relevance of this for historians is that, to avoid misunderstanding in their work, they must be alert for errors arising not only from different usages of words, but also from different conceptual systems.

A further consideration is the importance of context. In discussing the structures of communication, I assumed this was effected perfectly. In practice, of course, we do not achieve perfect communication. It must happen rarely, if ever, that all the conditions are fulfilled – that A and B think the same way, that they have the same command of language and choose words the same way, that they see the world the same way and bring it under the same set of concepts. Fortunately it is not necessary for everything to coincide exactly. Communication can fall well short of perfection and yet be effective. In extreme cases one sometimes communicates successfully with a foreigner even when one knows only a few words of a common language and when the other conditions (or the other connections in the four-term relation) fall equally short of fulfilment. What makes such communication possible at all in such unpromising conditions?

The answer is, simply, context. Once both speakers understand the situation – that A wants to buy sunglasses or find the way to the post office, for example – then a successful communication is (briefly) established. If we want to make contact with another mind, we need not only some similarity of symbolic usage and of conceptual systems, but the understanding by both parties of the situation – or, more generally, the context. This is not difficult for tourists, who usually find themselves in situations that are commonplace, if not stereotyped. It is much more difficult for historians, to whom I turn in the next section.

3   Communication and the Historian

Communication concerns historians at more than one level – in particular, at future, present and past moments. At every level, context is at least as important as the other elements I have discussed. We are, of course, only partly conscious of the context and of how it influences our thinking, speaking and acting, just as we are not fully aware of how we choose words and make reference.

Communication in the future affects historians, most of whom are writers

---

[7] J. L. Austin, *Philosophical Papers* (Oxford University Press, 1961), p. 184.

or teachers; a few work in the realms of the media or the arts. In all these capacities they will be concerned with making public their findings and the consequent ideas. They will have to initiate communication. In doing so they must assess the other minds with whom they wish to make contact, and then take into account the choice of words and style, the literary tropes and forms that will most appeal, the conceptual schemes of their audience, and the need to establish a common context. Some of this will be discussed in the next chapter.

With regard to the present, historians are both initiators and receivers of communication. In the last chapter I examined how their mind is formed by their own age and experiences, which range from the diffused influence of general ideas, conventions and fashions of the day (especially, nowadays, through the media) to the very particular help they obtain from their fellow scholars. No one is a purely passive recipient of messages; we also spend time talking and writing. These activities, too, help to shape one's mind and outlook. Anyone whose work calls for a good deal of formal, structured writing and speaking (as is the case with most historians) will, I believe, admit that these activities give the mind a certain form or quality; in maturity, it would not be easy to adopt a different way of thinking and speaking in order to become a comedian, a racecourse bookmaker, an actor or a poet. A lifetime of communicating (to sum up what I have said here and in chapter 6) is relevant to historians, for it largely shapes their mind – the essential organ of their task.

For all that, historians are concerned most with communication in the past. As I have already remarked, they are neither initiators nor (except rarely) recipients of communication; they are eavesdroppers, or phone tappers. Such intruders are not nearly so well placed to understand the message as either the initiator or its recipient, who are likely to have a much better grasp of word usage, reference, conceptual schemes and context. So often an eavesdropper can hear every word and yet utterly fail to understand the conversation. If this is a well-known fact of everyday life, how much more difficult is it when the conversation is not contemporary, but years, even centuries, old, and, in addition, is probably incomplete.

The historian's task is even more difficult, for there is more than one world of the past. I did not mean the various kinds of 'pasts' that Michael Oakeshott enumerates in his essay, 'The Activity of Being an Historian', since those 'pasts' are all created in the present.[8] I mean worlds that existed in the past, of which there were at least three at the same time. First, there is the world 'as it really was' at such and such a date – let us say England between 1640 and 1660. This is, surely, the world the historian is trying to reach. But,

---

[8] In *Rationalism in Politics and Other Essays*, p. 150.

second, there is the world as the people of the time *thought* it was. On some things they all agreed; on most they did not. One thing is clear from reading the sources: the world that the Stuarts saw was not that of Milton (for example, in 'Areopagitica'); nor was the world of Isaac Newton that of Abiezer Coppe or Gerrard Winstanley.[9] This rich medley makes a field day for the historian of ideas and *mentalités*. But, we may ask, did *any* of them see it as it really was? If we answer 'no', how do we find out how it really was? Can we filter out the few things on which they all agreed and reject those on which they differed? I think we should be left with very little. Moreover, some of these topics of general agreement (perhaps witchcraft, or the genesis of swallows in balls of clay, or a continuing decline of the world since the end of the Roman Empire) might run counter to our own prejudices. Universal consent is notoriously no guarantee of truth. Perhaps the difference between the second and the first worlds is that they saw a world containing witches, whereas we see a world that contained a belief in witches.

There is also a third world of the past – not the world as it *really* was, not the world as they *thought* it was, but the world as they *said* it was. It would be naïve in the extreme for anyone, let alone an eavesdropper, to suppose that what people say always exactly expresses what they think about the world. They may be acting, fooling or pretending; they may be deceiving or even lying outright; they may be quite unclear, as we so often are, about just what they do think. But they can put something into words, even if their ideas are confused, something that is appropriate to the occasion, though it may not (how often does it?) express their truest and deepest thoughts.

Thus between the first two is the relation between thought and the world – all the manifold problems that belong to the realm of epistemology. Between the second two is the relation between thought and language – most of the problems of linguistics. Taking the three together – world, thought and language – we have semantics. Finally, almost every particular piece of spoken or written evidence opens up the gap between language and speech, between the English (or French or Latin, etc.) language as a whole and its use by a particular speaker or writer on a particular occasion. If all these sets of problems arise in the course of normal communication – and there are enough of them to keep several academic disciplines in business – how much more difficult are they for communications made in the past, and only fitfully overheard by us.

As if all this were not baffling enough, there are additional complications. If thought, language and the world were as distinct in reality as they are in concept, it might not be too difficult to disentangle their interrelations.

[9] For the last two, see Christopher Hill, *The World Turned Upside Down* (Penguin, 1972).

But thought and language do not merely reflect the world in which we live; to a large extent they also create it. People think, feel and talk about the world, and what they think, feel and say helps to make the world. As Butterfield puts it: 'The ideas that men have about the events in which their life is involved are to be regarded as a dimension of the events themselves.'[10] For example, the stability of the state depends a great deal on what people feel about the state and its ethos, history and traditions. What do they feel about power, whether used against them or on their behalf, about their needs (for defence, justice, religion, perhaps), and about how the use of power relates to their personal hopes and desires? Consider how differently Germans felt about the Weimar Republic from their attitude to the realm of Kaiser Wilhelm II. Does that difference in feeling not explain in part the success of Nazism? Is not society too (more fundamental than the state) constituted and preserved by loves, loyalties, fears, antipathies and recognitions of authority? If this is true of feelings, is it less true of ideas? So do our thoughts help to make our world?

And what of language? Does that do no more than mirror the world? In 1946 George Orwell, in 'Politics and the English Language', rebutted this very point. He remarked that 'The English language...becomes ugly and inaccurate because our thoughts are foolish, but the slovenliness of the language makes it easier for us to have foolish thoughts.' The decline of our civilization and the decadence of our language reinforce each other as both cause and effect. But, he insists, the process can be reversed: 'If one gets rid of these habits one can think more clearly, and to think clearly is a necessary first step towards political regeneration.'[11] Orwell's argument is as relevant today as when it was written. 'In our time,' he says, 'political speech and writing are largely the defence of the indefensible.' This can, however, be done by distorting the facts, corrupting the emotions and twisting the logic. The effect on language employed to these ends is disastrous; further, 'if thought corrupts language, language can also corrupt thought.'[12] And corrupt thinking makes political evil that much easier. Since 1946 there has been no lack of evidence to support Orwell's case.

What German speaker can enjoy the beauties of a beechwood on a sunny day when he recalls its name – Buchenwald?[13] Thus thought and language help to constitute the world. This is an important consideration for the historian at each of the three moments of communication I have discussed – future, present and past.

[10] Herbert Butterfield, *George III and the Historians* (Collins, 1957), p. 41.
[11] In Sonia Orwell and Ian Angus (eds), *The Collected Essays, Journalism and Letters of George Orwell*, vol. IV (Penguin, 1970), p. 157.
[12] Ibid., pp. 166, 167.
[13] I owe this example to my daughter, Charlotte.

4   Semantic Levels and the Hermeneutic Circle

I have argued that thought, language and the world are three distinct entities, whose interpenetrations are confusing because each entity, in part, constitutes the other two. Since almost all the evidence is couched in one of the three – language – historians must use these mutual relations to draw conclusions about the other two. But is this possible? Are they deluding themselves that they ever do attain the other two – the thought and the world of the past? Can they ever escape from the prison of words?

The point arises obliquely from an essay on Freud in which Steiner argued that Freudian theory and practice are inescapably bound in such a net of words. 'The raw material *and* instrumentality of Freudian analysis are semantic – a duality which imposes serious epistemological dilemmas.' Briefly put, it's all words. As Steiner said, Freud hoped for neurophysiological confirmation of his theories, but none has yet been found. Thus there is no 'escape from the hermeneutic circle of language seeking to deal systematically with language'.[14]

Perhaps history too consists of no more than language dealing with language. To illustrate this question, I shall look at another nineteenth-century figure, one of the most influential who have ever written on history – Karl Marx. In his writings, but especially in *Capital*, Marx makes copious use of primary sources, mostly British parliamentary reports. These sources usually contain language at two semantic levels – the bald statements of the witnesses and the interpretative and explanatory remarks of the reporter, who is usually an inspector or a magistrate. The distinction is clear; often the witness and the magistrate inhabit quite different mental worlds, with marked disparities of both concept and usage. Alongside these he draws from a large number of secondary sources, especially economists such as Adam Smith, David Ricardo or J. S. Mill, but he also refers to political theorists, sociologists and historians. Here is a third semantic level. All three levels are used as evidence. But at the same time he writes theoretically, discussing, interpreting, paraphrasing and often mocking and refuting other theorists – Hegel, Proudhon, Feuerbach, and so on. This is a fourth semantic level, for now we have Marx's own voice talking about ideas – not alleged facts, as with the first three levels. Finally, his writing is full of allusions to and quotations from world literature. This is well illustrated in S. S. Prawer's *Karl Marx and World Literature*: 'One characteristic footnote begins with a passage from a Greek historian, Xenophon, sets this alongside a passage from a philosopher, Aristotle, and ends with remarks on the use of the terms

[14] George Steiner, 'A remark on language and psychoanalysis', in *On Difficulty and Other Essays*, p. 48.

δίκη and κέϱδος in the Greek tragic poets, notably Euripides.'[15] Here is surely another semantic level, distinct from the other four.

Marx was a great thinker and a great writer. As his translator, Ben Fowkes, says, he was 'a master of literary German'.[16] One could say of him what Steiner says of Freud: a 'major writer with relations to the German language of a sort and complexity which distinguish the great stylist.'[17] Such a writer can blend five (or more) semantic levels of language into a literary whole. The result, in both Marx and Freud, was to contribute to, as well as to draw from, a great literature.

After all this it may seem churlish to ask of these literary masterpieces whether they ever touch ground, or whether they are for ever in a mesh of language. If they blend language from five different kinds of source, and if each semantic level has its own echoes, resonances, assumptions and presuppositions in the speaker's own world of thought, then one wonders about the propriety of running all five into one – a sixth. For each of these levels offers a text with its own hermeneutic problems The final text may be great literature, but *is it true* (or at least falsifiable) in the historian's sense of being about the world as it really is or was? It has often been observed that Marxism and Freudianism exhibit many of the characteristics of a dogmatic religion. They are also amazingly long-lived. Could this be because neither of them has broken out of the hermeneutic circle, because they are language dealing with language? Is this why they are, as Popper points out, unfalsifiable?[18]

And now what of history? Is that, too, no more than language dealing with language at various semantic levels? There are, of course, non-verbal sources – archaeological, monumental, photographic, architectural, iconographic – and one can also draw upon the non-verbal arts of painting and music. Then there is memory, which is partly, but by no means wholly, a verbal source. So this, too, may help us to evade the prison of words. However, if we appeal to laws, either laws of nature or laws of society, the difficulty is that words are involved both in the statement of the universal and in the description of the particular. Moreover, whatever laws of society there may be (of economics, for example) are themselves largely derived from historical evidence. I conclude that it may be possible for history to escape from the hermeneutic circle, from the prison of language, but it is not at all easy. I think the problem remains; and it is aggravated by the fact that most empirical historians do not, or choose not to, see it.

[15] S. S. Prawer, *Karl Marx and World Literature* (Oxford University Press, 1978), p. 301.
[16] The Pelican Marx Library, *Capital: a critique of political economy*, vol. I (Penguin, 1976), p. 88.
[17] Steiner, *On Difficulty and Other Essays*, p. 48.
[18] See Karl R. Popper, 'Science: conjecture and refutation', in *Conjectures and Refutations* 5th edn (Routledge and Kegan Paul, 1974).

5 Expectations to be Met by the Historian

After all these problems of communication, I now turn to the next stage, the book to be written. Already it is making certain demands on the historian, as he or she wonders how to transform the mental construction into some tangible (or, rather, sensible) form that will communicate his or her thought to others. I have already touched on some of the obvious questions of limits (geographical, temporal and material) and of form (narrative, descriptive, analytical, global, etc.).[19] However, there are two rather more difficult puzzles arising from the nature of time: change and relativism.

Change gives rise to problems concerning the division of time, continuity and contemporaneity, and causes and convergences in time. Like other animals we live in the present; unlike other animals we can also bring the past and the future into our lives. Our understanding, perhaps our 'internal model', of the present world can be transferred to some imagined time and place remote from the here-and-now. In this way we plan our future, picture the past, and put ourselves into the fictitious worlds of the novel and drama. At the same time we try to make the necessary adjustments (such as seeing people clad in skins, doublet and hose or space-suits), but it is basically our own working model of the world (especially the human world) that we employ. What other have we?

Yet change is rarely incorporated in this model. We take pains to learn how the world is (for example, the way to the post office, how to fill in an income tax return, how to greet a guest), and we expect it to stay like that. When any part of it changes, we have to make a deliberate and inconvenient, sometimes painful, adjustment. To put it another way, we behave as if we were living in a horizontal slice of time. When we read a novel or envisage a forthcoming holiday we project a picture similar to the present but largely static. Perhaps this is because of our animal nature. One could imagine other beings who move freely to and fro in time, but who are perhaps tied to one spot; restricted spatially but not temporally, they would be in a contrary position to ours. Perhaps this is why we find it harder to envisage sequences than simultaneities. We never know our future; we forget our past and only with difficulty recover any of it. Although we know how to live in a world spread out at one point of time – 'horizontally', as it were – we have much less intuitive understanding of how the world moves and changes, at different rates, through time – as it were 'vertically'.

For various reasons, historians tend to work against the grain of human intuition and instinct, and are rarely content merely to describe a past society at one moment in time. The very concept of an 'event' or 'happening' (the

[19] See chapter 5, section 3; chapter 6, sections 1 and 6; and this chapter, section 3.

basic elements of their study) implies change, for when things remain the same there are no events to record. Since change implies movement through time, a 'before' and an 'after', historians are doubly concerned with time; first, with the past as distinct from the present and, second, with tracing movement over a period of time.

Historians' traditional solution is narrative: story seems to be a psychological device by which our minds, set in a horizontal world, can master the verticalities of time. The narrative may be crude, or limited, or even false, but following a story seems to be the one mode of historical thinking that comes naturally to human beings. (Could one imagine telling a story to an intelligent animal? At what age is a child capable of following a story?) However else historians try to structure the past – in reigns or centuries, in periods (ancient, medieval) or movements (Renaissance, industrial revolution), or in empires or civilizations – when they move away from narration (the simply vertical) or description (the simply horizontal) they encounter all sorts of difficulties.[20] Despite much debate, few of these difficulties have been permanently solved. Meanwhile the 'general reader' continues to prefer narrative.

The other problem arising from the nature of time is that of relativism, which results especially from the fact that we are inescapably confined to one small portion of time. Does this make it impossible truly to know the past, let alone the future? However much the most thorough researches make us believe we know it, surely our understandings are ineluctably fixed in the age that produced us. Are we not condemned to see any other age through the coloured and distorting lenses of our own society?

These doubts seem to have especially troubled historians around the turn of the century, especially those influenced by German historicism. English historians, then as now, were for the most part happy with a perhaps rather naïve empiricism.[21] But most Germans, who had been taught by historians to see each age in its own terms, with its own immanent values, felt it increasingly difficult to avoid the pitfalls of relativism. As G. G. Iggers puts it: 'Historicism as a theory had now [i.e. in the 1920s] arrived at its logical conclusion. If all truths and value judgments are individual and historical, then no place is left for any fixed point in history....All that remains is the subjective individual.[22] If all insights, values and *Weltanschauungen* are

[20] See, for example, comparison of Gibbon with Livy on this point in G. M. Young, *Gibbon* (Nelson, 1939), pp. 114–15. See also T. Stoianovich, 'An impossible "histoire globale"', in *French Historical Method: the 'Annales' paradigm* (Cornell University Press, 1976), for a discussion of some of the problems.

[21] For a defence of this attitude, see G. R. Elton, *The Practice of History* (Fontana/Collins, 1969). For a Marxist criticism of the English tradition, see G. Stedman Jones, 'History: the poverty of empiricism', or Eric Hobsbawm, 'Karl Marx's contribution to historiography', both in *Ideology in Social Science*, ed. Robin Blackburn (Fontana/Collins, 1972).

[22] G. G. Iggers, *The German Conception of History* (Wesleyan University Press, 1968), p. 243.

relative to their age and cannot be applied or transferred to another, then how can historians hope to understand another age or write of it free from the prejudices, preoccupations and assumptions of their own? What chance is there of telling it 'as it really was'?

This was the abiding anxiety of Wilhelm Dilthey, who made perhaps the most thoroughgoing attempt since Hegel to write a philosophy of history. In a speech on his seventieth birthday (1903) he said: 'The finitude of every historical phenomenon...hence the relativity of every sort of human conception about the connectedness of things, is the last word of the historical world view.'[23]

Others too came to despair of history as an objective branch of knowledge. Against this attitude I would argue that what Dilthey regarded as a weakness of historians – their humanity – is nothing of the sort. Certainly Dilthey realized the advantage of this humanity: that it is only because historians are themselves historical beings – plodders in Carr's procession – that they can understand history.[24] If we can cope with all the assumptions, implicit meanings and unspoken conventions of one complex society, we have some hope of understanding the irrationalities of another one. A disembodied rational mind, floating transcendent in the void, an angel or a fifth-generation computer, might make a great mathematician or chess-player, but never a historian. However, Dilthey feared that this very *Sitz-im-Leben*, this location in the flux of events, could not meet the challenge of relativism which to him and to many contemporaries was the reverse side of the coin. They feared that it would render objective historical knowledge impossible.[25]

I believe that there is evidence that human beings are capable of standing outside their social milieux with the attendant 'world-views' (*Weltanschauungen*). For example, Raymond Aron has pointed out the 'présence latente de l'esprit objectif dans chaque personne – the latent presence of objectivity in everyone', which rests on the language, concepts, monuments and techniques inherited from the past.[26] In all these things each of us is able to live, as it were, outside our own skins, to share our lives with our predecessors. Stronger evidence is provided by the inhabitants of Karl Popper's 'World Three'.[27] One need not go all the way with Popper simply to recognize that theories, problems, critical arguments, etc., have an objective existence independent of our minds, and therefore independent of any particular one

[23] Quoted in ibid., pp. 143–4.

[24] See E. H. Carr, *What is History?* (Penguin 1964), p. 36.

[25] See the discussions in, for example, H. Stuart Hughes, *Consciousness and Society* (MacGibbon and Kee, 1959), and Iggers, *The German Conception of History*. In *Wilhelm Dilthey: the critique of historical reason* (University of Chicago Press, 1978), Michael Ermath argues that Dilthey was heading towards a solution of the dilemma (pp. 334–8), but I think he fails to demonstrate this.

[26] Quoted by H.-I. Marrou, *De la connaissance historique* (Éditions du Seuil, 1954), p. 199.

[27] See chapter 3, section 5.

of us. Here again, precisely because we can live partly in this world of logical, mathematical, scientific, philosophical and aesthetic notions, we are capable of objectivity. Objectivity is not, of course, the same as truth; an objective notion may be true or false. But it was not so much the lack of truth as the lack of objectivity that Dilthey and others feared.

Objectivity is not threatened by the fact that 'to tell it as it actually was' is not possible, since the problem is not lack of evidence, or lack of insight or *Verstehen*. There is simply too much to tell. The human mind is not adequate to 'tell it as it is', even in the world of the present. A historian and a recording angel are two very different things. The analogy with science (which I made in section 1) holds here too. What we need is simply more knowledge.

Another reason for supposing that we are capable of objective thought is demonstrated in our love of a story, and the consequent pitching of history in narrative or dramatic form. Like Adam and Eve, we want to eat of the Tree of Knowledge because we wish to be like gods. We want to stand outside, to observe the drama, to follow the unfolding of plot, the interplay of character, the convergence of consequences. Narrative is thus not only the best way of dealing with problems of change; it also seems to be the best way of attaining that transcendence which is challenged by relativism – a challenge that I have suggested need not be taken at face value.

If narrative is the first demand made upon historians (not, of course, one they are always willing to meet), there are other demands – for interconnection, explanation and meanings – which are most obvious by their absence. Very crude, simple narratives are sometimes published for an unsophisticated audience, with titles like 'The Story of Flight' or 'The History of the Village of Magnum-in-Parvo'. The lack of 'horizontal' connections is particularly obvious in works of the first type, where a series of inventions are recounted as if in a void, with no reference to other events that could be a cause or effect of these apparently spontaneous inventions. Even more advanced 'histories' of science or technology have sometimes failed in this way. The lack of 'vertical' connections is even more lamentable in many a local history, where single events, separate from each other by decades or centuries, are simply written down without any suggestion of the possible relationship of one to another.

In addition, readers expect historians to explain why and how things happened as they did. The way in which this expectation is satisfied often reveals a lot about both historians and their public – or at least the public they envisage. One interesting exercise in comparative historiography is to note how the elements of a history seem, to one mind, to need explaining, while to another they are either too trivial or too obvious to require any explanation at all. That exercise would be a study in intellectual fashions. However, historians may adopt a particular mode of explanation, not because

of the needs and demands of their own day, but because they think it best
corresponds to the basic structure of the events of the past. What is basic
at one time (for example, economics) may not be so at another. The French
historian François Furet writes:

> It is not clear, for example, that the dynamism of French history from,
> say, the great expansion of the eleventh-twelfth centuries is economic
> in character: it may be that educational, cultural (in the broad sense)
> and state investment (the latter through the various public offices),
> play a more fundamental role here than increase in the natural
> product.[28]

Thoughtful historians will decide during, or even before, their researches
what sort of factors are fundamental to their period. It may be that overpopulation or religious enthusiasm or the interest rate seem to hold the key.
The more fundamental the factors, the greater their explanatory power.
Nevertheless, there is likely to be conflict: the events may appear most susceptible to one view, while contemporaries favour another. Gibbon would have
met with more obloquy in the nineteenth century for the irreverent handling
of Christianity in his fifteenth and sixteenth chapters than he did in the
eighteenth, and A. J. P. Taylor's *Origins of the Second World War* would have
been fortunate to find a publisher and a public during the course of that
conflict. Nor is this only a matter of political or religious prejudice. Today
explanations in terms of demography or technology are readily accepted; but
to account for the British Constitution or European imperialism in terms
of race is as unacceptable today as it was almost unquestionable a hundred
years ago.[29] It is not easy, then, for historians to offer an explanation that
accords both with the structures of events and with the mind of their public.

Similar remarks may be made about 'meaning', where there can also be
a tension between the demands of the historian's material and those of the
public. The public rightly expect the historian to justify taking up their time
with an account of something over several hundred pages. They want to
know what is especially significant about a particular narrative or description.
The concept of 'significance' or 'meaning' points to something else: as we
usually say, the significance or meaning of A is B. For example, a historian
recounting the history of Hermann Goering's economic activities might argue
that the significance of the great enterprise of the *Reichswerke* was that it played
a major part in Hitler's plans for a world war in the mid-1940s.[30] Or one

---

[28] F. Furet, 'Quantitative history', in *Historical Studies Today*, ed. F. Gilbert and
S. R. Graubard (W. W. Norton, 1972), p. 60.

[29] See, for example C. J. W. Parker, 'The failure of liberal racialism: the racial ideas of
E. A. Freeman', *The Historical Journal*, 24, 4 (1981), pp. 825–46.

[30] See R. J. Overy, *Goering – the 'Iron Man'* (Routledge and Kegan Paul, 1984), reviewed
in *The Times Literary Supplement*, 25 January 1985, p. 82.

might suggest that the meaning of the Enlightenment was that people had abandoned religious conflict and had a new faith in the powers of reason, or that the meaning of the miniskirt in the 1960s was that women had found a liberation from traditional roles.

The concept of 'meaning' is normally employed to relate the smaller to the larger, the apparently less to the apparently more important. Often nowadays the 'larger' is a theory from the social sciences; for example, the studies of poverty in nineteenth-century England are related to theories (for or against) of the creation of a proletariat. Sometimes the second term is very large indeed, as when the meaning of an event is given in terms of 'History' (by Marxists) or of God (by Christians). For historians the ultimate question about meaning is 'What is the meaning of history?' This is often asked of them, but perhaps they less often ask it of themselves. However, since a meaning points to something else, the meaning of history (as the sum of events) must be something beyond history – and on this, *qua* historian, the historian is no wiser than anyone else.[31]

In considering how to turn the historical construction into a sensible form that can be understood by others, historians must bear in mind these demands made by the public. As I shall demonstrate, there are other expectations too.

---

[31] See chapter 12, section 3.

8

Historiography or the Writing of History

1 History as the Use of Language

Epic poetry, astronomy, sublime hymns, erotic poetry, choral dance, tragedy, comedy, lyric poetry, and history; what, one may ask, is history doing here? Is she among the gifts of these songsters, daughters of Zeus and Mnemosyne, the goddess of memory? The answer is that history, like poetry and song, is a way of using language. Language has many functions: it recalls and conserves the past, it acts as a vehicle of the imagination, it conveys information, it stimulates emotion, it provokes to action, it gives a form and a measure to life. All these things are gifts of the Muses; Clio, the muse of history, is capable of doing each one of them herself. I have already considered some of these functions; the last three (concerning emotion, action, form and measure) will be touched upon in the remaining chapters.

In the last 200 years history has been recognized as both a scholarly discipline and a satisfying intellectual activity. No longer need a Catherine Morland complain: 'I often think it odd that it should be so dull, for a great deal of it must be invention.'[1] One unfortunate consequence, however, is that historians and public alike tend to look beyond the book to the events, to the interpretation too, and sometimes to the evidence (the topics of chapters 2, 6 and 4); and that these three aspects prove so interesting and throw up so many fascinating problems that people largely ignore the vehicle that conveys them – the book or article.

They have paid more attention to Clio's mother than to the lady herself. As George Herbert sang:

> A man that looks on glass,
>   On it may stay his eye;
> Or if he pleaseth, through it pass,
>   and then the heaven espy.

[1] Jane Austen, *Northanger Abbey* (1818), chapter 14; quoted by E. H. Carr at the front of *What is History?* (Penguin, 1964).

The more we have come to know about our past, the more we have neglected the written historical work. On the few occasions when people recognize this, they often complain that a work of history is no longer seen as a work of art, and deplore the dullness of the writing and the general lack of literary skills. Now it is true that more historians write like Bury than like Trevelyan, more like Ranke than like Gibbon or Macaulay. Whether this is to be regretted is a matter of some dispute: the general popularity of history both in education and with the general public, in spite of indifferent presentation, suggests that it does not.

However, the point goes far deeper than whether a work of history is, or should be, an aesthetic object. Today there is no question of purple passages and resounding sentences, even when we talk, as we may properly do, of 'the rhetoric of history'. What this phrase recognizes is that history is concerned with language. That is why Clio is a muse; she and her sisters command the various uses of language. Language is capable of many things, and, if history is not capable of everything language can do, at least it can fulfil the functions I listed in the first paragraph of this chapter.

Speaking mythologically I suggested that language is also vitally important to history because Clio is a muse. Hayden White has observed, 'in any field of study not yet reduced (or elevated) to the status of a genuine science, thought remains the captive of the linguistic mode in which it seeks to grasp the outline of objects inhabiting its field of perception.'[2] White's point is that, outside 'genuine science', we think about the world in terms of whatever linguistic mode we adopt to describe it. Of course we may grasp the world in other ways too: by art, mathematics or religious symbolism. Many scientists have sought to follow Galileo's belief in the language of mathematics:

Philosophy is written in that vast book which stands forever open before our eyes, I mean the universe; but it cannot be read until we have learnt the language and become familiar with the characters in which it is written. It is written in mathematical language, and the letters are triangles, circles and other geometrical figures, without which means it is humanly impossible to comprehend a single word.[3]

If we use language to grasp the world, however, we become prisoners of the ways in which we use it. History grasps the world almost entirely through language – and everyday language at that.

[2] Hayden White, *Metahistory: the historical imagination in nineteenth-century Europe* (Johns Hopkins University Press, 1973), p. xi.
[3] A. C. Crombie, *Augustine to Galileo* (Heinemann, 1961), vol. 2, p. 142. See also Stephan Körner on mathematization in *Categorial Frameworks* (Blackwell, 1970), pp. 44–50.

2   A History as a Text

The use of language in history can be appreciated at both the linguistic and the literary level. Listening to speakers or reading authors, one is aware that they achieve their effect by their choice of words, by the syntax of their sentences, and by their style – especially the 'tone' which indicates their intellectual and emotional attitudes to their material. The tone is easier to discern in a speaker, since one can see the expressions and gestures, and hear the modulations of the voice. But it is not difficult, with rather more attention, to discern the tone of a writer. The styles of Gibbon, Macaulay or Carlyle, for example, are unmistakable. In this century, well-marked styles are less evident, though there are exceptions: A. L. Rowse, A. J. P. Taylor and Lord Dacre (Hugh Trevor-Roper) can be readily distinguished. Indeed, few would accept Acton's ideal, whereby the writing made it impossible to tell where one author stopped and another began.[4]

At first sight it may appear unnecessary to do more than stress the importance of the use of language by a historian. A fair amount of work has been done on it. Perhaps more rigorous studies could be made by linguistic scholars, for a good deal that has been written on the subject consists of rather belletrist essays or occasional papers tossed off by historians (often at semi-social functions) in a mood of holiday from their serious work.

Certainly more could be done to investigate the spoken word, since the historical work is by no means always a book or article. A great deal of history is conveyed by word of mouth in classrooms, lecture halls, seminars and conferences, and on radio or television. In such communication, for the most part not read, and heard only once, the language must have more power than in a written work that may be read several times and pondered over on different occasions and in different contexts, thus reducing the power of language.

All these linguistic elements operate at a microcosmic level, pervading the book or lecture. The other level is that of the work as a whole. One can find Gibbon's characteristic syntax and style on almost any page of *The Decline and Fall*, taken at random, but to grasp its qualities as a work of literary art one has to consider the whole. To some extent every historian is aware of these architectonic problems – how the work should be planned; how many chapters it should comprise; what should be dealt with first; how the theme should be developed and rounded off, and so on. The result can vary greatly in skill from masses pushed together like a child's wooden blocks to the subtle blending and balance of a baroque church or a Haydn symphony.

---

[4] See Lord Acton's letter to the contributors to the *Cambridge Modern History*, quoted in chapter 5, section 2.2.

However, there seems to be more to it than building. A number of writers (among whom perhaps the most distinguished is Hayden White) have begun to look more closely at historiography as a literary art.[5] It would be unprofitable to try to repeat what people can say better for themselves, but, to give some idea of the issues, I shall take some of the leading points from White's major work.[6] I have already quoted the basis of his argument: that in subjects like history our thinking is held within the linguistic frame with which we apprehend reality. Thus he asserts that history is at once poetic, scientific and philosophical. In what ways it partakes of the nature of the first two perhaps does not by now need explaining. A little more may be said about the third. The idea that history as the course of events (*res gestae*) raises philosophical problems (about progress, meaning, purpose, and so on) is not new; it goes back to the Old Testament, if not further, and continues in a tradition of philosophy of history to (at least) Arnold Toynbee in our own day. That history as the report of events (*historia rerum gestarum*) also entails philosophical problems has a shorter ancestry but today a greater popularity. Questions of cause, explanation, objectivity, truth, generalization, quantification, and so on, are much debated. But the notion that history as a verbal discourse provokes yet another set of philosophical questions has perhaps only recently come to our attention.

White argues that there was no great difference in the nineteenth century between the writers and the philosophers of history; the philosophers merely made explicit what was implicit in the writers. In his book he studies four historians (Michelet, Ranke, de Tocqueville and Burckhardt) and four philosophers of history (Hegel, Marx, Nietzsche and Croce). Each of these, he insists, was also a great philosopher of language.

White maintains that as soon as historians confront their evidence, and before they apply to it their conceptual (and presumably technical) apparatus, they must 'prefigure' the field. This is an essentially poetic act; they must constitute what they are studying as an object of mental perception. We might say, 'They have to see it in a certain way', but that is too vague. White is more precise. He draws a close analogy with language. He reminds us how a language is used to articulate a certain domain. Anthropologists of language like Benjamin Whorf, and scores of his successors, have done this with rather remote peoples. Nowadays we are probably more familiar with

[5] For example, Stephen Bann, 'Towards a critical historiography: recent work in philosophy of history', *Philosophy*, 56, 217 (July 1981), pp. 365–85; Roland Barthes, 'Historical discourse', in *Structuralism*, ed. M. Lane (Jonathan Cape, 1970), pp. 145–55; Robert H. Canary and Henry Kozicki (eds), *The Writing of History: literary form and historical understanding* (University of Wisconsin Press, 1978); Hayden White, *Tropics of Discourse: essays in cultural criticism* (Johns Hopkins University Press, 1978); Hayden White, 'Historicism, history, and the figurative imagination', *History and Theory*, 14 (1975), *Essays on Historicism*, pp. 48–67.
[6] White, *Metahistory*.

the operations of artificial languages, like those used with computers – BASIC or FORTRAN. The general points are the same, however. Before a given domain can be interpreted, the language-user must be clear about (1) the discernible figures that inhabit it, (2) the classification of these figures into types of phenomena, (3) the kinds of relationships they bear to one another. In short, we must be clear about what things there are, how they may be classed, and how they stand to each other. Only then can a domain be handled in a language. (One thinks of Wittgenstein's point that we must first agree in judgements.)

The historian, says White, does not have to *make* a language, but has to prefigure his or her material, roughly as a language deals with *its* material. As he puts it:

> the historian's problem is to construct a linguistic protocol, complete with lexical, grammatical, syntactical and semantic dimensions, by which to characterize the field and its elements *in his own terms* (rather than in the terms in which they come labeled in the documents themselves), and thus to prepare them for the explanation and representation he will subsequently offer of them in his narrative.[7]

First White considers ways in which prefiguring can be done by the historian, for this action determines not only the domain (that is, what is to be dealt with) but also the concepts to be used (that is, how it is to be handled). Three of these ways of prefiguring are straightforward – 'naïve' in Schiller's sense; the fourth is oblique and sophisticated – Schiller's 'sentimental'. He attaches them to four tropes (or figures of speech): metaphor – the representational way; metonymy – the reductive way; synecdoche – the integrative way; and irony – the self-conscious and sceptical way. These, I repeat, are fundamental; they represent how the historian sees the material (according to White) before beginning work on it.

The historian then uses, simultaneously, three distinct ways of explaining and making sense of it: emplotment (for example, tragedy, satire, etc.); formal argument (for example, formist, which emphasizes the uniqueness of things, or organicist, which represents discrete phenomena as constituting an organic whole, as was the practice of nationalist historians like Treitschke or Stubbs); and ideological implication (for example, radical or conservative).

It has not been my purpose here to give anything like a full account of White's theories, which are worked out in a lengthy but readable book. All I want to do is to indicate the various dimensions of one literary-critical approach to a work of history.

It may, however, be worth spending a little more time on some of the

---

[7] Ibid., p. 30. The italics are White's own.

issues that White raises both in his *Metahistory* and in a later essay, 'Historical Text as Literary Artefact'.[8] He argues that there are a limited number of plot structures (tragedy, comedy, romance, satire, etc.) 'by which sets of events can be constituted as stories of a particular kind.' The choice among these is made by the historian: 'how a given historical situation is to be configured depends on the historian's subtlety in matching up a specific plot-structure with the set of historical events that he wishes to endow with a meaning of a particular kind.' By choosing a familiar form the historian can 'make sense of a set of events that appears strange, enigmatic, or mysterious in its immediate manifestations.'[9] By rendering familiar the unfamiliar, the historian performs a calming and healing function upon our puzzled and anxious minds.[10] But historians do more than make sense of given events; according to White, they impose relationships upon the historical field and even 'constitute their subjects as possible objects of narrative representation by the very language they use to describe them.'[11]

If there is any truth in this, then the historian has been undervalued, for historiography is a literary activity that is not merely constructive or decorative but creative in the full sense of the word. It creates its own subjects, determines their relations, and explains their meaning. If this 'in no way detracts from the status of historical narrative as providing a kind of knowledge', as White asserts, then may we not ask 'knowledge of what?'[12] Must we abandon our belief in a 'real past'? Louis O. Mink argues that we should 'abandon...the idea that there is a determinant historical actuality, the complex referent for all our narratives of "what actually happened," the untold story to which narrative histories approximate.'[13] One feels that here a good case has been carried too far, and that both White and Mink would be well advised to consider the stubborn realities of historical evidence. As Olafson says of White's approach, 'the claim of history to speak the truth about the past typically seems to go by the board.'[14]

There are, moreover, other criticisms to be brought against White. First, clearly not all works of history are cast in a narrative form. Yet it has been argued that all historiography implies narrative. Lawrence Stone seems to suspect it.[15] Gallie seems more sure of it: 'I have...argued that whatever

---

[8] This is printed both in White, *Topics of Discourse*, and in Canary and Kozicki (eds), *The Writing of History*.

[9] Canary and Kozicki (eds), *The Writing of History*, pp. 48–9.

[10] See the point discussed in chapter 10, section 6.

[11] Canary and Kozicki (eds), *The Writing of History*, pp. 56–7.

[12] Ibid., p. 49.

[13] Louis O. Mink, 'Narrative form as a cognitive instrument', in ibid., p. 148.

[14] F. A. Olafson, *The Dialectic of Action: a philosophical interpretation of history and the humanities* (University of Chicago Press, 1979), p. 38.

[15] 'The revival of narrative: reflections on a new old history', in Lawrence Stone, *The Past and the Present* (Routledge and Kegan Paul, 1981).

understanding and whatever explanations a work of history contains must be assessed in relation to the narrative from which they arise and whose development they subserve.'[16] Nevertheless it is not difficult to point to other, non-narrative, models for historical works. Kieran Egan, following F. M. Cornford, has argued that Thucydides shaped his history as a myth-determined tragedy.[17] Burckhardt's *The Civilization of the Renaissance in Italy* is the elaboration of an idea. Le Roy Ladurie paints Breughel-like portraits of a community (*Montaillou* or *Carnaval*). Many works of economic or quanti-tative history aim to follow scientific models. Others, again, develop a rational argument – for example, Alan Macfarlane, *The Origins of English Individualism*.[18] None of these is, prima facie, a narrative.

It should also be pointed out that not all modes are always apt. White himself admits that one can hardly emplot the story of President Kennedy as a comedy.[19] Nor could the history of the First World War be told as comedy or romance, though easily as tragedy or satire.

F. A. Olafson, has commented on the difficulties of scale: a history usually demands a larger canvas than does imaginative literature.[20] Indeed, he might have noted that historical accounts of very different scales have to be reconciled; the end of the Roman Empire may take up a few pages in a textbook or several volumes of Gibbon. Yet every such account (like maps of various scales) must be accurate within its own limits. This seems to be practicable only on the assumption that there is a real historical field to be mapped, and that the various accounts are veridical.

More tellingly, Olafson points out that in history, unlike literature, there is rarely or never an agent who recognizes what is going on. 'As a plurality of consciousnesses is introduced into even the most central areas of dramatic agency, as it is in history, the likelihood that any one of them will be able or disposed to experience it as having the mode of unity that is proper to a tragedy or a comedy becomes more and more problematic.' He concludes that this 'must call into question any assumption to the effect that the plot structures of literature will be transferable without further ado to historio-graphy.'[21] In a footnote he adds that White's *Metahistory* 'conspicuously fails to take into account the erosion that generic plot-structures undergo when they are transferred to the real historical event.'[22]

---

[16] W. B. Gallie, *Philosophy and the Historical Understanding* (Chatto and Windus, 1964), p. 9.

[17] See Kieran Egan, 'Thucydides, tragedian', in Canary and Kozicki (eds), *The Writing of History*: 'it is so profoundly infected with a particular myth-determined preconception that it should be classed as a tragedy' (p. 64).

[18] Alan Macfarlane, *The Origins of English Individualism: the family, property and social transition* (Basil Blackwell, 1978).

[19] Hayden White in Canary and Kozicki (eds), *The Writing of History*, p. 48.

[20] Olafson, *The Dialectic of Action*, p. 80.

[21] Ibid., pp. 80, 81.

[22] Ibid., p. 271.

Against the imposing of plot structures on history Olafson recognizes that 'the deepest commitment of the historian must be to evidence rather than to any particular form of unity which he may think he discerns in the materials with which he deals.' His own theme centres on the importance for history (and other humane studies) of 'what human beings, whether fictive or real, have done and said and believed and desired.'[23] History, for Olafson, is to be understood primarily (though not entirely) in terms of how the agents saw the world of their actions – in terms of their beliefs, concepts and descriptions.

Olafson's thesis therefore challenges that of Hayden White, despite the fact that both regard history as a humanistic and literary endeavour rather than as a social science *manqué*. However, White has raised important questions, some of which I have touched on elsewhere in this book is discussing 'fact', 'event', 'imposed or inherent relations', 'significance', 'meaning', 'making and conveying sense', 'explanation' and 'the reality of the past'. A fair conclusion is that White's arguments are much more applicable to historians of the last century (about whom he writes in *Metahistory*) than those of the present one. His theory is fruitful but one-sided, since it does not cover all works of history. He has opened a number of serious questions, but has not closed them.

There are two good reasons for paying attention to the literary characteristics of a history book, instead of reading it just for pleasure and information. The first is that the more we understand how a historian has done the work the better we can penetrate to what that work is about – the world of the past 'as it actually was'. To use George Herbert's analogy again, if we pay some attention to the glass through which we look, the better we shall understand what we are looking at.

Second, whatever their differences, Hayden White, Kieran Egan, Louis Mink and Frederick Olafson agree that history is written in traditional forms that are deeply familiar to the public – whether it be comedy or tragedy (White), myth (Egan), narrative (Mink) or a commonsense understanding of human intentions (Olafson). To these the public responds promptly and yet with definite expectations – for example, that comedy should end in reconciliation. If we pursue this line of thinking we may attain a clearer understanding of the influence of history upon its public. A historian may write from many different motives, not all of them acknowledged or even conscious. His language, his style, his construction, his modes of explanation will be adapted to these ends.

[23] Ibid., pp. 19, 34.

3   Histories of Historiography: a Fresh Approach

Herbert Butterfield drew attention to the benefits to be derived from the history of historiography.[24] To *Man on his Past* he added the subtitle: *A Study of the History of Historical Scholarship.* Since this work appeared in 1955 more historians have followed his advice. Historiographical surveys range from the rather thin series of *Problems in European Civilization*, to the more thorough works of Pieter Geyl on Napoleon (written before Butterfield's book), J. McManners on the French Revolution, R. C. Richardson on the English Revolution, M. Anderson on the eighteenth century, and so on.[25] Another approach is to study historians in the context of the mentality of their age, and to regard the history of historiography as part of the history of ideas. This is the approach of J. W. Burrow, Christopher Parker and others.[26]

The structure I am following in this book might, however, furnish a guide to a more thorough and perhaps more comprehensive approach to the history of historiography. By careful differentiation it may also help to avoid confusion. In the Prologue I sketched out what I take to be the structure of historical activity – that 'relation which determines its peculiar nature'.[27] There are six stages representing the structures of a process, rather than of a condition: the events of the past; the evidence; the construction in the historian's mind; the historical communication; the public mind; and historical actions. I shall examine these in relation to the history of history and of histories.

What corresponds to the first stage, the events themselves, is historians' topics. Some topics may in the historical field have been 'really there' – such as the advancing frontier in nineteenth-century America, or the First World War. Others are less certain: there are reasons to doubt whether there really was such a phenomenon as the Carolingian Renaissance in the ninth

---

[24] See chapter 6, section 4. Also Herbert Butterfield, *Man on his Past* (Beacon Press, 1960), p. vxii and *passim*.

[25] *Problems in European Civilization* (D. C. Heath); Pieter Geyl, *Napoleon: for and against* (Jonathan Cape, 1949); J. McManners, 'The historiography of the French Revolution', in *The New Cambridge Modern History*, vol. VIII: *The American and French Revolutions, 1763–93*, ed. A. Goodwin (Cambridge University Press, 1965); R. C. Richardson, *The Debate on the English Revolution* (Methuen, 1977); M. S. Anderson, *Historians and Eighteenth-Century Europe, 1715–1789* (Clarendon Press, 1979).

[26] J. W. Burrow, *A Liberal Descent: Victorian historians and the English past* (Cambridge University Press, 1981); C. J. W. Parker, *History as Present Politics*, Winchester Research Papers in the Humanities (King Alfred's College, Winchester, 1980); C. J. W. Parker, 'The failure of liberal racialism; the racial ideas of E. A. Freeman', *The Historical Journal*, 24, 4 (1981); C. J. W. Parker, 'English historians and the opposition to positivism', *History and Theory*, 22, 2 (1983).

[27] Prologue, section 4; chapter 1, section 1.

century, an English Revolution in the seventeenth or a Great Depression in the nineteenth.[28] It is, indeed, histories of such topics, possibly real, possibly factitious, that Butterfield urges upon us and that so many publishers and editors have followed. Few, however, have been as precise as Butterfield himself. In putting the case for 'the history of the historiography of the whole subject' in *George III and the Historians*, he warns that it could result in 'a measureless amorphous mass if the topic itself did not have an essential core, or if it could not be resolved into a hard piece of subject-matter, amenable to analytical treatment.' This core is 'the question of the King's intentions at the moment of his accession'.[29] All too many surveys of historiography fail to specify the central core of the topic, and thus leave the reader confused and without a focus. These works, of very variable quality, much in vogue and familiar to every student of history, are the histories of historiography that correspond to my first stage.

The second stage is the evidence. Here at least two types of history could be of use – histories of evidence, and histories of the treatment of evidence. What immediately suggests itself is a work that traces how the evidence for different periods and subjects became available for historians: the recovery of classical manuscripts in medieval and Renaissance times, the collections for English history made by Cotton in the early seventeenth century and Harley in Queen Anne's time, or the documents collected for Louis XIV by Colbert, the publishing of treaties by Rymer, the slow calendaring of the papers by the Public Record Office, the opening of the Vatican Archives, the work of the Historical Manuscripts Commission, and so on. The work would include one or two melancholy chapters on evidence that has been lost, as in the destruction of classical libraries – Alexandria in AD 309 or the burning of the Hôtel de Ville of Paris in 1871, up to the archives lost in British, German and Russian cities during the Second World War. Such events are usually mentioned obliquely in histories of the historiography of topics – as in Butterfield's *Man on his Past*. Nevertheless, the subject is important enough to merit scholarly study in its own right.

On a similar theme a shorter, but perhaps livelier book could be written on changing views of historical evidence. As I have argued, evidence is not an absolute concept but is always evidence *of* something *for* someone. In the past, small fossils were regarded as 'devil's toenails' and mammoth skulls as remains of giants. Some quite amusing chapters could be written on the changing interpretations of evidence. More instructive would be an account of the many things – post-holes, industrial machinery, Languedocian cadastral surveys, lists of baptisms, marriages and funerals, place-names, street

[28] See chapter 2, section 3.
[29] Herbert Butterfield, *George III and the Historians* (Collins, 1957), pp. 39, 40.

plans, business papers – that historians have learned to use as evidence. Some of these were formerly not considered to be evidence at all; others were regarded as evidence for a specific subject – for example, church records for genealogies – without any suspicion that they could be used for such other purposes as historical demography. Again, one must not ask whether something is evidence but rather what it is evidence of, and for whom.[30]

Yet perhaps the most valuable exercise in the historiography of evidence would be to trace the development of the techniques of handling, preserving and making available the various kinds of evidence (not only documentary) that the historian needs. From palaeography to computer science is a remarkable journey.

My third stage is the historian's mental construction. Here again there is more than one story to be told. The most common approach is biographical, or semi-biographical. As I have already remarked, biographies and autobiographies of historians tend to be disappointing, since they relate a good deal of the outer portion of their lives, such as where they went or whom they met, but neglect the most interesting part of their lives (at least to us) – what went on inside. Obviously this is the more difficult to discover, but it is not impossible. Even so, most of what has been done so far concentrates more on their passive than on their active experiences. By studying historians' correspondence, and still more their diaries, notes, journals, working papers and other private documents, where they have been preserved, one can discern the influences of their world. Such influences, as I argued in chapter 6, operate through public affairs, professional contacts, education, private friendships, and so on. When historians are set neatly into the context of their age, they provide material for the historian of ideas or (more fashionably nowadays) of mentalities or of meanings.[31]

To say this is by no means to decry the valuable work done by Burrow, Parker and others. Yet I think it might be worth while giving more emphasis to historians' thinking in its more positive aspects – not only the sort of prefiguring of the field that Hayden White describes, but also recognizing and identifying entities, attributing significance, classifying, generalizing, and, above all, interpreting and explaining. It has often been pointed out that a good historian follows clues like a detective, exercising a kind of logic that is neither deductive nor inductive.[32] All these are essential skills, many

[30] See chapter 4.
[31] See W. J. Bouwsma's article, cited in chapter 6, section 6.
[32] See chapter 4, section 1. See also R. M. Chisholm, *Theory of Knowledge* (Prentice-Hall, 1966), p. 2.

of which (especially explanation) have been discussed at great length by philosophers.[33]

These issues might well benefit from being treated historically as well as philosophically. Perhaps my brief remarks on the types of explanation in the *Anglo-Saxon Chronicle* indicate what I mean.[34] As with other histories of historiography, one can learn something useful about the subject matter (let us say about historical generalization) as well as about our predecessors in the profession. I believe there is a coherent story to be told of historical techniques of this kind. A historian's mind, as it works on the evidence and constructs an account, is neither a *tabula rasa* nor a mere reflection of experiences, any more than is that of a mathematician, a painter or a sociologist. And there already exist histories of *their* professional skills. So why not a history of, say, historical explanation?

My fourth stage is the historical work. There are many histories of histories that deal with the subject matter or with the historian. However, if one follows the lead of Hayden White, Stephen Bann, Louis Mink, Roland Barthes, Lionel Gossman and others, and considers the importance of the linguistic and literary aspects of historical work, then one might profitably consider a historical study of such books in their capacity as works of art.[35] How are they constructed, how do they achieve their effects? A history of poetry is not the same thing as a history of poems or a history of poets, though they overlap. If one can have a history of poems or of paintings, why not a history of histories, that is, of works of history, considered as literary vehicles, as aesthetic wholes? Again, a start has been made by Hayden White in his examination of four historians in *Metahistory*.

The fifth stage is the public mind. It is sometimes informative to discover for whom particular historians were writing. One difference between William of Malmesbury and A. J. P. Taylor, or between Bishop Bossuet and Eric Hobsbawm, is that they wrote with different readers in mind. Whether a useful history could be written of the development of the historical public I do not know. I am pretty sure, however, that a good story could be told of what effects historians have intended to produce on their readers. That they all desired no more than to impart disinterested information is not probable. How many histories have been written in the cause of nationalism,

[33] For example, the Dray–Hempel controversy. There is a good discussion of this in R. F. Atkinson, *Knowledge and Explanation in History: an introduction to the philosophy of history* (Macmillan, 1978). Many of the relevant articles are printed in P. Gardiner (ed.), *Theories of History* (The Free Press, 1959) and *The Philosophy of History* (Oxford University Press, 1974), and in W. H. Dray (ed.), *Philosophical Analysis and History* (Harper and Row, 1966).

[34] See chapter 6, section 4.

[35] For Bann, Barthes and White, see section 2. See also L. Gossman, 'History and literature: reproduction or signification?', and Louis O. Mink, 'Narrative form as a cognitive instrument', in Canary and Kozicki (eds), *The Writing of History*.

for example? It is not always the worst histories that could be labelled sheer propaganda.

The last stage in my schema is that of historical action. The deeds of men and women, especially but not only those in power, constitutes history (*res gestae*). Many of these deeds are influenced by how these people see themselves in the context of history. One has only to think of the British in 1940 encouraged by popular historians like Winston Churchill and Arthur Bryant, or the Russians in 1941 who were urged to fight for Mother Russia rather than communism.[36] And of Ireland ever since 1690 – or even 1648.

Sociologists have remarked that someone should make a study of the impact upon society of sociology and sociological knowledge. Equally some thorough investigations might be made (by historians and perhaps by sociologists) of the effect of history upon society. Books and articles have appeared and assumptions been made about the significance of certain views of the past. Yet there is room both for a number of monographs and for an overall synthesis (with conceptual and analytical investigations) on how history-as-belief feeds back into history-as-action. Some interesting books have already been written in this area.[37] Many of these, however, merely describe influences of the past. It is more useful to estimate how these influences led to certain actions and so helped to make history.

I offer these suggestions, first, to indicate what has been done and what is yet to be done in the history of historiography; and, second, to try to sort out the different kinds of history that might come under this rather broad concept. I hope that the first will prove a stimulus and the second a clarification.

4   Language and Mental Construction

I now return to the concept of structure – in this case, the structure of the historical work. Whether spoken or written, it is a construction in words, and the function of words is to communicate. For the historian, words also have the function of conserving: documents conserve information about the past, notes and card indexes conserve findings for later use, books conserve

[36] See chapter 11, section 1.
[37] See, for example, the works cited in footnotes 26 and 27 of this chapter. Also J. W. Burrow, '"The village community" and the uses of history in late nineteenth-century England', in *Historical Perspectives: studies in English thought and society in honour of J. H. Plumb* ed. Neil McKendrick (Europa Publications, 1974); Mark Girouard, *The Return to Camelot: chivalry and the English gentleman* (Yale University Press, 1981); J. R. Hale, *England and the Italian Renaissance* (Faber, 1954); Christopher Hill, 'The Norman yoke', in *Puritanism and Revolution* (Heinemann, 1966); Richard Jenkyns, *The Victorians and Ancient Greece* (Basil Blackwell, 1980); J. G. A. Pocock, *The Ancient Constitution and the Feudal Law: a study of English historical thought in the seventeenth century* (Cambridge University Press, 1957).

ideas for future generations. But words' ability to conserve is a consequence of their ability to communicate. Much information could be preserved in the Linear A of Crete or the inscribed seals of the Indus Valley, as in other lost writings and languages, yet since no one can read them the words fail to communicate, and nothing is conserved. Should we ever learn to read them, as Champollion did the Egyptian hieroglyphs or Chadwick and Ventris Linear B, then communication and conservation will be simultaneously effected.

Past events, which are mostly not verbal, are preserved in the form of present evidence, which is largely verbal. But both language and events have a social context, and written evidence does not explicitly convey either of these past contexts. They have to be re-created by the historian's intelligence and imagination. This total construction of past events is by no means wholly verbal. Much rational and constructive thinking is pictorial; a good deal of it must be below the level of words – pre-verbal or infra-verbal. The problem-solving processes of a historian's mind – moving from clue to clue, selecting the significance of this, rejecting that and reaching a tentative conclusion – are not unlike those of a mathematician or a detective. They are literally too quick for words, but they can usually be articulated after-wards. If they cannot, the historian (or detective) may talk about 'hunches' or 'sixth sense'; one may feel sure of something but cannot say why. Very probably there is good reason, but it remains obstinately below the level of consciousness or verbalization.

Thus the historian's construction of the past – the pivot of historical knowledge and the centre of this book – is an activity of the creative imagina-tion. How much of it is verbal probably differs with individual psychologies. This construction stands between history$_1$ and history$_2$ – between history-as-events and history-as-record, or between history and historiography. If the construction is never produced in written or spoken form, then history$_2$ fails to appear.

However, when this knowledge does emerge – in the course of lectures, dissertations, books, and so on – it must normally be put into words. This is not to neglect the part played by diagrams and illustrations in books, or the interesting problems that arise in a classroom or a television studio when various non-verbal sounds and sights are used to convey historical knowledge. Many aspects of communication by language are, *mutatis mutandis*, relevant here.

In chapter 7, section 2, I considered the slightly complex four-term relation of symbolic communication. Most other visual means employed in books or lectures are also symbolic, including maps, diagrams and political cartoons. Although paintings and photographs may purport to be representa-tional, some are so well known as to verge on the symbolic – such as Henry VIII, standing arms akimbo, or the Light Brigade at Balaclava; or, among photographs, Hitler dancing in triumph at Compiègne in 1940, the US marines hoisting the Stars and Stripes at Iwo Jima, or the naked child, burnt with napalm, running down a road in Vietnam. Many sounds too are used in broadcasting as symbols rather than representations (drums, gunfire, birdsong, brooks). It is only when pure representation is employed that different considerations may apply. Representations of the past range from films, photographs and tape recordings, to paintings, drawings and sculptures, to pageants, mock battles and theatrical performances. Some are obviously more directly representational than others, but even with the most lifelike and unsophisticated we need to be aware that all is not as it seems. It is not so much a question of accurate imitation of the past – 'This Roman legionary has forgotten to take off his wristwatch', 'That slavegirl's skin shows the marks of a bikini' – but rather that the contexts are different. Every word, picture and symbol has its own public and private context, its own social and psychological resonances; and so had every past event. Clearly it is impossible to ensure that resonances in the present are the same as those in the past.

Attempt at accurate reconstruction must, however, still be made. In trying to convey a mental construction of the past to the public, historians must use every skill at their disposal, in their use of words and aural and visual aids. In addition, they need the active co-operation of their audience (listeners or readers), who must make for themselves a corresponding mental construction, and who must exercise their intelligence and imagination in order to recover some part of the past. Thus, just as the historian's own construction stands between past events and present book, between history and historiography, so the historiography (whether as book, lecture, diagram or pageant) stands between the historian's mental construction and those of the audience.

It is now clear why the writing of history is so demanding an art. It must look back to the construction in the historian's mind and look forward to similar constructions in the minds of the public. The book (or whatever) must embody as accurately as possible the historian's ideas and findings; that requires one structure. Equally it must meet the demands of whatever literary or rhetorical forms seem most apt for conveying them to others, and encouraging those others to make the necessary imaginative and intellectual effort; this requires another structure. Both structures have to be incorporated simultaneously in the work of historiography. What we call 'good history', a clear, coherent and penetrating vision of the past, succeeds in the first respect. What we call 'a good work of history', an attractive, stimulating and readable book, is effective in the second respect. To succeed on both counts is almost impossible. Of the historians whose literary powers arouse our intellectual and imaginative co-operation – Gibbon, Macaulay, Burckhardt, Treitschke, Pirenne, Bloch, Braudel – how many convince us that the past was really like that? And of those scholars who display a deep understanding of the past – Ranke, Maitland, Namier, Butterfield – how many are masters of the literary arts? The answer in each case is 'very few'. Historians of lesser achievement lean so far towards one pole that they miss the other altogether, while really bad ones come nowhere near either. Finally, we must never forget that history is not just a matter of intellectual and imaginative construction; it looks beyond both historian and public, for history begins and ends in action.

9
From Historiography to the Mind of the Public

1 Expansion and Contraction

In tracing the process of history through six stages one can discern a regular expansion and contraction rather like breathing. Events occur in the real world, a place of many dimensions (stage 1). As evidence (stage 2) they are reduced to three dimensions – mind, symbol, referent. In the historian's mental construction (stage 3) they are further reduced to two dimensions – mind and referent. Then comes the expansion. When the historian's thoughts issue in words or other symbols (stage 4), the past events take on a three-dimensional form – of mind, symbol and referent, as in stage 2. But again the message has to be taken up by its recipients, and this communication (like those considered under the heading of 'evidence' in chapter 4) is a four-term relation (as shown in chapter 7, section 2). At this point the minds involved are different from those at stage 2; only the historian's mind is common to both the earlier and the later types of communication. Therefore the connections made between symbol and referent are likely to be different; the contexts, both psychological and sociological, will certainly be different. The public does not understand the history exactly as the historian does. All this is again reduced to two dimensions as it constitutes the various historical constructions in the minds of the readers or hearers, for they too are now thinking about past events. Again there are the two dimensions of mind and referent as at stage 3. This expands again into three- and multi-dimensional forms, as historical knowledge is popularized, disseminated and acted upon. This will be the subject of the following chapters. Here I shall explore the transition from the work of history to its reception by the public.

2 Every Man his own Historian

History is not a remote academic discipline; it is something of which nearly everyone is aware and in which most people take some interest.

The continuing concern with the Second World War, amply demonstrated on bookstalls and television, is evidence enough. On the other hand, a few minutes' conversation will reveal that the picture of the past held by the average man or woman is widely different from that of the professional historian. Nevertheless, in at least one important respect, every man is his own historian.

In earlier chapters I suggested how historians arrive at their particular understanding of the past. Non-historians, however, attain their knowledge in rather different ways. The first is by memory. Memories may be naïve, unreliable and totally lacking in academic rigour. Nevertheless, for older people especially, they provide a picture of an earlier age which was manifestly different from the present. Others find these memories particularly interesting if they include recollections of important public events. For all its obvious shortcomings as a form of knowledge of the past, memory surpasses every other in vividness and in the authenticity of firsthand experience – 'I was there.'

Knowledge of the past given by memory is contingent and very limited in both time and space. The second source of such knowledge, formal education, is in principle unlimited in either respect. It is also deliberate, planned and organized, and possesses an authenticity that is academic rather than personal. What is taught in schools and universities is commonly more reliable and more coherent, but it lacks the vividness and sense of reality given by memory. History is taught at all levels, from primary school to postgraduate courses, and at all ages from infancy onwards. Moreover, the intellectual demands of the subject matter and the intellectual capacities of the students have a very wide range. There remains room for thorough and seemingly endless discussion of both the aims and the methods of teaching history at any level.

The third way in which we attain knowledge of, or beliefs about, the past is less organized, less continuous, less coherent and without overt aims – though usually it is by no means aimless. It is the casual snowfall of information fluttering down to the average man or woman from a wide variety of sources. These include works of formal history in books and journals, historical fiction, guidebooks to historic cities and sites, exhibition catalogues, and other sources, not primarily historical but nevertheless purporting to convey information about the past. They also include the writings and speeches of journalists, publicists and politicians, works of art, radio and television programmes both factual and fictional, and drama and films, which do not aim primarily at giving information, but use the past for other purposes. From all these sources we pick out ideas that arouse our interest and put them together as best we can. If the first way to knowledge is centred on the authenticity of experience, and the second on the intellectual development of a formal education, this third way is largely built upon emotion. Such emotions include patriotism (Bunker Hill), revulsion (Auschwitz), wonder (the Parthenon or the Taj Mahal), sympathy (Mary, Queen of Scots) or admiration (Mahatma Gandhi or Abraham Lincoln). Curiosity may be aroused by artefacts (an old gun or a soldier's cap) or by oral accounts of family memories of battles, air-raids, demonstrations, and so on. An enthusiasm is thereby aroused in many people for a knowledge of history that their formal education never gave them.

If we put aside memory, which plays only a small if vital part in our knowledge of the past, we are left with the problem of the gap between the scrupulous researches of historians and the casual historical gleanings of ordinary people. Although there is a chasm between them, these two groups do have some things in common, including an interest in the past. They also live in the same age and society at exactly the same distance in time from a particular moment in the past. Most important is the common need to attain a vision of the past and to bring this vision into their present-day lives. Like historians, ordinary people must build up their own mental con-struction of the past, exerting to the utmost their own powers of imagination and intellect to the same end. They will not build exactly the same con-struction as historians, if only through lack of time, but what they build must be their own, not another's. Any historical construction must be one's own, first because one must honestly employ one's own mental powers to make it (not borrow someone else's) and, second, because the construction must be adequate to one's own life as and where and when one lives it, not to another's. Thus every man must be his own historian.

3   The Communication of Knowledge

Being one's own historian does not mean that one does not need to draw on the knowledge of the professional. There is, again, a question of com-munication, hence one of re-creation. It was necessary in previous chapters (chapters 4 and 7) to point out that historical research involves communica-tion. But it is hardly necessary to do this when discussing the dissemination of historical knowledge, for at this stage many people (teachers, publicists, authors) make their living by communication. These I shall speak about later, but first I shall consider a more direct relation, that between historians and a wider general public. It is characteristic of history, unlike many other disciplines, that most of its practitioners write for the general public; history, indeed, speaks to ordinary people in a way that, say, geology or astrophysics does not. One reason is that its subject matter comes closer to our actual experience; we all know wars and elections in a way that we do not know continental drift or red shifts. Another reason is that historians use ordinary, not technical, language. This has often been stressed by writers on the nature of history, and rightly so, for 'scientific jargon' places a barrier between scientists and others. But the question lies deeper than language. Körner makes a clear distinction between 'commonsense and theoretical attributes in scientific thinking'.[1] All quantitative sciences use idealized theoretical concepts; only in limited contexts and for limited purposes can they be identified with the corresponding commonsense concepts. Any branch of enquiry that does so he calls 'double-layered'. History, however, is single-layered: 'In its traditional form, it tries to describe sequences of events as they have occurred, and has no use for a simplified ideal world as described by an axiomatic or less strictly organized theory.'[2]

Thus, in subject matter, language and concepts, history is close to all of us; Gibbon remarked that it is accessible to every intelligence.[3] Before the rise of history as a profession in the second half of the nineteenth century it was normal for historians to write for the general reader. Gibbon's claim is supported by the incident recounted by G. O. Trevelyan in his biography of his uncle, Lord Macaulay. On its publication in 1849 one man read the *History* to his neighbours. At the end a vote of thanks was passed to Macaulay 'for having written a history which working men can understand'.[4] Indeed, both Gibbon and Macaulay claimed to write for a wide public of both sexes.[5] Later it became less obligatory for a historian's best work to have a wide general appeal, or even to be intended to. One may cite as examples such acknowledged masterpieces as F. W. Maitland's *Domesday Book and Beyond* or Sir Maurice Powicke's *King Henry III and the Lord Edward*. On the other hand, Emmanuel Le Roy Ladurie finds quite a wide international readership for his *Montaillou*.

When professional historians write for the general public, they, of course, become communicators as well as historians. Thus many of the comments made about communicators apply to historians too. For simplicity's sake, I shall examine communication direct between the historian and the general reader.

One must consider first the minds at either end of this procedure; then *what* is to be communicated – that is, the message; third, the mode of communication – that is, the code, as well as the problems of encoding and decoding. Finally, one must take account of all the emotions involved, for the success of the communication depends very largely on these. They include the sense of purpose of both parties to the enterprise and their satisfaction in it, especially relating to the very fact that they *are* in communication.

---

[1] Stephan Körner, *Categorial Frameworks* (Basil Blackwell, 1970), pp. 47–8.
[2] Ibid.
[3] *Autobiography* (Dent, 1911), p. 144.
[4] G. O. Trevelyan, *The Life and Letters of Lord Macaulay* (Oxford University Press, 1932), vol. II, p. 173.
[5] See chapter 1, footnote 22.

Then there are emotions appropriate to the message itself, perhaps of urgency or intellectual exertion, or to finding the solution to a problem, or to composing or following a narrative or a reasoned argument. Some emotions relate to the mode of communication; for example, the pleasure derived from a clever use of language, or from the architectonic and other literary skills of construction, or the dramatic and psychological skills of setting scenes, developing plots or portraying character.

Over these many aspects of communication – the minds, the message, the encoding and decoding, the various emotions – writers have only limited control. They can govern (at the most) only their own end of the communication – their own mind, message, choice of language, emotional experiences and aesthetic structures. But they have no control over the minds of their public – their power, content and scope; no control over the way their message is decoded; no certainty even that other minds are capable of receiving their message; above all, no control over the emotions involved in others' study of history, and of their own work in particular. Can they do more than pass on words and concepts? Can they convey that sense of a whole society that gives both coherence and life to their understanding and reconstruction of a part of the past? Wholeness and vitality are both essential to a successful historical construction. It is not enough for historians to attain them themselves, though many do not get so far. They must convey them to their readers and this is the art of writing history.

To illustrate the complexity, suppose, for example, that a historian's subject is the assassination of the Archduke Franz Ferdinand in Sarajevo on 28 June 1914. This event stood at the intersection of what we may call horizontal and vertical axes. To grasp its significance we must know what was happening that day – the arrangements in the town for the day's ceremonies, the activities of a secret society, the moods and actions of members of the Serbian and Austrian governments, the attitudes of the great powers, and so on. This contemporary context stretches further and further outwards, and yet throughout it all that one pistol shot echoed. We must also know the vertical axis, the preceding and succeeding events. If we wish to trace its causes we must know something of the history of the Balkans, of the fierce national struggles of the Serbs, the decay of the Ottoman Empire, the anxieties of the Habsburgs which had developed since the Turks were driven from Vienna in 1683, the expansion and jealousies of Romanov rule in Russia since Peter the Great, and so on. All this might be known to a historian on that day in June who would, however, not know what events were to result from that shot. Today we can understand the full significance of that assassination; it has acquired its meaning from its context in the stream of history – the vertical axis.

The two contexts that meet at this point are incorporated into the historian's own mental construction. Further complexities are involved when this mental vision is transformed into physical form as a manuscript, typescript and printed book. To produce a readable account even for other historians is a formidable task. Moreover, as the skills and techniques have advanced since the days of Michelet and Macaulay, so the outlook of the professional historian has moved away from that of the non-historian, and communication to a wider audience is therefore more difficult.

Often a historian may wish to write for a more specific readership: the average schoolchild, the sixth-former, the first-year undergraduate, the reader of popular paperbacks, the adult student. Pedagogical structures must then be considered. It is difficult to ascertain what the recipient already knows, what needs to be mastered first, what illustrations, repetitions, examples, analogies or self-testing exercises should be employed, and along what lines the reader will progress.

At this point many historians decide to go no further, and leave the task to the professional communicator. The historian has already had to play several roles – archivist, investigator, detective, critic, creative thinker, literary artist – and is commonly reluctant to adopt the role of teacher, journalist or publicist, unless this is possible without departure from familiar ways of thinking and writing. A distinguished professor of history once expressed frank disbelief when I spoke of the need to learn how to teach history. There are no skills to be taught, he insisted; you know your history and you just tell them. This chapter can have little meaning to such an outlook. It implies a view of facts like that attributed to those doyens of French positivist history, Langlois and Seignobos, of whom Marrou said: 'A leurs yeux, l'histoire apparaît comme l'ensemble des "faits" qu'on dégage des documents; elle existe, latente, mais déjà réelle, dans les documents.'[6] It is as though 'facts' were nuggets of precious metal to be quarried from the rock and then passed from hand to hand.

Yet if history needs to be adapted from the scholarly thinking of professionals to the less erudite minds of general readers, students and children, this is labour from which historians may be permitted to excuse themselves. But they should realize that it needs to be done and that it is no easy task. For it is not only a question of superior erudition. Many learned scholars in other disciplines are naïve in their understanding of history. The gap is not between the dull and the clever or the ignorant and the learned, but between the non-historian and the historian.

This is visible all too often when the two come together. There is no great meeting of minds. Discussion is heavily dominated by academics; the approach to the subject is rather that of the university than of the school

---

[6] Henri-Irénée Marrou, *De la connaissance historique* (Éditions du Seuil, 1954), p. 49: 'In their eyes history appears as the collection of facts that are extracted from the documents; it exists in the documents, latent but already real.'

or the general public; it is academic standards and methods that are taken for granted, not pedagogical ones. Schoolteaching is assumed to be merely an inferior type of university teaching; yet in fact, schoolteaching is usually a more skilled activity. Through academic snobbery, many academics miss a valuable opportunity of discovering the nature of their own subject. There are few better ways to understand how complex history is than to attempt to teach it to a wide range of capacities. Academics do not oversimplify the past; they are well aware of the complexities of events. But history is more complex than the events themselves – as I am attempting to demonstrate in this book. Academics are also aware that there can be different interpretations (though many see these as divided only between the right ones and the wrong ones), but very few are aware of the subtleties, the nuances, and the many stages and levels of historical knowledge. A good schoolteacher is usually more aware of this than the academic, if only because he or she has to deal with history at many different levels of sophistication. Teachers are more likely, therefore, to understand that history is not a set of positivistic 'facts' but rather a series of personal visions, each of which have been created by hard work, thinking, imagining and empathizing.

History is an exacting task for the intelligence, as for the imaginative and creative faculties. It is solitary work that can be done only by the individual, not by being taught so-called 'facts' to be memorized. The imparting of facts can no more result in history than it can produce a drama or a scientific hypothesis. It is worth emphasizing that this is true for both the professional historian and the schoolchild or student writing a history essay. Almost everything that has been said in the last six chapters about the one applies also to the other: selection and evaluation of evidence, forging a mental construct, use of rhetoric, literary structure, awareness of potential readership. History, like mathematics, art or poetry, must be thought out for oneself.

Creation does not spring only from the intellect, however; it also requires a driving force. It is relevant to ask what are the driving forces of a good historian, whether a schoolchild or a university professor. (Some of the ways in which interest may be casually aroused have already been discussed.) There may be a passion or curiosity for knowledge; or a desire to establish the truth; or an urge to bring order to confusion. Perhaps there is a nostalgia for a vanished world, a longing to re-create and experience the immediacy of sound and smell and touch; or a compassion for long-dead people seen in a photograph. Or is there, as with E. P. Thompson's artisans, a desire to rescue people from the enormous condescension of posterity?[7] Above all, perhaps, the student of history may be driven by an urge to defy human fate, to reassert humanity in defiance of death. There is a conviction that

---

[7] See E. P. Thompson, *The Making of the English Working Class* (Penguin, 1968), p. 13.

death is wrong; that we were not made for it. The desire for immortality expresses itself in many human activities – in art, in moral action, in philosophy. It also emerges in the desire to know human history, in total perhaps, but certainly in detail; hence especially (as remarked in chapter 7, section 5) the appeal of historical narrative.

4 History in Education and Popularization

How is history conveyed, both formally and informally, in such a way that it satisfies these human needs? Formally, it is transmitted by education, which gives rise to the pedagogical problem of why history should be taught, what part of it should be taught and at what stage in education, and how the knowledge is to be imparted. The questions 'what', 'when' and 'how' are, of course, dependent on 'why', for, if that is not satisfactorily answered, the question 'whether' may be answered in the negative. Informally, history is conveyed by popularization, which itself shows the widespread demand for history. The questions 'whether' and 'why' do not arise here, but 'what' and 'how' still do. The answers will be different from those relating to formal teaching, since the situations are different. For example, the recipients are likely to be more mature, but their efforts will be less sustained.

Decisions about all these questions will be taken by educationalists and teachers in the first case, and by editors, producers, directors, writers, illustrators and actors in the second. About the work of these 'middlemen' there are two points to be made, one relating to vision, the other to structure.

We must remember that they are in the middle between producers and consumers, between the scholars who research and write and the public who watch, listen and read. If they are mere bearers of a message, they are little different from a radio, telephone or carrier pigeon. But if they (as teachers, writers, actors) are to be a medium for history, they have a responsibility to understand the message, to make judgements about what they are trying to do and how they are to do it. These things would be impossible if they were only tracks in the process of communication, but they are stations, where the train must halt.

We recall that the pattern of communication is: initiator–encoding–text--decoding–recipient. These middlemen of history must not see themselves as the text, or even as bearers of the text (no more than messengers). They must be at the end of one process and at the beginning of the next, both recipients and initiators. The pattern of the communication of history is not:

Initiator → Encoding → Text → Decoding → Recipient
(Historian)   (Middleman)   (Public)

But this:

$$\text{Initiator} \rightarrow \text{Encoding} \rightarrow \text{Text} \rightarrow \text{Decoding} \rightarrow \text{Recipient}$$
(Historian)   (Middleman)

And then:

$$\text{Initiator} \rightarrow \text{Encoding} \rightarrow \text{Text} \rightarrow \text{Decoding} \rightarrow \text{Recipient}$$
(Middleman)   (Public)

The decoding at the first stage and the subsequent encoding at the second stage must be performed by the teacher, writer, actor, and so on. These are mental activities that require an understanding of the original message by means of a successful decoding of the historian's encoding, and an equal understanding of how that message is to be passed on, by a fresh encoding, to the inexperienced minds of their pupils or public. Like historians, communicators must do their research and establish a mental construction, and then labour to put it all into a coherent physical form to reach their hearers, viewers or readers. Their mental construction of the past will be constituted partly by the qualities of their own mind, partly by the evidence – which, for communicators, is the historian's publication rather than documents. In contrast to the historian, however, they must know their audience quite specifically, and must carefully frame their communications (whether spoken, written, demonstrated or acted) to the interests, life experience and intellectual capabilities of the recipients. They must communicate not words, not a message, not even ideas alone, but a complete vision. Unless they possess a clear vision of the past, they cannot successfully communicate. For example, a good actor does not simply walk on to the stage and repeat the lines that Shakespeare wrote for Hamlet; he has his own vision of Hamlet as a character and of *Hamlet, Prince of Denmark* as a play. Yet actors must not indulge in ego-trips either; they have responsibilities to both the author and the audience.

Similarly, if teachers of English literature do not have their visions, pupils are likely not only to fail to formulate *theirs* but never to realize that it is possible to attain such a vision. The study of Shakespeare then remains no more than the memorizing of notes on plot, character and prosody. The analogy with history is obvious.

The teaching of history is even more demanding. It is not enough to respond only to the various pedagogical demands, or to the increasingly heavy academic burden resulting from the growth of historical knowledge in range, depth and subtlety. If history teachers are not merely to echo other people's thoughts, or use 'scissors-and-paste' techniques, they must find time, interest and energy to think out in structure and in detail a whole, coherent construction of the period or problem of the past they are dealing with. For those who do succeed in this exacting task, one of their rewards is that their work gives them a better insight into the whole complex nature of history than many more illustrious historians have.

I have already pointed out that a number of structures are involved in the process of history: at the level of events there are at least two, along the horizontal and the vertical axes of time; at the level of understanding there is the complex structure of the historian's mind working on the evidence at one end of the vertical axis to create a structured historical visualization. Then there is the literary or rhetorical structure of the historian's publication. Now we have to consider yet another set of structures – those of the middleman, the teacher or popularizer.

How can the material be structured so that the recipients – pupils or public – may build on firm foundations a sturdy and coherent edifice of historical knowledge? Teachers in schools or universities have the opportunity of imposing a formal structure on students' minds, stretching over a period of several years. Although some organizations have provided schools with structured syllabuses extending over some five years or more, there are few if any agreed syllabuses at the level of college, polytechnic or university. Syllabuses, it should be noted, specify *what* should be taught rather than how. Is it possible so to arrange the parts of the course that they support each other and constitute a whole whose character is determined by the nature of the relationship of its parts? This is the test of a structure, as opposed to a mere arrangement.

Three considerations seem to conflict. The first is that, since historical events occur in temporal sequence, the course should follow a chronological pattern. However, this is a structure only, perhaps, to a Hegelian philosopher of history – hardly to a schoolchild. The second is that the recipient minds are growing. Should one, therefore, teach the simplest things to the youngest, the more complex to the older children? Such a course is well adapted to the structure of a child's mental development, but it may play havoc with the coherence of the material taught. The third is that human affairs may have a sort of inherent logic, like mathematics, so that the most important things have to be understood first. These may be political or (for Marxists and others) economic affairs. Should one, then, teach politics (or economics) first, economics (or politics) second, then social history, then the history of ideas, then history of art, for example? All three considerations have logical force; somehow they have to be reconciled in any history syllabus. And this is to say nothing of the future complications that arise when one considers range (local, national, European or world history), or means, such as availability of staff and resources, and access to places of interest or research. These problems are most acute in schools, but they are by no means absent from higher education.

What of 'general readers', non-historian adults, who are often more interested in history than students but whose historical studies lack the structures of formal education? The relevant considerations are rather different. Adult minds do not develop as fast as a child's (think of the growth in mental powers between eight and eighteen compared to that between thirty-eight and forty-eight). Their knowledge of the past will not be acquired in the chronological order of events (unless they impose on themselves an almost impossibly rigid system). Obviously they cannot postpone knowing about their own and their parents' time (the Second World War, Suez, Vietnam, the oil crisis) until they have worked their way through Greece and Rome, the Dark Ages, and so on. Similarly, they are not likely to begin with one fundamental aspect and then proceed logically from base to superstructure, as Marx would have it. Their historical studies may well begin only when their interest is aroused by changes in technology or art or ideas.

Rather I would postulate that the growth of historical knowledge in people who are neither professional historians nor students under instruction is determined by chance, interest and the formation of understanding: that is, by the accidents of where they go, whom they meet, what they see; by a book, a problem, a television programme, or a political argument or an economic disaster that may stimulate them to think, perhaps about cause and effect in history; and the sort of mental structures and outlook that, as engineers, businessmen, nurses, and so on, they bring to their historical studies. As I have already suggested, ideas and information descend in a largely random way, like snowflakes in a blizzard, upon the historical thinking of non-historians. What hope have they of building a coherent structure of historical knowledge, when it must be based upon so many chance occurrences and when it lacks the deliberate patterning of a formal education? To attain this is not at all easy for the student pursuing a course of history at school or university. It might seem almost impossible for the average man and woman, who, needless to say, constitute the majority.

Yet many such non-historians do nevertheless build up a very sound (that is, deep and well-structured) knowledge of history. In addition, history is not an abstruse subject; almost everyone has some ideas (however crude, muddled or erroneous) about the past. Even more important, perhaps, is that history is made by the actions of millions of average men and women, and that their notions of their historical situation play a part in their actions. If, therefore, their knowledge of history is of such consequence, how is it structured?

10
The Reception of History
by the Public Mind

1 Structure for the Non-historian

For non-historians the need for a structured knowledge of the past is even more pressing than for professional historians or those in the process of education. Unlike these, non-historians must build a structure for themselves. When they go back behind the various pedagogical, literary and professional stages that I have discussed in recent chapters to the events themselves, how can they arrange them mentally in a coherent pattern that will itself have the qualities of a structure *and* will correspond to the structure of events? Leaving aside considerations of chance, interest or life experience, what they want to know above all is what is significant, what is fundamental, what possible pattern could there be in the apparent chaos of the almost infinite number of events in the past. Much of what they read, moreover, is inconsistent. How can the contradictions be reconciled?

A similar problem faces teachers or popularizers, who must frequently make a brief summary of an area of the past, perhaps by way of introduction or background to a more detailed study. They perceive an immediate need to grasp the basic structure of events over a period of decades or centuries, or over a continent or civilization. How can they convey such an understanding to their audience in a few words? What is it essential for the audience to grasp about ancient Rome or early modern Europe before, or alongside, a detailed study of the Roman revolution of the first century BC or the English one of the seventeenth century AD? They must be able to represent these structures on any scale, according to whether they want to outline a millenium, a century, a decade or even a year (as, perhaps, in the case of the Bolshevik Revolution).

I have discussed the possible structure of historical events in chapter 2. Here it is more relevant to consider what is *taken* to be the structure. Judgements about structure generally focus on the concept of causality in some form or other. These are different from judgements of value, since the best is not always the most effective. For example, one might judge that fifth-century Athens or fifteenth-century Florence embodied in their thought and their works of art some of the highest human values. One might then regret that the military and political power of Philip of Macedon or Charles V put an end to them, just as Stalin put an end to the great flowering of arts in Russia during the first quarter of this century. It is not inconsistent with an estimation of these arts to recognize that the power of kings, emperors and dictators can be more efficacious in setting the course of history than intellectual or artistic genius.

The average person, I believe, judges the fundamental causal forces of history to be roughly those of his or her own experience. The historian, with wider knowledge, may well judge differently. People may believe that all historical causes are of the same kind as those of the twentieth century. Some may take the pessimistic view that there are no consistent causes: that things happen largely or wholly by chance and mankind is the sport of fortune – 'As flies to wanton boys are we to the gods.'[1] Another popular view is some form of determinism. This still implies that our fate is out of our hands, but that there are recognizable and consistent causal forces: these, in descending order of impersonality, may be technology, economics or political power. To some people it is almost self-evident that the most powerful effects are wrought by such discoveries as fire, the polished axe, the wheel, metallurgy, gunpowder, the printing press, nuclear fusion, the integrated circuit. To others, by no means only Marxists, it is the production and distribution of wealth that is at the root of human affairs; to still others it is the power of kings and governments.

Much less in vogue today is the belief in the superior effectiveness of spiritual or rational forces. It has been argued that human progress chiefly depends on advances in morals and sensibility – mostly by various thinkers of eighteenth-century France, such as the Abbé de Saint-Pierre, Étienne de Condillac or the Marquis de Chastellux.[2] H. T. Buckle, however, argued that progress depends entirely on the intellect, not on morals.[3] More often it has been an article of faith with Jews and Christians that history is guided by the will of God or by human response to his goodness (roughly the outlooks of the Old and New Testaments). Both of these views are rather out of fashion. Then there are two ways of looking at the power of reason. The less common is that of Kant or Hegel: that there is a rational force (nature or reason) which directs affairs and which, being rational, can be rationally understood, after considerable effort, by the human mind. The more common rationalist view is that human intentions are, for the most

---

[1] *King Lear*, IV. i. 35.

[2] For an interesting discussion, see John Passmore, *The Perfectibility of Man* (Duckworth, 1970).

[3] H. T. Buckle, *History of Civilization in England* (1957; Grant Richards, 1903), vol. 1, chapter 4, p. 130.

part, sufficiently effective for human beings to be able to plan and direct their affairs with reasonable expectation of success. This optimism is found especially with technocrats and Americans. However, it also inspired the French Revolution, as well as the Russian, the Chinese and a number of Third World revolutions of this century.

These sorts of views arise when one follows rather superficial impressions; if one gives the matter more thought, one is likely to be receptive to more academic influences. Those who make a lifelong study of human affairs (historians, social scientists) should have a deeper insight into them. Historians, in particular, have no excuse for parochial thinking. They, above all others, should know that not all centuries were like the twentieth, but that some 5000 years of civilization have exhibited a very wide variety of economic, political, social, religious and artistic patterns of life. Historians, at least, should not fall into the anachronism of attributing to all other centuries the modes of causation of the twentieth. That Spengler did just this demonstrates that he was as poor a historian as he was a philosopher.[4]

2   Five Approaches to Structuring

Leaving aside the structuring of history by social scientists (for example, Comte, Weber, Talcott Parsons), one may discern among historians alone at least five distinctive approaches: the ideal, the literary, the selective, the fundamentalist and the pluralist.

The ideal approach resembles that of the social sciences in that it is dominated by a theory. Many products of the *Annales* school fall into this category, especially the two major works by Fernand Braudel, *The Mediterranean and the Mediterranean World in the Age of Philip II* and *Civilization and Capitalism, 15th–18th Century*. Other examples are Arnold Toynbee's *A Study of History* and Immanuel Wallerstein's *The Modern World-System*. The literary mode of structuring, especially in the prefiguring of the field in terms of tropes, has been described by Hayden White and others.[5]

Each of these two categories (unlike the next three) furnishes examples of structures imposed upon the materials.[6] It is obvious, on the one hand, that the imposition of a theoretical structure upon a set of data poses grave threats to truth and accuracy. It is equally obvious, on the other hand, that those sciences that are the most idealized and abstract are commonly the most advanced. Even the most stubborn of empiricists must recognize that it is impossible to think or write about history at all without some sort of

---

[4] See Heller's remarks quoted in chapter 6, section 1.6.
[5] See chapter, 8, section 2.
[6] See chapter 1, section 3.

structuring, while insisting that this is permissible only in so far as we can correctly discern some inherent structure in the events. The issue, in one form or another, has been debated since the last century at least in the case of history; with science in general it goes back to Galileo, as Körner remarks, if not to Plato.

It is not necessarily wrong to impose a structure upon historical events, provided that Körner's warning about negligibility is heeded.[7] On the one hand are theoretical statements couched in a more or less ideal language, as in physics or chemistry; on the other are empirical statements couched in a natural, non-idealized language. One may properly identify the first set with the second, but only within certain limits and for certain limited purposes. How to demarcate the limits of this identification is, as Körner says, an empirical question to be settled by trial and error.[8] In the sort of theory-dominated historiography that one finds in Braudel, Toynbee or Marx, certain words and concepts (arising from the theory) are used to refer to phenomena that other more empirical historians would describe or conceptualize in other ways. Thus one may properly use such expressions as 'conjuncture' or 'class conflict' to characterize phenomena that others describe differently, provided one is careful to state the limits of this identification. The trouble is that, as Körner remarks, history is normally a single-layered activity that employs natural language only.[9] If a theory is imposed upon it, replete with theory-laden terms and concepts, then the average reader, and even many historians, suppose that these terms and concepts are being employed in the normal way; they do not realize that at this point history is being rendered a double-layered activity. If they realize this, and at the same time heed the warning about the limits of identification, then much conflict and confusion can be avoided.

The other three methods of structuring – the selective, the fundamentalist and the pluralist – are concerned not with imposing a structure but with discerning a structure inherent in the events; so at least they claim. The selective approach is outlined in *Feudal Society*, where Marc Bloch discusses the various points of view from which medieval civilization can be studied. He insists that he has 'no thought of claiming any sort of illusory primacy', for his chosen viewpoint: 'A society, like a mind, is woven of perpetual interaction. For other researches, differently oriented, the analysis of the economy or the mental climate are culminating points; for the historian of the social structure they are a starting point.'[10] I take this to imply that

[7] But see section 5 for some of the risks. For negligibility, see Stephan Körner, *Categorical Frameworks* (Basil Blackwell, 1970), p. 47.

[8] See Körner, *Categorial Frameworks*, chapter 4. See also above, chapter 9, section 3.

[9] Körner, *Categorial Frameworks*, p. 48.

[10] Marc Bloch, *Feudal Society*, trans. L. A. Manyon (Routledge and Kegan Paul, 1965), vol. I, p. 59.

one may discern a number of structures in a period of history and that historians are free to choose which they will write about. Bloch explicitly denies that one is more fundamental than another; it is a matter of which structure one selects to work upon.

In distinction from the selective approach, the fundamentalist type is based on the insistence that one structure is fundamental to society, and that all others are variously dependent upon it or subordinate to it. This rather dogmatic type is most familiar in Marx and his followers, who claim not only to have discerned the true structures of history but to be able to discern which is the basic one.

The pluralist view, like the Marxist and unlike Bloch's, accepts that there is a fundamental structure to history. Unlike the Marxist, however, it accepts the possibility that different structures may be fundamental at different times. On this I have already quoted François Furet.[11]

My own opinion is that it would be desirable, but perhaps not possible, to accept Bloch's view. It would spare us a certain amount of conflict if we regarded it as no more than a matter of taste which sort of structure we take to be fundamental in human affairs – at least, at any one time. This is rather like the fiction that all guests at a function are equally welcome though we know that, in reality, the host and hostess prefer some to others. Regretfully I must decide that both the thinking and the acting of history demand more. While it is perfectly possible for historians to restrict their interests to one sort of structure (for example, the mental climate) of a given period, when they are dealing with the period as a whole they must decide what is fundamental to that period and what is dependent or subordinate. Was it economic events and conjunctures (crises such as overproduction by manufacturers, shortages of footstuffs, lack of specie, exhaustion of soils, for example) that were fundamental to the Thirty Years War? Or power-structures and rivalries? Or matters of religion? The general historian cannot ignore the issue.

Similar considerations apply to historical action, which occurs in the practical world. Political problems of whether to effect desired changes by reform or revolution, of whether to gain an end by battles or diplomacy, problems of peaceful coexistence or hostile confrontation, of international revolution or socialism in one country, of consensus or conflict: all of these may turn on decisions about the fundamental structures, about the basic forces impelling human affairs. Do we put our trust in God, or in justice and the liberal decencies, or in the democratic process, or social and economic necessity, or the human will, or brainwashing and the control of minds, or in force and violence? The answer, if it is to be based on more than blind faith, should rest on, or at least be consistent with, a rational

[11] See chapter 7, section 5.

conviction derived from a study of human affairs in history. I shall return to this point in the next chapter.[12]

3   Some Functions of History

Some decision about the structures of history is essential not only for the academic historian but also (and perhaps even more) for anyone engaged in practical affairs; for the former studies history, but the latter makes history. Michael Oakeshott has argued that a distinction should be made betwen various attitudes to the past, especially between the 'practical' and the 'historical'. 'The practical man,' he says, 'reads the past backwards. He is interested in and recognizes only those past events which he can relate to present activities. He looks to the past in order to explain his present world, to justify it, or to make it a more habitable and a less mysterious place.' By contrast, 'the activity of "the historian" may be said (in virtue of its emancipation from a practical interest in the past) to represent an interest in past events for their own sake, or in respect of their independence of subsequent or present events.'[13] On the one hand he denounces the 'practical' attitude of the past as the chief undefeated enemy of history (that is, of the activity of the professional historian); on the other, he admits that the 'practical' attitude is not illegitimate. He resolves the difficulty by pointing out that the practical past 'is not the enemy of mankind, but only the enemy of "the historian"'.[14]

I wish to go further than this rather grudging admission and insist that a concern with the past is essential to any thinking person. A practical concern, on most occasions, furthers our understanding of the world around us and so helps guide our actions. If the historian is distinguished from the practical person in being interested in the past for its own sake, not for how it relates to present concerns, then the two people should not be separated. The view of historians is objective; they see the past as having its own inherent value, (every age is equally near to God, as Ranke put it). They enjoy it for its own sake, and their understanding is free from present concerns.[15] It is just this objectivity, this wider view, this freedom from the intellectual and emotional pressures of today's demands, that can be of most value to non-historians in their practical affairs. Thus, almost paradoxically, it is when history is furthest removed from the practical that it is of most value to the practical person.

[12] Chapter 11, section 2.
[13] Michael Oakeshott, 'The activity of being an historian' (1955), in *Rationalism in Politics and Other Essays* (Methuen, 1967), pp. 153, 155.
[14] Ibid., p. 165.
[15] Ibid., p. 166.

Of course, we should not use the past as 'a field in which we exercise our moral and political opinions, like whippets in a meadow on Sunday afternoon'.[16] Nor should the past be regarded as nothing more than a source of stories, whether romantic (*Gone with the Wind*) or frightening (*Holocaust* or *The Killing Fields*) – not even when these stories are, or claim to be, true (*The Reason Why* or *The Last Days of Hitler*). Nor should history be used by politicians and propagandists to justify current policies – for example, the British expeditions to Suez in 1956 or to the Falklands in 1982, policies which common sense might find it hard to defend. J. H. Plumb argues that the function of history is to bring about the death of the past: 'Nothing has been so corruptly used as concepts of the past. The future of history and historians is to cleanse the story of mankind from those deceiving visions of a purposeful past.'[17] Sound history, not legend or romance or propaganda, is of real concern to everyone's practical needs. For that reason, too, every man should be his own historian.[18]

From the political function of history I turn to its social function. Here it is useful to remember the distinctions between historical events (history$_1$) and historical accounts (history$_2$). The former have an overwhelming social function, for the present condition of any society is shaped by its past. It is important to discover, at any given time and place, not whether, but how much and in what ways a society has been shaped, and (more important) how much and what sort of latitude remains for present initiatives. As Marx observed, 'Men make their own history . . . not under circumstances they themselves have chosen. . . . The tradition of the dead generations weighs like a nightmare on the minds of the living.'[19] Perhaps no one has offered bolder answers to these questions than Marx himself. Fernand Braudel too has worked out the effects of 'structures' and 'conjunctures' upon the present – that, is upon the sixteenth-century present (see section 2).

These questions lead us to consider the functions of history-as-account. The most important function of history$_2$ (as I suggested in the last chapter) is to help every man or woman to make practical decisions on the basis of the fullest, most objective knowledge. But history$_2$ also serves as a source of delight, wonder, horror and intellectual interest to a large number of leisure occupations, from paperback romances, plays, films and tourism, to amateur historiography and archaeology. In these cases the soundness of the historical knowledge matters less than in the first one. It would be fascinating to pursue the topic of history in leisure, but lack of space compels me to turn to more serious functions of historical studies.

[16] Ibid., p. 165.
[17] J. H. Plumb, *The Death of the Past* (Penguin, 1973), p. 16.
[18] For the other reasons, see chapter 5, section 3 and chapter 9, section 4.
[19] Karl Marx, 'The Eighteenth Brumaire of Louis Bonaparte', in *Surveys from Exile*, ed. D. Fernbach (Penguin, 1973), p. 146.

4   History in the Service of Social Science

The services rendered by history to the social sciences raise some interesting issues. Purists on both sides have tried to avoid any such co-operation, which they regard as corrupting. However, theories and concepts from the social sciences – jurisprudence, economics, political science, anthropology, sociology and even linguistics – have penetrated the world of history and have been profitably used by historians. Conversely too, all the social sciences, in so far as they are more than exercises in abstract theory, must consider actual occurrences. This has long been the case with political scientists. Aristotle caused accounts of the constitutions of 158 Greek cities to be collected, and his *Politics*, especially books IV–VI, shows his mastery of the facts. So with economists: both Adam Smith's *The Wealth of Nations* and Karl Marx's *Capital* contain much factual material and some economic history. Economic theorists tended to use economic history as little more than a storehouse of examples until the mid-twentieth century. Outside Marxist thought, little was done to bring them together in a systematic way until the emergence of the new economic history of the 1950s and 1960s. This may be seen as a bid from the theoretical side to take over the historical, even within economic history. Temin writes: 'The new economic history (known also as econometric history or cliometrics) differs from the old by being a member of the classical economics family, not the historical economics clan.'[20] As Temin's book shows, there is now a closer link between economic theory and economic history.[21]

Until the early years of this century, anthropology and sociology made considerable use of historical material. When Malinowski made 'fieldwork' fashionable, the functional method of observation (if not always participant observation) spread to sociology, and history was ignored.[22] Much the same became true of linguistics with the structuralist revolution of Saussure, Trubetskoy and Jakobson, and the replacement of the diachronic or philological approach with the synchronic or structural: or, as one might say, looking at language horizontally instead of vertically.

In spite of such theories there has been an increasing *rapprochement* between history and sociology, especially since the early 1960s. A good deal has

---

[20] Peter Temin (ed.), *New Economic History: selected readings* (Penguin, 1973), p. 7.

[21] For an interesting survey of their relationships, see N. B. Harte (ed.), *The Study of Economic History: collected inaugural lectures, 1893–1970* (Cass, 1971). A valuable short article is J. Habakkuk, 'Economic history and economic theory', in *Historical Studies Today*, ed. Felix Gilbert and Stephen R. Graubard (W. W. Norton, 1972).

[22] For a review of the present position, see 'Anthropology in the 1980s', in T. K. Rabb and R. I. Rotberg (eds), *The New History: the 1980s and beyond: studies in interdisciplinary history* (Princeton University Press, 1982).

been written on this which there is no need to discuss here.[23] Much of the literature is concerned with the impact of the social sciences upon history. Our concern here is with the services that history can render the social sciences. The possibilities of more than one time-scale, raised in one form by Lévi-Strauss,[24] make an interesting set of problems for sociologists and philosophers, but history, not time, is our business.

I discern at least three ways in which history has been, and can be, useful to the social sciences. The first, the oldest, is by supplying 'facts' to be used in support of theories. This nineteenth-century practice, against which most social sciences rebelled around the turn of the century, is now rather discredited by both social scientists and historians; by social scientists because it does not conform to the more theoretical approaches of the twentieth century, and by historians because its use of examples disregards their period and context. It is futile to study 'revolutions' from Corcyra in the fifth century BC to China, Cuba, Vietnam and Africa in the twentieth century AD and suppose that you are talking about the same thing.

More useful is the discussion of change (together with accompanying concepts of growth, evolution, development, progress). Sociology, economics and political science were encouraged to modify some of their theories by the need to take account of change (and hence of time) in two spheres. One was the inadequacy of functionalism and other equilibrium models to explain change within a society. (Even the most primitive societies turned out not to be homeostatic systems.) The other was the rapid political and economic changes that took place in Asia and Africa after the Second World War with the decline of European empires. In dealing with such processes, history can offer far more than mere 'facts' to its sister disciplines. Many economic and sociological models were not constructed to take account of rapid processes of deep-seated changes, but this is just what history is good at. What is narrative, the most basic form of history, if not an account of a series of connected changes? Thus historians can help their colleagues not with raw material but with well-tried methods and concepts.

The third kind of assistance that history can offer is more subtle. In 'Time and Theory in Sociology' Herminio Martins argues with much cogency that

---

[23] One might begin with the useful little book (with a good bibliography) by Peter Burke, *Sociology and History* (Allen and Unwin, 1980), and with two stimulating essays: Lawrence Stone, 'History and the social sciences in the twentieth century', in *The Future of History*, ed. Charles F. Delzell (Vanderbilt University Press, 1977); and Eric Hobsbawm, 'From social history to the history of society', in *Historical Studies Today*, ed. Felix Gilbert and Stephen R. Graubard. Braudel has long argued for a partnership rather than a mere *rapprochement*. See F. Braudel, *Écrits sur l'histoire* (Flammarion, 1969); in English, *On History* (Weidenfeld and Nicolson, 1980).
[24] C. Lévi-Strauss, *The Savage Mind* (Weidenfeld and Nicolson, 1972), pp. 256–62. See also Herminio Martins, 'Time and theory in sociology', in *Approaches to Sociology*, ed. John Rex (Routledge and Kegan Paul, 1974).

sociology is properly a second-order mode of enquiry or 'meta-discipline' like logic and epistemology, 'a reflection of pre-given constructs'.[25] This implies that it must reflect upon itself in a critical and responsible way – as he puts it 'historicophilosophically'. It is in this crucially important function of understanding itself that sociology, I would argue, needs history most. As Martins points out, it has proved sterile to separate philosophy from history in the case of natural science: 'Any adequate conception of scientific knowledge must involve a deep understanding of its history.' This is all the more true of social science. Martins concludes that 'Reflexive, even philosophically reflexive, sociology involves a substantial effort at the systematic understanding and reappraisal of the history of sociological thought.'[26]

How far history can help sociology to understand itself on the whole remains to be seen. A history of sociological analysis, edited by Bottomore and Nisbet, traces the inner history of the subject by showing how schools and thinkers have helped its development.[27] Historians, however, could bring a greater subtlety to the task, with their experience in processes, in working along the vertical axis of time. But I think their contribution would be even more valuable because of their skills with the horizontal axis; that is, their ability to grasp an age as a whole, to understand how the various parts interact. In Bloch's words (quoted in section 2), 'A society, like a mind, is woven of perpetual interaction'. Sociological analysis, as distinct from social thought, could therefore profitably be made a subject of study by historians.

A good example of a historian's account of social thought is H. S. Hughes's *Consciousness and Society*. Rather more challenging to a historian would be to write a broad-based account of the history of the more rigorous concepts of sociological analysis on which Bottomore and Nisbet rightly lay stress.[28]

5   Comparison in History

Many books straddle the divide between history and sociology – books that could be categorized as works of historical sociology and sociological history. These include the many studies of the English working class in the nineteenth century and of American slavery;[29] studies of social movements such as

---

[25] See H. Martins in *Approaches to Sociology*, ed. Rex, p. 284.

[26] Ibid., p. 287.

[27] T. Bottomore and R. Nisbet (eds), *A History of Sociological Analysis* (Heinemann, 1979).

[28] See H. Stuart Hughes, *Consciousness and Society: the reorientation of European social thought, 1890–1930* (MacGibbon and Keee, 1959); see also Bottomore and Nisbet (eds) *A History of Sociological Analysis*.

[29] See, for example, E. P. Thompson, *The Making of the English Working Class* (Penguin, 1968); E. D. Genovese, *Roll, Jordan, Roll: the world the slaves made* (Deutsch, 1975).

early modern peasant risings, modern peasant wars and modern rebels, and their political consequences;[30] and Lawrence Stone's massive studies of a social class and of family mores.[31]

Some of these authors are historians employing concepts from the social sciences. There is no reason why they should not use all the historian's skills we have discussed in this book. When, however, they are writing a study that is primarily comparative, problems arise. Such problems are seen more clearly when social scientists write historical sociology or historical political science. Such I take to be the works of Barrington Moore and Theda Skocpol.

The question of comparison in history is large and complex. Of course, since the beginning of historiography historians have drawn comparisons. Herodotus is full of them.[32] Plutarch in his *Parallel Lives of the Greeks and Romans* made explicit comparisons of a Greek with a Roman. Methodical comparison was considerably developed by sociologists in the nineteenth and early twentieth centuries (notably Comte, Spencer, Durkheim and Weber) but was not much used at that time by historians, in spite of earlier examples in Enlightenment history. Perhaps the greatest comparative work of the Enlightenment, Montesquieu's *L'Esprit des lois*, is not history. A historical was combined with a comparative approach, for example, by Freeman on politics, by Maine on law, and by Müller on philology, but on the whole comparison ran against the nineteenth-century currents of romanticism, historicism and idealism, with their emphasis on the unique and the particular. The use of comparison with a more central historical concern is seen in Bishop Stubbs's lecture 'The Comparative Constitutional History of Medieval Europe'.[33] Perhaps, however, the *locus classicus* of the comparative approach to history is Marx's statement in the Preface to the first edition of *Das Kapital*: 'The country that is more developed industrially only shows, to the less developed, the image of its own future.'[34] There is a whole philosophy of history in that one sentence.

A serious attempt by a distinguished historian at a comparative method

[30] Robert Mousnier, *Peasant Uprisings in Seventeenth-Century France, Russia and China* (Allen and Unwin, 1971); Eric R. Wolf, *Peasant Wars of the Twentieth Century* (Faber, 1971); Eric Hobsbawm, *Primitive Rebels: studies in archaic forms of social movement in the 19th and 20th centuries*, 3rd edn (Manchester University Press, 1971); Barrington Moore, Jr, *Social Origins of Dictatorship and Democracy: lord and peasant in the making of the modern world* (Penguin, 1969); Theda Skocpol, *States and Social Revolutions: a comparative analysis of France, Russia and China* (Cambridge University Press, 1979).

[31] Lawrence Stone, *The Family, Sex and Marriage in England, 1500–1800* (Weidenfeld and Nicolson, 1977; Penguin, 1979); *The Crisis of the Aristocracy, 1558–1641* (Oxford University Press, 1965).

[32] See, for example, II, 35, or VI, 60.

[33] In William Stubbs, *Lectures on Early English History*, ed. Arthur Hassall (Longmans Green, 1906).

[34] Karl Marx, *Capital* (Penguin, 1976), p. 91.

of history was adumbrated, but not worked out, by Marc Bloch in an article published in 1928, 'A Contribution towards a Comparative History of European Societies'.[35] Since 1959 comparative history has enjoyed the respectability bestowed by a learned journal, *Comparative Studies in Society and History*.

Unfortunately comparative history, and its need for a rigorous analysis, is too big a subject to be discussed here, but while I am considering the functions of history – in particular that of serving the social sciences – I would note that comparative history raises many of the issues involved. Some are discussed by Skocpol.[36] In a laudable attempt at a more rigorous approach than most writers on the subject, she suggests that comparative historical analysis can be directed by the logical methods of J. S. Mill – his 'method of agreement' and 'method of difference'. But if we delve further into logic we find that things are not so simple. Mill based his methods upon the so-called law of universal causation: 'that there are such things in nature as parallel cases; that what happens once, will, under a similar degree of similarity of circumstances, happen again, and not only again, but as often as the same circumstances recur.' Or again, 'For every event there exists some combination of objects or events, some given concurrence of circumstance, positive and negative, the occurrence of which is always followed by that phenomenon.'[37]

Such a law of universal causation cannot be proved. It may be a working assumption in the natural sciences, but it is more questionable in the social sciences. Indeed, as Kant argued, causality of any kind may be a category of the understanding, our way of looking at things, something that we impose upon reality. Can we be absolutely certain in human affairs that what happens once will, in similar circumstances, always happen again? Can we be sure that we know and can specify, independently of the result, exactly what are the 'similar circumstances'? We cannot predict when, or even whether, a marriage will break down, a rebellion occur, a war break out. It may be argued that in any particular case we never know enough of the relevant facts to do so, but if we did we could. Yet this seems very doubtful. Is it possible, without tautology, to state in advance the exact conditions which, where fulfilled, will always bring about such occurrences? I believe not.

Yet if a law of universal causation could be established in the social sciences (Skocpol implies it by resting her case on Mill), and if Mill's arguments

[35] Reprinted in Marc Bloch, *Land and Work in Medieval Europe* (Routledge and Kegan Paul, 1967). See also the issue of the *American Historical Review* 85, 4 (October 1980), entitled 'Comparative history in theory and practice'.
[36] Skocpol, *States and Social Revolutions* pp. 33–40.
[37] J. S. Mill, *A System of Logic*, in *Collected Works of John Stuart Mill* (University of Toronto Press, 1973), vol. VII, book III, chapter 3, $1, p. 306; book II, chapter 5, $2, p. 327.

were valid, we should, indeed, have to be sure not only of what were the facts, but that we knew which facts were relevant, and that the facts in the original case were exactly the same as those in subsequent cases – which 'always followed', as Mill said.

Each of these conditions presents some difficulty. For reasons that are obvious to anyone with experience of historical research, one can never be sure of knowing exactly what was the case about any episode in the past. There is always the possibility that more evidence will come to light or that present interpretations are erroneous, or both. The growth of historical knowledge is at best an asymptotic process. Sometimes it can go widely astray, as Butterfield has shown.[38] In respect of the relevance of facts, one must consider the advances in historical method and the widening range of historical subject matter since the positivistic and politics-orientated historiography of the beginning of the century. There remains hardly any activity, from business promotion to breastfeeding, from faith-healing to fairy-tales, that has not been made the subject of historical research, not only for its own sake but also for the light it throws on other activities of its age. All this tends to show that human activities hang together, that 'a society, like a mind, is woven of perpetual interaction.'[39] To determine the limits of relevance in historical matters (where we are always groping in the twilight if not in the dark) is almost impossible. It is a matter of determining the 'negligibility of the neglected'.[40] Can we be certain that what we neglect in any particular case is negligible?

It is even more difficult to establish that the facts are the same. We must be sure that the subsequent phenomenon is the same as the original one; we also must be sure that the attendant 'concurrence of circumstances' is the same as before. But the subsequent phenomena will occur at different times and places from the original. In those respects they cannot be the same. Mill's argument would be valid only if they were essentially the same – that is, if the spatio-temporal differences could be ignored. Since Einstein's theory of relativity this is to be doubted even in the natural sciences. It is even less probable in human affairs. For example, it is notorious that those planning a war, a marriage, a rebellion, a raid on the stock market or an election campaign are rarely unaware of the success or failure of earlier attempts at such things; thus, in this important respect at least, the second occurrence can never be the same as the first.

My argument so far has been consistent with a positivistic attitude to facts; as if 'facts' were self-contained entities like Greek atoms that could be hewn out by the historian and handed over to the social scientist, rather as

---

[38] See above chapter 6, sections 1 and 2.
[39] Bloch, *Feudal Society*, vol. I, p. 59.
[40] Körner, *Categorial Frameworks*, p. 47.

chemicals are taken from jars in a laboratory for use in experiments. The whole tenor of this book inclines against this view. It would be nearer the truth, as I see it, to say that facts are concepts, enshrined in words, of what is the case.[41] This is in addition to, and different from, the truth that Bloch indicated when he said, 'Historical facts are, in essence, psychological facts.'[42] Thus for historians, perhaps more than any others, the truth must be seen in the context of time and place. Since they cannot enter that spatio-temporal location, they must endeavour to re-create it as accurately and as fully as possible in their own mind. Social scientists must do the same. Like everyone else, they must be historians in the sense that they must make such a mental construction for themselves.[43] However, most social scientists do not have the time, even if they had the inclination, to do this essential historical work. For social scientists work differently from the historians. They start with a hypothesis about some model or type or ideal to which they wish to fit a number of occurrences of what they take to be essentially the same thing – a war, a peasant revolt, a feudal relationship, a currency inflation, and so on.[44] By the very nature of the case, these must be removed from their different historical contexts, as specimens are picked out by tweezers in a laboratory, and tested against the model. Although this is a legitimate way of working, it is not a historical method.

Max Weber and Marc Bloch, and more recently Peter Burke and Theda Skocpol, are among many, both scientists and historians, who have sung the praises of comparative history.[45] There is no doubt that it stimulates our thinking; it opens up new possibilities, suggests new problems, and helps to refine our concepts. Much can be gained – but only at the price of thinking unhistorically. Although it is sometimes worth it, it is important to recognize the price that one is paying (as few of its enthusiasts appear to do). The greatest danger of comparative history is of imposing man-made structures upon the past instead of patiently trying to discern the inherent structures.

To conclude: just as historians cannot borrow methods from the social sciences without danger to their understanding, so social scientists cannot obtain material from historians without the risk of getting false or shoddy goods. Historians can certainly serve social scientists, but only to a limited extent and not with their best material. Historical truth cannot be purchased

[41] See chapter 4, section 6.
[42] Marc Bloch, *The Historian's Craft* (Manchester University Press, 1954), p. 194.
[43] See section 1; also chapter 5, section 3, and chapter 9, section 2.
[44] Cf. the first sentence of J. Habakkuk, 'Economic history – economic theory', referred to in section 4.
[45] See, for example, Skocpol, *States and Social Revolutions*, and Burke, *Sociology and History*, pp. 33–7.

at second hand; it can be gained only by the essential historical method of imaginative and intellectual re-creation of a whole.

6 History as Giving Meaning

The function of history has mostly been seen here as meeting a hunger for greater knowledge and understanding. But it may also meet a need for meaning. It may be argued that it is not among the functions of history, but rather of philosophy or art or religion, to give meaning. Nevertheless many, perhaps most, people today lack both a firm religious faith and a thought-out philosophy. Many too (not necessarily the same ones) feel themselves adrift in a chaotic and threatening universe. It has always been a function of art to organize its material into a meaningful whole. The material of the historiographic art, it might be argued, is the events of human life, even the most outrageous and alarming. History, then, seems to have the power to exorcize these demons by placing them in a coherent, ordered and purposeful work of art. This may not always be possible. In spite of reading many books, I am still bewildered and distressed by a failure to understand how the Nazis could have come to power in a deeply civilized country and have been able to commit such atrocities. Like many of my generation, I suspect, I have not yet come to terms with the evil that is symbolized by Auschwitz, Treblinka, Babi Yar... Yet other people or other subjects have been more fortunate. On the whole it does seem that history, whether narrative or not, can exert an intellectual control, and (even if subconsciously) give some reassurance that rational sense can be made of this mad world, that cosmos can be made out of chaos. One is tempted to employ the title (though in a way quite remote from the author's intention) of Theodor Lessing's book, *Geschichte als Sinngebung des Sinnlosen* – 'History as Meaning Given to the Meaningless'.[46]

A meaningless world inhibits action. If nothing makes sense, why do anything? But if, on the other hand, history does help to give a meaning to human life, then it also has certain practical consequences. To these I turn in the next chapter, while deferring further discussion of meaning to the final chapter.

[46] See G. G. Iggers, *The German Conception of History* (Wesleyan University Press, 1968), p. 240. For some discussion of 'man as a creator of meanings', see William J. Bouwsma, 'Intellectual history in the 1980s; from history of ideas to history of meaning', in *The New History*, ed. Rabb and Rotberg.

11

From the Public Mind to Action in History

1 Practical Consequences of Knowing History

In the two preceding chapters I discussed the formation of historical knowledge in the mind of the public, and considered some of the structures and functions of that knowledge. Now I turn to the practical consequences. Many of these consequences depend upon comparisons between the past and the present; hence the extended discussion of comparison in history in the previous chapter. How does knowledge of the past help us decide what to do? In our private affairs we consult our experience when we have to make a decision. Of course, unless we are rock-ribbed conservatives we do not let ourselves be guided entirely by precedent. We also take into account considerations of, for example, morality, common sense or emotional disposition. But personal experience is, perhaps, the greatest source of practical information. Hence the advantage of talking things over with friends.

Although history is not of much help in our private lives, in public affairs we seem to be as dependent on history as on memory in private affairs. If politicians making decisions are moved by emotion, they rarely admit it unless the emotion is a very popular one. Like private individuals, they may be guided by principles of justice or common sense, but, unlike the rest of us, they may also be guided by party policies – which are often neither just nor sensible. Both in public and in private matters, however, we consult our experience when making decisions. For public matters, experience is often the same as history; or, more precisely, we are largely influenced by our beliefs about the past.

Decisions about public affairs are made by governments, both national and local, by international bodies like the United Nations, and by non-governmental public institutions. Increasingly they are also made by what are, technically, private institutions, such as banks, building societies, corporations and public limited companies. This is because many of their decisions affect the public outside the organization itself, and they are therefore affected by both government policy and public opinion (for example, about the environment), the latter in its turn much influenced by the media. This gives only a hint of the complications of public decision-making in a modern society. Yet beliefs about the past have some part in most, if not all, of these decisions.

A few of these beliefs about the past may be personal, but still influential if their holder is powerful. One may think of the British prime minister Eden's belief in 1955–6 that Colonel Nasser was a dictator resembling Hitler or Mussolini who had to be opposed by similar methods. This belief, one may suppose, drew much of its power over Eden's mind from his searing experiences in foreign affairs some twenty years before.[1] Such a belief is experiential rather than historical. Beliefs about the past are also obtained from the records of a government or institution. When a practical problem arises, one of the first actions is to 'send for the files' to see what was done last time. Such office records will be very valuable, for they are probably the only source of relevant information, apart from the (perhaps unreliable) memories of a few who were involved before. They have the great disadvantage, however, of not being history, but only information about the past. Records are not history because they have not emanated from the mind of a historian and so have not been seen in long perspective; they are often too recent for the consequences of what they record to have revealed themselves. Since they are written usually only from one viewpoint based upon one set of (probably unexamined) assumptions, they are not balanced by accounts from different or even conflicting perspectives. nor have they been set in the wider political, economic, social and intellectual context that gives them proportion and reveals their significance.

Apart from these non-historical sources of belief about the past, what of the part played by history as a source of beliefs that have a bearing upon action? One such influence of history is concealed and implicit. In any society tradition and precedent weigh heavily upon the present. As Marx put it, 'We suffer not only from the living but from the dead. "Le mort saisit le vif!"'[2] In a modern Western society, however, where the study of history has an important cultural role, we are able to view the past with some objectivity and hence, as J. H. Plumb argued in *The Death of the Past*, to liberate ourselves from it. This does not mean that we ignore the past; rather, by understanding how we are related to the past, we can hope to take it rationally into account. Any rational action is preceded by an assessment, however, cursory, of the situation in which we propose to act; otherwise we act on impulse or instinct, not rationally. In making such an assessment we consciously take several factors into account. But we do so against a

[1] See *The Memoirs of Sir Anthony Eden: Facing the Dictators* (Cassell, 1962); also *Full Circle* (Cassell, 1960).
[2] Karl Marx, *Capital* (Penguin, 1976), p. 91.

background of unspoken assumptions that are not in the forefront of our consciousness, though they could be brought into awareness if necessary. Part of this background is the general mental climate of the age. And in this mental climate or *mentalité* of a modern society history, like science, plays a considerable part.

History also influences us in a much more obvious, explicit way, when we seek in the past a situation similar to the present as a guide to action, either positive or negative. It is surprising how closely British and French military thinking between September 1939 and April 1940 matched that of the First World War. Although the historical parallel was obvious, the events of May 1940 showed the unreliability of the analogy. Upon being attacked by the Germans in 1941 the Russians, both in policy and in propaganda, made much of the parallels, not only with Napoleon's invasion, but also with the attacks upon Muscovy by the Teutonic knights in the Middle Ages. After the fall of France in June 1940 Napoleonic parallels replaced those of the First World War in British thinking, which regarded Britain's situation as close to that of 1803–4. C. S. Forester's 'Hornblower' novels and Sir Arthur Bryant's two volumes of history of the wars of 1793–1814 drew much of their popularity from this analogy. The general point, however, has often been made that the interest, both of historians and of public, is most aroused by those periods of the past that seem to resemble our own day. Hence Croce's famous (if exaggerated) remark that 'all history is contemporary history' – an elevation of the practical as against the historical past, in Oakeshott's terms. Anything we can learn from the past may help us solve baffling present problems; on the other hand, to draw the wrong lessons from the past may be more disastrous than ignoring it altogether. Hence the importance of the question of comparative history.

Another subtle way in which history may influence our actions relates to how we see history as a result of formal or informal historical education (discussed in the previous chapter). It is a matter not of belief about particular historical events but rather of the deeper assumptions that are subtly and implicitly conveyed by the history we have learned. These include values – for example, patriotism or internationalism; metaphysical tenets about the fundamental nature of the universe – a fortuitous concourse of atoms, or a rational design, or a developing but comprehensive process; sociological tenets about the fundamentals of human society – whether it is based on homeostasis or progress or the conflict of opposites; and judgements of meaning – of the individual human life, of a sect or nation, of humanity, or even of all living things. In the absence of a well-reasoned religion or philosophy of life, these unexamined implications are all the more powerful in their influence. Does history show that war is more effective than peace, strife than justice, hatred than love, materialism than idealism? It may be retorted that history is in principle not capable of answering such questions.

Teachers and disseminators of history do, however, answer them, if only implicitly – implicitly but no less effectively.

What we believe to be our knowledge of the past is, then, derived from memory, from records and, above all, from history. Before I approach the final stages of my suggested schema, as historical knowledge shapes action, and action in turn makes history, I wish to consider a number of problems that arise.

2 Actions and History: Twelve Questions

I shall now address myself to several questions that must not be ignored, whether or not they can be answered. As well as considering questions that cannot be answered, we should also look critically at those we take to have been answered and examine how well they have been answered – whether by an exhaustive study, a series of guesses or an unthinking prejudice. This issue is particularly important when (as here) we are dealing with practical questions upon whose answers we base our actions; in other words, how history is made.

Although these questions about actions and history are posed in a general way, it does not follow that one question has only one answer: the same question may have different answers according to time or place. With regard to free will, for example, people may be in control of their destinies at one time but not at another. In an early spring young plants may shoot up and unfold their leaves, only to be blighted by a late frost.

Here, then, are twelve questions that, I believe, demand to be answered.

(1) The first relates to what is confusingly called the issue of free will and determinism. The question is not whether our actions are free, but whether the human race is free to make its own history. There are, of course, two other possibilities. If we are not free in this way, it may be because the course of history is under the control of a stronger will or force than our own. A second possibility is that the universe is ultimately chaotic and so neither we nor anything else can determine what is to happen.[3]

(2) The second question relates to the practical use of a knowledge of history. If the human race is free to make history, there may be some use in such knowledge. If either of the other two possibilities is the case, then history could have no practical use, though it might still be a matter for contemplative or aesthetic activity.

---

[3] It is sometimes asserted that this view receives support from the principle of indeterminacy in physics, postulated first by Heisenberg; it does not. See K. R. Popper, *Objective Knowledge* (Oxford University Press, 1972), pp. 303–4, and *The Logic of Scientific Discovery* (Hutchinson, 1972), pp. 246–50.

(3) There is no doubt that many non-human factors influence and restrict our actions; physical laws, for example. Does any one of these play an overwhelmingly important, even if not a wholly determining, part in history? Some people have thought so. One may suggest geography (for Montesquieu, Braudel or Toynbee), disease (Zinsser), sunspots and climate (Le Roy Ladurie or Lamb), and so on. If we can identify any one non-human factor as preponderant, can we also determine how much it weighs at any particular point?

(4) If the first three questions were answered in a way that was favourable to our freedom, how can we explain the unintended results of so many human actions? Many of these actions may be free and rational, regarding both ends and means, yet their consequences may be quite other than was desired. Wars, revolutions, bank crashes, overpopulation and tourism all offer examples of the free rational actions of a number of people together resulting in quite the opposite of what was intended. Is nuclear defence another example? Can we hope to understand, and, by understanding, learn to avoid what seem to be the cruel tricks of fate? Or is there really a malign force in ourselves or in the universe which we have yet to identify, let alone master? On the other hand, may we hope for a benign force that turns our various bad deeds to a common good, like Adam Smith's 'hidden hand'? There are, of course, the answers proposed by Hegel and Marx: that humanity makes itself by this very process of rational activity with unintended results. One can see how a dialectical argument can be made from it. Hegel or Marx may be right. But in the late twentieth century we are, perhaps, less inclined to optimism of this kind.

(5) If hopeful answers have been given to the previous questions, and if we have decided (on whatever grounds) that a substantial part of history is open to free and effective action, we see ourselves as, at least potentially, in command of our own destinies; what we decide to achieve we *can* achieve. (This intoxicating notion manifested itself, perhaps most of all, in France in 1789.) How, then, do we act?

A rational action, I suggest, has four parts: first in importance is the end, the aim or goal; next is our current situation; third is the means by which we hope to transform the present situation into the future desired state of affairs; fourth is the driving force that moves us to action. Each of the first three should be the object of a rational judgement. The first and the third are susceptible to choice. The second most definitely is not. It must be coldly and clearly assessed. To allow any element of desire or choice to affect the assessment can cause the whole enterprise to fail. This danger arises from the fourth factor, which must be controlled but not stifled.

This brings us nearer to the part played by historical knowledge in the making of history; in short, to the role of history$_2$ in history$_1$.

(6) What part, then, does history$_2$ have in the rational effective activity

that has been postulated as the major determinant of the course of human affairs? Do our beliefs about the past influence our choice of action, or more specifically, our choice of ends, our assessments or our choice of means? In principle, they would probably most affect our understanding of our present situation. In practice, there seems little doubt that many people allow such beliefs also to influence their choices of both ends and means. Here they are on rather shakier ground because of their dependence on the validity of comparative history. One may well understand how one reached the present situation without supposing that the sequence of events will be repeated, but if one uses history in choosing either an end or a means to that end then one is likely to be making the dubious assumption that certain past events can be repeated in the future.

(7) If we decide that beliefs about the past do affect our judgement of any of these elements of action, we must ask how important is the accuracy of such beliefs. In many practical problems a knowledge of the latest science or technology may be more useful than a knowledge of the past – even of the past of science and technology. In those many decisions where we *are* influenced by our beliefs about the past, however, it seems desirable that those beliefs should be as reliable as possible. Hence I would argue again that every man be his own historian.

(8) Although we may build up knowledge with a view to rational action, in making, as well as studying, history we have to take account also of the irrational. How do we allow for and come to terms with irrational behaviour, both our own and other people's? Secondly, how do we deal with the unexpected and apparently irrational consequences of rational actions? Thirdly, how do we deal with consequences that are equally unpredictable but are not quite irrational because they are not incomprehensible? Comprehensibility and explicability are not, in history, to be equated with predictability – though they may be in science.[4] Can a knowledge of history help solve these problems of the unpredictable?

(9) Can we learn anything from history? Two ways of doing this have been suggested. Speculative philosophers of history, from St Augustine to Toynbee, have argued that we can understand the course of history as a whole. If we were to do so, then we could use this understanding to help decide what to do. It is now widely held, however, that such an intellectual feat of grasping the whole is impossible. The other view, which comes from the opposite end of the empiricist–idealist spectrum, is the belief in comparative history that I have already discussed. In spite of some people's enthusiasm, it seems that there are, in practice, two difficulties. Using Mill's

---

[4] See Popper, *The Logic of Scientific Discovery*, pp. 59ff., and *The Poverty of Historicism* (Routledge and Kegan Paul, 1961), p. 133. See also R. Harré, *An Introduction to the Logic of the Sciences* (Macmillan, 1960), p. 107, for the functions of a science.

terminology, can one be even reasonably sure of recognizing the same phenomenon when it recurs; and can one be equally sure of recognizing the 'sufficient degree of similarity of circumstances' that accompany its recurrence?[5] Nevertheless, many people do assume, perhaps without giving much thought to it, that we *can* learn from history, and they act accordingly; not always wisely or successfully.

(10) If history is of doubtful use in the choice of ends and means, though valuable in situation assessment, then has it any deeper lessons to teach? It seems that people do, even if subconsciously, draw such lessons. However, as I have suggested, they are learning from historians rather than from history, and how the purveyors of history tell the story, or should tell it, is much disputed. For example, should they, openly or implicitly, embody their own value judgements in what they say? Such a practice in the last century (for example, by Macaulay, Carlyle, Michelet or Treitschke) came under attack at the turn of the century. History was, or should be, a science; there should be no more value judgement in a work of history than in a chemical experiment. Ranke's claim to relate the past *wie es eigentlich gewesen* became a general watchword. Then things changed again. Since, roughly, the Second World War historians have acknowledged, perhaps rather regretfully, that it is not possible to write value-free history, but they will none the less be as objective as they can.

(11) However, if historians shun the posture of moral superiority (preferring to take Creighton's side in the famous Acton–Creighton correspondence), do they write history from a non-moral point of view? Since history, like the daily press, seems to prefer bad news to good, a great deal of historical writing consists of an 'objective', that is non-moral, account of many morally dubious activities.[6] The concentration camps do not, perhaps, need to be explicitly condemned, but when the diplomacies of a Frederick the Great, a Bismarck or a Kissinger are recounted with no reference to their moral obliquity this obliquity may not be perceived at all or, worse, may be considered acceptable.

Thus the best intentions of historians may result (as is so often the case with good intentions) in what they would not desire; namely, a slide from a non-moral attitude in historians to attitudes in their readers that are, first, amoral, and then, perhaps, immoral. And this matters because morality is directly concerned with action. I am not accusing historians of teaching immorality, or even amorality, but I think there is a question whether non-moral historiography may not blunt the finer moral sensibilities of the men and women whose actions will make history.

---

[5] See J. S. Mill, *A System of Logic*, in *Collected Works of John Stuart Mill* (University of Toronto Press, 1973), book III, chapter 3, § 1, p. 306. See above chapter 10, section 5.

[6] Cf. Edward Gibbon, *The Decline and Fall of the Roman Empire*, chapter 3: '. . . history, which is, indeed, little more than the register of the crimes, follies, and misfortunes of mankind.'

(12) My final question, then, is whether history should play as large a part as it does in shaping our judgements and so guiding our actions? Would it be better to act on moral or aesthetic or religious grounds? None of these involves judgements about the past which, at best, rest on rather shaky foundations. In the practical sense, that is for the making of history, is a knowledge of history at best useless, at worst harmful? Should the study of history be confined to the distant past, with no place for contemporary history? Still more, should history be a contemplative activity? What would Aristotle say to that, with his views on contemplation and on history?[7] History$_2$ has indeed a role in history$_1$. But should it have?

---

[7] See *Nicomachean Ethics*, X, 1177–9, and *The Art of Poetry*, chapter 9.

12

From Historical Action to the Making of History

In this chapter I conclude my study of the course of history through its various stages of event, evidence, reconstruction, publication, popular belief, and then action and the making of history. The sixth stage merges into the first stage, and the tune is resumed *da capo*. One important difference is that in stage 1 historical events were viewed in the past, whereas now they are viewed in the present. We can see how history is made because it is being made here and now under our very eyes.

1   The Past in the Present

What part, then, do the past and our knowledge of it play in present events? I begin by positing that human actions are rational deeds performed in the double context of a natural world and a human or cultural world. In so far as these deeds are rational, they rest, to a greater or lesser extent, upon a knowledge of the past (as was discussed in chapter 11, section 2). But the usefulness of such knowledge does not stop there. We may assume that human actions are directed into the future with a view to changing the state of the world – either by bringing about changes that would not otherwise have taken place or (less often) by preventing changes that *would* otherwise have taken place (like the accelerator and the brake in a motor car).

The natural and cultural contexts in which actions take place both support and limit those actions. When our actions are concerned with the natural world we need to understand how and to what extent that world may be changed. A farmer may choose the crops, but cannot alter the climate; a builder may choose materials and methods, but not the hazards of war or weather that the building may have to withstand. Developments in natural science and technology (where an understanding of the past has played an important but minor role) have enlarged the scope of action, but have not removed the natural limits.

It is otherwise with the cultural context. Compared with palaeolithic man, we are much less constrained by the natural world but much more dependent upon our richer cultural context. Here the influence of the past is all-pervasive and subtle. Unthinkingly, we tend to accept the world as it is. According to the perspective from which it is viewed, this may be the height of folly or the profoundest wisdom. As the saying goes: 'The fool tries to adapt the world to himself; the wise man adapts himself to the world. All progress is due to the fools.'

Much of human behaviour is not rationally directed action, but rather the unreflecting following of custom, tradition, convention, habit.[1] This is necessary because we lack time and energy and knowledge to give to everything we do a lot of careful thought, and to secure the agreement of others. Nevertheless, in such unreflecting behaviour we are largely directed by the past. Since the past was, in many respects, different from the present, ways of behaving that were suitable to yesterday's conditions may not suit today's. A case where this point was quickly taken is the revolution in moral attitudes that followed the introduction of reliable contraceptive methods. An equally radical change in attitudes and behaviour was called for by the invention of nuclear weapons (a change that Einstein urged in the late 1940s), but soldiers and politicians have been rather slower to grasp the irrelevance of yesterday's behavioural norms.

In the absence of evidence to the contrary it is easy to assume that 'human nature' is always the same. One of the most valuable lessons to be learned from history is that human behaviour, customs, norms and attitudes have differed in many ways; that human society has taken widely varying forms; and that most things need not be as they are but are susceptible to change. Eastern travel by scholars in the late seventeenth and early eighteenth century had a profound effect upon European intellectuals by showing that civilization could take very different forms. It contributed largely to the Enlightenment, as Paul Hazard showed in *La Crise de la conscience européenne*.[2] The enormous development of history in the nineteenth century had an equally liberating but unsettling effect upon the European mind.[3] By increasing our rational comprehension of the cultural world in which we live and act, history co-operates closely with the social sciences. Historical knowledge is therefore useful in encouraging habit, superstition and myth to be replaced as guides to action by rational understanding and responsibility.

Indeed, rational knowledge, rationally grounded and rationally expressed,

[1] See J. H. Plumb, *The Death of the Past* (Penguin, 1973).
[2] English edition, *The European Mind, 1680–1715* (Penguin, 1964).
[3] See, among a host of books on nineteenth-century thought, the works of Hayden White and G. G. Iggers, cited above (Prologue, sections 2 and 3, footnotes 4 and 6); the inaugural lecture of Lord Acton (June 1895), in Lord Acton, *Lectures in Modern History* (Fontana, 1960), pp. 35–6; and the Rede Lecture at Cambridge in 1977 by Professor R. W. Southern, 'The historical experience', *The Times Literary Supplement*, 24 June 1977.

may well be at a premium in the coming information revolution that is being ushered in by the integrated circuit. Computers have for some time been used in certain kinds of historical research, such as economic history or demography, which deal with large quantities of numerical data. The introduction of computers that operate symbols rather than numbers now makes it possible to handle forms of knowledge that are expressed linguistically rather than numerically.[4] Historical knowledge is not among the first of these forms, but much of it will surely be so before long. This will be hastened with the development of the so-called 'natural language' systems in artificial intelligence.

It may seem that I am here contradicting all that I have said about the historical imagination and the need for the full powers of the human mind to be employed in historical construction. But this is not so. There is, of course, always a danger that the construction of 'knowledge-based' or 'expert' systems can lead to a fossilization or restriction of knowledge. Physical and biological scientists who use such systems are prepared to take the risk, for the gains clearly outweigh the losses. Is there any reason to suppose that the reverse will be the case in the more complex and subtle kinds of knowledge like history? The more obvious objection is that historical knowledge, at its best, is beyond the reach of any man-made machine, and that probably no artificial intelligence will ever reach the heights that human beings can attain in religion, philosophy, science and the arts. Yet, while this is true, even greater heights may well be attained by people who can, as it were, stand on the shoulders of machines. If artificial intelligences could take over the more tedious part of the work in each of these spheres, the human mind could be freed for even greater achievements – including achievements in historical knowledge.

How much of what I have said here is useful foresight and how much is idle speculation will doubtless be revealed in the next decade or so. But whatever happens in the development of artificial intelligence I believe that we should increase our rational understanding of history, both of historical occurrences and of historical knowledge. Such a rational understanding should, in turn, lead to more rational actions – in other words, to a more rational making of history.

Knowledge of history has certainly grown enormously in the last two centuries, and it continues to grow. There seems to be far more than we can cope with, even if we confine ourselves to what is strictly relevant to the matter in hand. Is it not even more important that, as well as amassing knowledge, we should have a clear understanding of the nature, scope,

---

[4] For a good discussion of these, see the articles on quantification by David Herlihy and Allan G. Bogue in *The New History: the 1980s and beyond: studies in interdisciplinary history*, ed. Rabb and Rotberg (Princeton University Press, 1982).

limitations and ordering of our knowledge? For action is based on knowledge, and, on the whole, one may assume that better knowledge will lead to better action. A similar point was made in 1857 by Buckle, who argued that the progress of civilization has been due to advances in knowledge rather than in moral insights.[5] Although I believe that there *have* been advances in moral insights, I am sure that we desperately need further moral progress, yet the growth of knowledge will not wait for it. I hope that this book will contribute to a clearer insight into at least one kind of knowledge. It may also assist in clearer moral insights. Even if it does not, I cannot believe that it will delay them. Rather I hope that a more rational ordering of our knowledge of the past will contribute to a better future.

2 The Making of History

At the beginning of this chapter I said that when we reach stage 6 of my historical schema we can see how history is made because it is being made under our very eyes. I have already examined history-as-event and distinguished four elements: the constituent parts, the articulations and interrelations, the moving forces of change, and the nature of the whole.[6] I shall now try to analyse history that is happening now.

First, it may be convenient to distinguish the terms 'occurrence', 'event' (with its lengthier forms, 'trend' and 'movement'), 'behaviour' and 'action'.[7] The loosest of these is 'occurrence', which I take to refer to anything that happens in the natural or human spheres. More commonly used in history is 'event', which normally refers to a human rather than a natural occurrence or string of occurrences. As I have shown (chapter 3, section 4), it is not distinguished by any inherent quality, but is picked out by observers as worthy of note. Most occurrences are ignored by most people; one that attracts the attention of a number of people may be regarded as an event. It may be made up of many occurrences; hence, for purposes of analysis, any event may be broken down into lesser events or sub-events, as a war into battles, or a battle into assaults, retreats, cannonades, and so on. An event has no dimensions of its own, it is simply whatever people consider an event. 'Behaviour' and 'action' both refer to what human beings do. It is not possible to draw a hard-and-fast line between them, but, roughly, we can say that actions are the product of rational thinking, while behaviour springs rather from habit, convention, custom or emotion. A piece of

---

[5] H. T. Buckle, *History of Civilization in England* (Grant and Richards, 1903), vol. I, chapter 4.
[6] See chapter 2, sections 3, 4, 5, 6 respectively.
[7] See also chapter 2, section 5; chapter 3, section 4.

behaviour may be a reasonable thing to do on that occasion, but it has not been thought out on that occasion; on the other hand, it may be quite unreasonable. There is no need further to distinguish behaviour from action. To do so is useful for psychologists, but the rough-and-ready analysis that is needed for history requires no more than to treat behaviour as a defective or inferior form of action.

The analysis of action reveals four constituents: the goal, the assessment, the means and the drive. In any action we aim to achieve something, usually an alteration in the state of the world or of ourselves. The selection of this *goal* depends upon the recognition of, and preference for, some value. The second element is the *assessment* we make about the state of the world in which we find ourselves, and perhaps of the future (different) state that our action is likely to bring about. In this we recognize the context of our action. Such an assessment is based on the best of beliefs at the time. Nevertheless, these beliefs may be false and the assessment erroneous. Historians, coming later, tend to believe they have a more correct view of the context of an action in the past. For example, we know what Napoleon did *not* know on the morning of 18 June 1815, namely that Blücher had not retired northwards after Ligny, but was marching westwards to join Wellington. 'Nonsense,' snapped the emperor. 'The Prussians and English cannot possibly link up for another two days after such a battle' – or so, at least, he is alleged to have said.[8] But historians do not always know better, since sometimes the agent may understand his or her own time as no later age can. (Obviously I can give no example.) In any case, the success or failure of an action may depend upon the accuracy of the agent's belief about its context.

The third constituent of action is the *means* the agent chooses for the purpose of attaining the goal, of bringing about the desired result. In a battle, the goal is victory, and the means adopted to this end is the tactics. Choice of means is almost purely intellectual, so it is in this that the historian gets closest to the historical action. One has only to stand on the battlefield of Culloden to see how greatly mistaken was Prince Charles Edward to decide to leave the slopes before the battle and to meet Cumberland on the plain. The fourth constituent is the *drive*, the nervous energy and emotion that carry the proposed action into effect. This is what we recognize as the will.

It is worth remarking that one can formulate a different philosophy of history according to which of these four elements one emphasizes. Adam Smith and Karl Marx considered that people are chiefly guided by a desire to get rich or to avoid poverty. Many nineteenth-century historians believed the pursuit of national glory was the key factor in history. On this view, one can understand history best by discovering what people have most desired (the goal). Another approach assumes that people have always had

---

[8] Quoted from Elizabeth Longford, *Wellington: the years of the sword* (Panther, 1971), p. 547.

much the same goals, but that their success has increased with the growth of knowledge available to them. This view is particularly favoured by historians of science and technology. Historians of ideas and of *mentalités*, practitioners of 'intellectual history', have been able to throw light on how people in the past saw the world around them, and hence on what sort of assessments they made of the context of their actions. Keith Thomas's *Religion and the Decline of Magic* or Christopher Hill's *The World Turned Upside Down* are good examples.

The more purely rational study of means, the consideration of what it is reasonable to do in a given situation, was the basis of R. G. Collingwood's philosophy of history. He was at pains to stress both that history was only possible by rethinking the thoughts of the historical agent, and that these thoughts had to be rational. 'Of everything other than thought, there can be no history,' he wrote; '...the record of immediate experience with its flow of sensations and feelings, faithfully preserved in a diary or recalled in a memoir, is not history.'[9] He insisted that 'the historian must re-enact the past in his own mind', and illustrated it by the example of a study of the Theodosian Code:

> he must envisage the situation with which the emperor was trying to deal, and he must envisage it as that emperor envisaged it. [This is the agent's assessment.] Then he must see for himself, just as if the emperor's situation were his own, how such a situation might be dealt with; he must see the possible alternatives, and the reasons for choosing one rather than another. [This is the choice of means].[10]

Collingwood explicitly referred to two of the four constitutents of action: the third (the aim) is implied in the phrase 'was trying to deal'; the fourth (the drive) is taken for granted in a vigorous ruler. Collingwood, then, stressed rationality as the key to history.

Yet another view finds this key in the drive or will. It achieved some philosophical respectability with Schopenhauer, who identified it with Kant's 'thing-in-itself' or noumenon. However, it has been too popular with twentieth-century dictators to be given much serious consideration nowadays. 'However grave the crisis may be at this moment,' Hitler proclaimed in his last broadcast to the German people on 30 January 1945, 'nevertheless it will be finally overcome by our unalterable will.[11]

My own view is that the first constituent, the goal, is the most important. In the case of Hitler, for example, there is little doubt of the effectiveness of his will, of the skilful choice of means to his ends, or of his accurate

[9] R. G. Collingwood, *The Idea of History* (Oxford University Press, 1961), p. 304.
[10] Ibid., pp. 282–3.
[11] See J. P. Stern, *Hitler: the Führer and the people* (Fontana, 1975), p. 69.

assessment of the political situation, both domestic and foreign, of the 1930s. His political success, as Stern reminds us, was unprecedented in German history and his military success was unparalleled in the history of modern Europe.[12] But beyond all this the key to Hitler's impact upon the world is his choice of goals, the values that he preferred.

A further possibility is that there may be other, non-human, causes of change. If older stories used witches and demons and evil spirits to explain unforeseen disasters, and, less often, benign spirits or 'hidden hands' or miracles of God to explain unforeseen good fortune, more recent historiography and social science make use of impersonal forces for similar explanation of the inexplicable. Indeed, reification is found not only in Marxism but also in Durkheim, who insisted that 'social phenomena are things and ought to be treated as things.'[13] If history is full of accidents, if what eventuates is quite contrary to what was intended, how are we to explain this 'play of the contingent and the unforeseen'? Must we postulate the existence of other entities in the world which exert mysterious forces and bring about unforeseen effects? Or should we exorcize all Germanic 'ideas' or modern economic or social 'forces' along with the ghosts and witches of the pre-scientific world? Is there anything else on earth except human beings and nature? Does history consist of anything but people and their actions? If not, do we need to bring in impersonal forces and pseudo-persons (states, classes or parties) to explain our muddles, just because we do not fully understand ourselves and our effects upon each other? My own preference is for an answer in terms of 'Ockham's razor': *Entia non sunt multiplicanda praeter necessitatem* – entities must not be multiplied unnecessarily. The question remains open, but I think it should not be ignored.

The whole texture of history (the total existence of mankind) is woven of the relations between people, their actions and their interactions. This point was made more cogently by Marx than by most other historians or philosophers, but he oversimplified the relations and underplayed the interactions. Accurately to discover and to portray these complexities is the unending task of the historian. To improve such relations for the future is the task of us all. As this endeavour increases our understanding of human beings and human relations, so we may hope our insight into the past will also be improved. If some such improvement has been due to Marx's analysis of relations, we may hope for greater progress from an analysis of the action and interaction. It is here, in the realm of historical movement and the course of change (how and why things happen as they do), that Marx was arguably less successful, for future events did not conform to his predictions. So certainly we need to improve our understanding of the structure of human

[12] Ibid., p. 16.
[13] E. Durkheim, *The Rule of Sociological Method* (Free Press, 1964), p. 27.

relations, but we have a greater need correctly to analyse the structure of human action and interaction. In practice, this means (*inter alia*) that the structure of the historian's understanding and account of history should approximate even more closely to the structures, both static and dynamic, of the real past.

3 Going Beyond History

History, then, is a struggle to understand ourselves by a particular means: through our past actions and passions, what men and women have done and suffered through the ages. The historian's activity is, as I have tried to show, at once rational, imaginative and creative. Its criteria of truth are both empirical (though not quite like a natural science) and critical (though not quite like a philosophy). Its objectivity arises, as in all sciences and philosophies, from the agreement of (inevitably) subjective judgements. This is particularly true of the social sciences, which also attempt to understand people by examining what they do. Moreover, in history and the sciences, much more than in philosophy and art, we seek not only to understand but also to explain.

One of the foundations of historicist thought – a foundation that finally collapsed and brought down the whole edifice – was the belief that history is self-explanatory, that 'history is the sole guide to the understanding of things human.'[14] But if history-as-events (history$_1$) is not self-explanatory then history-as-account (history$_2$) cannot hope to explain it without drawing on sources outside itself. Although it was generally conceded, after the collapse of historicism in the first half of this century, that meaning is not to be found in history, the awkward problems of meaning still remain.

These problems are not so much the hermeneutic problems of the meanings of texts, on which a great deal of energy and ingenuity is expended, as the more historical and metaphysical problems of the meanings of events, of the actual course of history. As I suggested above (chapter 7, section 5), the reading public expects historians to show the meaning or significance of what they relate; a mere chronicle will not do. Further (in chapter 10, section 6), I pointed out that the need for meaning is more than the intellectual or aesthetic demand for a satisfactory piece of history-writing; meaning relates to action, and people need meaning for the sake of action. What is the point of rational action to an agent who sees the world as totally meaningless? As has often been noticed by those philosophers and theologians who study our present discontents, the demand for meaning is fundamental

---

[14] See G. G. Iggers, *The German Conception of History: the national tradition of historical thought from Herder to the present* (Wesleyan University Press, 1968), p. 270; cf. F. Auerbach, *Mimesis* (Princeton University Press, 1968), pp. 443–4.

to our being. Yet this deeper, spiritual demand is also made of historians, and they cannot wholly ignore this responsibility. Can anything be done to ease the tensions at this crux of history-as-account with history-as-events, for it is here that historical knowledge bears most heavily upon historical action? I shall attempt a little clarification.

The concept of meaning is generally held to be an attribute of something done or something said. The meaning of an action is, largely though not wholly, that which the agent intends. The meaning of a word, sentence or text is what it signifies or conveys. But, as already noted, the meaning of both deed and word is largely constituted by the context. Moreover, meaning always points to something else. To the question 'What is the meaning of A (whether a word or a deed)?' the answer can never be 'A', but 'B' or 'C' or 'D'. . . Nothing can be its own meaning; something else must supply it.

Since a word or deed acquires a necessary part of its meaning from its context, and that context is usually the culture of the society within which the deed is done or the word is spoken, one can see the force of Bouwsma's remark that cultural anthropology 'is centrally concerned with the construction and symbolic expression of meaning in every dimension of human activity'.[15] For it can be argued that the most important function of a culture is to give meaning to the words and deeds, and hence the very lives, of the men and women who inhabit that culture. For a number of reasons, the culture of the late twentieth-century Western world does not readily give any reassuring stability and resonance of meaning. For one thing, it is 'pluralistic'; it contains a wide variety of philosophies, religions and value-systems that are by no means mutually compatible. For another, it is in the process of rapid and fundamental change and upheaval – something that is psychologically unsettling. Thirdly, it may be too self-conscious. Bouwsma speaks of 'man as a creator of meanings', and Clifford Geertz says man is 'an animal suspended in webs of significance he himself has spun'.[16] But in the face of private or public disaster – in Dresden, Hiroshima, Vietnam, Kampuchea, Uganda, Beirut – is it enough to say that human beings make their own meanings?

I should wish to argue that, if nothing can be the meaning of itself, then history cannot supply its own meaning, and existential human beings, beings-in-history, cannot find their own meaning in history. They cannot explain themselves; no more can history as a whole explain itself; hence the collapse of historicism. Thus what must be sought is the meaning not only of the sum of history, of history as a whole, but also of every passage in the course of history and of every account of those events. Such meaning

---

[15] See William J. Bouwsma, 'From history of ideas to history of meaning'. in *The New History*, ed. Rabb and Rotberg, p. 289.
[16] Ibid., pp. 289–90.

must be, if anywhere, not in but outside history; historiography cannot be a self-sufficient activity. If the meaning of history is not within history, then, assuming that human life has any meaning beyond the factitious meanings that we make up for ourselves, we are left with two choices: either the meaning lies outside us and is wholly unknowable, or we are not wholly contained in history. This is a problem that we must each answer for ourselves. I shall indicate my own preference, but first I wish to conclude my schema of history.

As stage 6 becomes stage 1 and present action fades into past history, so thinking about history comes to an end, or rather to a T-junction. One way it issues into history$_1$, into events. The other way it issues into philosophy – into epistemology, questions about how we know and what we know; into metaphysics, questions about the nature of human beings (both as historical subjects and as historical objects), about the nature of the human world, about the reality of groupings and forces, and how these seem to come together and create history, and about causation in general. It issues into other questions, philosophical or religious, about the nature of the universe, about values – their origins, their characteristics, their range in time and space, their role in human affairs; above all, into these problems about meaning. All these questions must be explicitly acknowledged by historians, for they have a place in history in both aspects, as events and as account. But history can provide no solution. They take us beyond history into philosophy, art, religion – or, perhaps, further. For our minds must remain open. Closed circuits may be suitable for television, but not for systems of thought.

My own conclusion is something like this. History consists of what men and women do and suffer in a four-dimensional world, time being the fourth dimension. The material of history is their actions, which are real and of intrinsic – even transcendent – importance. The structure of history is the relationships among human beings. But men and women themselves somehow escape being totally enclosed in the world of four dimensions. One wall of their dwelling is open to infinity. We are greater than history.

Epilogue

As I said on the first page, history has, perhaps, too many structures. If, then, I have devoted this book to applying the concept of structure to history, my aim has not been to increase the number of structures. Rather have I hoped to explore and clarify the concept, and so to use it to demonstrate how the various elements of history (denoted by my six stages) relate to one another in one overriding structure.

I have sought to show how both the course of history and the knowledge of history belong to a single process – a process that, in its movement, follows a regular, constitutive pattern that may properly be called its structure. In the course of tracing the process through the six stages of the schema, structures have been discernible at each stage. Moreover, I have suggested that each of these stages may be more clearly understood if the structure proper to that stage is recognized and used. In working through these stages I have come across a number of problems. In only a few cases have I suggested how these may be tackled. To attempt them all would demand far more time, space and ability than any one person is likely to dispose of. Yet I believe it may have been useful to indicate where certain questions are relevant.

Thus what I have attempted is not to answer the questions, but to locate them. I should wish to claim no more for this book than to have drawn a rough sketch-map of the terrain. Greater accuracy must inevitably be achieved on a different scale, with the attendant loss of perspective. In the places where particularly challenging questions lurk I could have written 'Here be dragons'. If at times I have aimed a blow or two at these beasts, I have on the whole been content solely to give warning.

Such a sketch-map may be inadequate in scale, detail or content. Yet I believe it to be of prime importance to identify and indicate the essential features of the terrain (the six stages), to show how they stand in relation to one another, and to grasp how the character of the whole is thus determined. This whole includes both history$_1$ and history$_2$. If my chief concern is to offer a clearer understanding of the nature of historical knowledge, it is apparent that this primarily epistemological problem cannot be divorced from metaphysical and empirical questions about the nature of historical events, nor from sociological and psychological questions about the formation and the effects of such knowledge in individual minds. I have tried to take account of these considerations.

One thing that makes the study of history so baffling and yet so intriguing is that, when we try to tackle any one problem at any degree of philosophical depth, we find that it draws in a number of other philosophical problems like a tangled skein of wool. One of the main purposes of this book is to locate and fix these problems in their proper place, so they can be dealt with one at a time. Then, with the help of the concept of structure, it should be possible to achieve a better understanding of our understanding of history.

Two questions, however, continue to challenge any tendency to complacency. One is whether it is at all possible in history, as in the natural sciences, to build up a self-consistent, rational and objective body of knowledge, which, while not beyond criticism at any point, is generally accepted as the best approximation to the truth that is at present available. Is it even desirable to attempt this with history? Or does such an undertaking merely indicate a failure to grasp the peculiar nature of historical knowledge? The other question relates to the role of language in history. For the course of history consists largely of actions, not words, and the study of history, I feel, should be an empirical not a literary exercise. Yet, as I have tried to show, language is so important at each stage of the historical process, with every landmark of the terrain, that it is permissible to doubt whether historical knowledge can ever free itself from linguistic and literary influences. Can history, in Steiner's words, ever 'escape from the hermeneutic circle'?[1]

Finally, I hope that this book will not be thought to have answered questions or solved problems. It is in no sense an end to any thinking, but an attempt at clarification. I should wish it to be both an aid and a spur to ever more rigorous and adventurous thinking about the nature of history and of our knowlege of it.

[1] See chapter 7, section 4.

Index

its achievements 102–6
its contribution 97–100
its functioning 100–2
its nature 89–97, 119
mind, of non-historian 3, 4, 24, 76,
  81, 84, 115, 119, 135, 141–2,
  144, 146–8, 149–50, 151–2
mind, structure of 10, 11–12
Mink, Louis O. 135, 137
model 1, 4, 11, 13, 15–16, 96, 100,
  106, 124
Muses 130–1
myth *see* folk-lore

Namier, Sir Lewis 19–20
narrative 16–17, 20, 43, 111, 125,
  127, 153

Oakeshott, Michael 97, 119, 162
objectivity (objective mind) 27, 43–4,
  126–7, 178, 187, 191
'Ockham's razor' 186
Ogden, C. K. and Richards, I. A.
  115–18
Olafson, Frederick A. 135–7
Orwell, George 121

Parker, Christopher, J. W. 79, 138,
  140
particulars, historical
  see also identity 32–3
past, the 26–7, 45, 56
  idea of 46, 48–9
  influence of 181
  practical uses of 162–3, 172–5,
    177–8
  varieties of 119–20
philosophy 1, 2, 189–91
place-names 63
Plumb, J. H. 163, 173
Popper, Sir Karl R. 51, 53–4, 97–8,
  99, 115, 123, 126, 175, 177
Powicke, F. M. (Sir Maurice) 50, 149
present, the 26–7, 45, 56, 180
presuppositions 91–3

process, processes *see* evidence,
  processive
purpose 43

Ranke, Leopold von 42, 78, 162
rational, rationality 181–2, 185, 191
reality, degrees of 33–4
reasoning, historical
  see also judgement 56, 58–9
relativism 124, 125–6
representation 143–4

Saussure, Ferdinand de 164
schema, of historical activity 1, 2,
  5–6, 23, 26, 138, 146, 180,
  189, 190
sciences, auxiliary (techniques) 62, 65,
  67, 68, 81, 86
selection
  of evidence 85–6
  of subject 84–5
self-consciousness, national or
  communal 3, 41–2
semantic levels 122–3
Skocpol, Theda 167, 168, 170
Smith, Adam 164, 176, 184
sources 77, 79, 80, 84, 85–6, 123
space 28, 29, 34, 35
Spengler, Oswald 96–7, 159
statements 53–4, 72–3
Steiner, George 122–3
structure
  concept of 7–25 *especially* 7–8, 11–15,
    190
  definition of 7, 25, 30, 104, 107, 138
  of historian's construction 88, 106,
    107, 108–13, 114
  of historical activity *see* schema
  of historical education 155–6
  of history$_1$ 30, 34–7, 43, 88, 106,
    114, 157, 160–1, 183, 189
  of history$_2$ 23–4, 88, 106–7,
    142–5, 190–1
  imposed 7, 15–23, 108, 125, 137,
    159–60, 170
  inherent 7, 8–11, 108, 160–1, 170
  for non-historian 144, 157–9